# Siberia and the Soviet Far East

# WORLD BIBLIOGRAPHICAL SERIES

General Editors:
Robert G. Neville (Executive Editor)
John J. Horton

Robert A. Myers                    Ian Wallace
Hans H. Wellisch        Ralph Lee Woodward, Jr.

**John J. Horton** is Deputy Librarian of the University of Bradford and currently Chairman of its Academic Board of Studies in Social Sciences. He has maintained a longstanding interest in the discipline of area studies and its associated bibliographical problems, with special reference to European Studies. In particular he has published in the field of Icelandic and of Yugoslav studies, including the two relevant volumes in the World Bibliographical Series.

**Robert A. Myers** is Associate Professor of Anthropology in the Division of Social Sciences and Director of Study Abroad Programs at Alfred University, Alfred, New York. He has studied post-colonial island nations of the Caribbean and has spent two years in Nigeria on a Fulbright Lectureship. His interests include international public health, historical anthropology and developing societies. In addition to *Amerindians of the Lesser Antilles: a bibliography* (1981), *A Resource Guide to Dominica, 1493–1986* (1987) and numerous articles, he has compiled the World Bibliographical Series volumes on *Dominica* (1987) and *Nigeria* (1989).

**Ian Wallace** is Professor of Modern Languages at Loughborough University of Technology. A graduate of Oxford in French and German, he also studied in Tübingen, Heidelberg and Lausanne before taking teaching posts at universities in the USA, Scotland and England. He specializes in East German affairs, especially literature and culture, on which he has published numerous articles and books. In 1979 he founded the journal *GDR Monitor*, which he continues to edit.

**Hans H. Wellisch** is Professor emeritus at the College of Library and Information Services, University of Maryland. He was President of the American Society of Indexers and was a member of the International Federation for Documentation. He is the author of numerous articles and several books on indexing and abstracting, and has published *The Conversion of Scripts* and *Indexing and Abstracting: an International Bibliography*. He also contributes frequently to *Journal of the American Society for Information Science*, *The Indexer* and other professional journals.

**Ralph Lee Woodward, Jr.** is Chairman of the Department of History at Tulane University, New Orleans, where he has been Professor of History since 1970. He is the author of *Central America, a Nation Divided*, 2nd ed. (1985), as well as several monographs and more than sixty scholarly articles on modern Latin America. He has also compiled volumes in the World Bibliographical Series on *Belize* (1980), *Nicaragua* (1983), and *El Salvador* (1988). Dr. Woodward edited the Central American section of the *Research Guide to Central America and the Caribbean* (1985) and is currently editor of the Central American history section of the *Handbook of Latin American Studies*.

VOLUME 127

# Siberia and the Soviet Far East

David N. Collins

*Compiler*

**CLIO PRESS**

OXFORD, ENGLAND · SANTA BARBARA, CALIFORNIA
DENVER, COLORADO

British Library Cataloguing in Publication Data

Collins, David N.
Siberia — (World Bibliographical series; v. 127).
I. Title   II. Series
016.957

ISBN 1–85109–157–2


Clio Press Ltd.,
55 St. Thomas' Street,
Oxford OX1 1JG, England.

ABC-CLIO,
130 Cremona Drive,
Santa Barbara,
CA 93117, USA.


Designed by Bernard Crossland.
Typeset by Columns Design and Production Services, Reading, England.
Printed and bound in Great Britain by
Billing and Sons Ltd., Worcester.

# THE WORLD BIBLIOGRAPHICAL SERIES

This series, which is principally designed for the English speaker, will eventually cover every country in the world, each in a separate volume comprising annotated entries on works dealing with its history, geography, economy and politics; and with its people, their culture, customs, religion and social organization. Attention will also be paid to current living conditions – housing, education, newspapers, clothing, etc.– that are all too often ignored in standard bibliographies; and to those particular aspects relevant to individual countries. Each volume seeks to achieve, by use of careful selectivity and critical assessment of the literature, an expression of the country and an appreciation of its nature and national aspirations, to guide the reader towards an understanding of its importance. The keynote of the series is to provide, in a uniform format, an interpretation of each country that will express its culture, its place in the world, and the qualities and background that make it unique. The views expressed in individual volumes, however, are not necessarily those of the publisher.

## VOLUMES IN THE SERIES

1 *Yugoslavia*, John J. Horton
2 *Lebanon*, Shereen Khairallah
3 *Lesotho*, Shelagh M. Willet and David Ambrose
4 *Rhodesia/Zimbabwe*, Oliver B. Pollack and Karen Pollack
5 *Saudi Arabia*, Frank A. Clements
6 *USSR*, Anthony Thompson
7 *South Africa*, Reuben Musiker
8 *Malawi*, Robert B. Boeder
9 *Guatemala*, Woodman B. Franklin
10 *Pakistan*, David Taylor
11 *Uganda*, Robert L. Collison
12 *Malaysia*, Ian Brown and Rajeswary Ampalavanar
13 *France*, Frances Chambers
14 *Panama*, Eleanor DeSelms Langstaff
15 *Hungary*, Thomas Kabdebo
16 *USA*, Sheila R. Herstein and Naomi Robbins
17 *Greece*, Richard Clogg and Mary Jo Clogg
18 *New Zealand*, R. F. Grover
19 *Algeria*, Richard I. Lawless
20 *Sri Lanka*, Vijaya Samaraweera
21 *Belize*, Ralph Lee Woodward, Jr.
23 *Luxembourg*, Carlo Hury and Jul Christophory
24 *Swaziland*, Balam Nyeko
25 *Kenya*, Robert L. Collison
26 *India*, Brijen K. Gupta and Datta S. Kharbas
27 *Turkey*, Merel Güçlü
28 *Cyprus*, P. M. Kitromilides and M. L. Evriviades
29 *Oman*, Frank A. Clements
31 *Finland*, J. E. O. Screen
32 *Poland*, Richard C. Lewański
33 *Tunisia*, Allan M. Findlay, Anne M. Findlay and Richard I. Lawless
34 *Scotland*, Eric G. Grant
35 *China*, Peter Cheng
36 *Qatar*, P. T. H. Unwin
37 *Iceland*, John J. Horton
38 *Nepal*, John Whelpton
39 *Haiti*, Frances Chambers
40 *Sudan*, M. W. Daly
41 *Vatican City State*, Michael J. Walsh
42 *Iraq*, A. J. Abdulrahman
43 *United Arab Emirates*, Frank A. Clements
44 *Nicaragua*, Ralph Lee Woodward, Jr.
45 *Jamaica*, K. E. Ingram
46 *Australia*, I. Kepars
47 *Morocco*, Anne M. Findlay, Allan M. Findlay and Richard I. Lawless

48  *Mexico*, Naomi Robbins
49  *Bahrain*, P. T. H. Unwin
50  *The Yemens*, G. Rex Smith
51  *Zambia*, Anne M. Bliss and J. A. Rigg
52  *Puerto Rico*, Elena E. Cevallos
53  *Namibia*, Stanley Schoeman and Elna Schoeman
54  *Tanzania*, Colin Darch
55  *Jordan*, Ian J. Seccombe
56  *Kuwait*, Frank A. Clements
57  *Brazil*, Solena V. Bryant
58  *Israel*, Esther M. Snyder (preliminary compilation E. Kreiner)
59  *Romania*, Andrea Deletant and Dennis Deletant
60  *Spain*, Graham J. Shields
61  *Atlantic Ocean*, H. G. R. King
62  *Canada*, Ernest Ingles
63  *Cameroon*, Mark W. DeLancey and Peter J. Schraeder
64  *Malta*, John Richard Thackrah
65  *Thailand*, Michael Watts
66  *Austria*, Denys Salt with the assistance of Arthur Farrand Radley
67  *Norway*, Leland B. Sather
68  *Czechoslovakia*, David Short
69  *Irish Republic*, Michael Owen Shannon
70  *Pacific Basin and Oceania*, Gerald W. Fry and Rufino Mauricio
71  *Portugal*, P. T. H. Unwin
72  *West Germany*, Donald S. Detwiler and Ilse E. Detwiler
73  *Syria*, Ian J. Seccombe
74  *Trinidad and Tobago*, Frances Chambers
76  *Barbados*, Robert B. Potter and Graham M. S. Dann
77  *East Germany*, Ian Wallace
78  *Mozambique*, Colin Darch
79  *Libya*, Richard I. Lawless
80  *Sweden*, Leland B. Sather and Alan Swanson
81  *Iran*, Reza Navabpour
82  *Dominica*, Robert A. Myers
83  *Denmark*, Kenneth E. Miller
84  *Paraguay*, R. Andrew Nickson
85  *Indian Ocean*, Julia J. Gotthold with the assistance of Donald W. Gotthold
86  *Egypt*, Ragai, N. Makar
87  *Gibraltar*, Graham J. Shields
88  *The Netherlands*, Peter King and Michael Wintle
89  *Bolivia*, Gertrude M. Yeager
90  *Papua New Guinea*, Fraiser McConnell
91  *The Gambia*, David P. Gamble
92  *Somalia*, Mark W. DeLancey, Sheila L. Elliott, December Green, Kenneth J. Menkhaus, Mohammad Haji Moqtar, Peter J. Schraeder
93  *Brunei*, Sylvia C. Engelen Krausse, Gerald H. Krausse
94  *Albania*, William B. Bland
95  *Singapore*, Stella R. Quah, Jon S. T. Quah
96  *Guyana*, Frances Chambers
97  *Chile*, Harold Blakemore
98  *El Salvador*, Ralph Lee Woodward, Jr.
99  *The Arctic*, H.G.R. King
100  *Nigeria*, Robert A. Myers
101  *Ecuador*, David Corkhill
102  *Uruguay*, Henry Finch with the assistance of Alicia Casas de Barrán
103  *Japan*, Frank Joseph Shulman
104  *Belgium*, R.C. Riley
105  *Macau*, Richard Louis Edmonds
106  *Philippines*, Jim Richardson
107  *Bulgaria*, Richard J. Crampton
108  *The Bahamas*, Paul G. Boultbee
109  *Peru*, John Robert Fisher
110  *Venezuela*, D. A. G. Waddell
111  *Dominican Republic*, Kai Schoenhals
112  *Colombia*, Robert H. Davis
113  *Taiwan*, Wei-chin Lee
114  *Switzerland*, Heinz K. Meier and Regula A. Meier
115  *Hong Kong*, Ian Scott
116  *Bhutan*, Ramesh C. Dogra
117  *Suriname*, Rosemarijn Hoefte
118  *Djibouti*, Peter J. Schraeder
119  *Grenada*, Kai Schoenhals
120  *Monaco*, Grace L. Hudson
121  *Guinea-Bisson*, Rosemary Galli
122  *Wales*, Gwilym Huws. D. Hywel E. Roberts
123  *Cape Verde*, Caroline S. Shaw
124  *Ghana*, Robert A. Myers
125  *Greenland*, Kenneth E. Miller
126  *Costa Rica*, Charles L. Stansifer
127  *Siberia*, David N. Collins

# Contents

INTRODUCTION ................................................................ xi

GENERAL WORKS ................................................................ 1

TRAVELLERS' ACCOUNTS ........................................................ 5
    Up to 1800   5
    From 1800 to 1916   10
    From 1917 onwards   22

TRAVEL GUIDES ................................................................ 30

GEOGRAPHY ................................................................ 32
    General   32
    Maps and atlases   34
    Climate   36
    Physical geography   37
    Special features   38
    Regions   39

FLORA AND FAUNA ................................................................ 44

ENVIRONMENTAL PROBLEMS AND PROTECTION ..................... 48

PREHISTORY AND ARCHAEOLOGY ......................................... 50

HISTORY ................................................................ 55
    General   55
    From the earliest times to 1580   58
    From Ermak's conquest to 1799   59

# Contents

From 1800 to 1916   65
During the Revolution and civil war, 1917 to 1922   68
Since the end of the civil war, 1923–   76

ETHNOGRAPHY ........................................................................ 79
General   79
Individual peoples   87

LANGUAGES ............................................................................ 99
General   99
Altaic languages   101
Uralic languages   103
Paleosiberian languages   103

FOLKLORE AND ORAL LITERATURE ..................................... 106

RELIGION ............................................................................... 110
General   110
Buddhism   111
Christianity   111
Shamanism   116

SOCIAL ISSUES ...................................................................... 119

EXILE AND IMPRISONMENT ................................................. 121
From the seventeenth century to 1916   121
The post–1917 period   126

POPULATION, SETTLEMENT AND URBAN DEVELOPMENT ..... 132
From the seventeenth century to 1916   132
The post-1917 period   134

EDUCATION AND SCIENCE ..................................................... 139

POLITICAL DEVELOPMENTS ................................................... 140
Regionalism   140
Communist Party and Soviet administration   142

ECONOMY ............................................................................... 143

AGRICULTURE ....................................................................... 147
Herding and stockraising   148
Forestry   149

ENERGY, FUEL AND MINERAL RESOURCES ........................... 152

INDUSTRY .............................................................................. 156

TRADE ................................................................................. 158

TRANSPORT AND COMMUNICATIONS .................................... 159
    Air transport   160
    Rail transport to 1916   160
    Rail transport from 1917   163
    Road transport   166
    Water transport   166

LITERARY WORKS ABOUT SIBERIA ......................................... 168

BIBLIOGRAPHIES.................................................................... 178

ENCYCLOPAEDIAS AND REFERENCE WORKS......................... 183

PERIODICALS.......................................................................... 185

INDEX OF AUTHORS ............................................................... 187

INDEX OF TITLES ................................................................... 197

INDEX OF SUBJECTS .............................................................. 209

MAPS OF SIBERIA .................................................................. 218

# Introduction

Unlike most of the books in this series the present volume is not about a country, but about a region. There are several reasons for preparing a complete bibliography of this particular region.

For a start, the area commonly known as 'Siberia' to people outside the USSR is immense in size, occupying much of the Eurasian landmass. It stretches from the Ural mountains in the west to the Pacific Ocean in the east, from Mongolia in the south to the Arctic Ocean in the north. Its very size demands that it be accorded separate treatment. Secondly, there has never been a collection of English-language bibliographical material relating to all facets of the region. A rapid browse through the work will quickly make the reader aware of the rich and varied nature of publications available over a whole range of subject areas. Thirdly, it has become an ever more important part of the Soviet state in view of its incalculably rich natural resources and its strategically vital situation, facing as it does the United States to the north and China and Japan to the south and east.

Interestingly, Siberia also constitutes a focal point where four religious traditions (aboriginal shamanism, lamaist Buddhism, Russian Christianity and Islam) meet. Its plains and forests have been a battle-ground between three distinct socio-economic systems: the forest and tundra hunter-gatherer societies, the fluid nomad cultures of the steppes based on the rapidity of the horse, and the stolid Slavic arable farmers of the forest–steppe margins. Muscovite, Imperial Russian and Soviet domination of the region makes it a unique repository of data for the investigation of colonial and imperialist expansion.

Deep-frozen mammoth carcasses unearthed here have been found to be remarkably preserved when defrosted. The earliest Americans reached the New World from Siberia, and the many minority peoples inhabiting the area provide a fertile ground for ethnographic and linguistic investigations, especially as they are just beginning to emerge into a state of national and political activism akin to that already well developed among the indigenous peoples of the USA and Canada. Lake Baikal, the largest volume of fresh water in the world, contains numerous examples of unique flora and fauna, whose conservation is now attracting the attention of the world scientific community, not to speak of the ardent Siberian champions of this jewel of nature. A fascinating imaginative literature is just emerging, full of hints of the mystery, legend and clear pine-scented air of a land which, if properly developed, can provide adventure for tourists and mountaineers as well as data for scientists. In short, Siberia is a fascinating subject of enquiry in many areas of human experience.

Westerners generally have a very poor image of Siberia. Mere mention of the name conjures up images of ice, exile and imprisonment. It appears to have no attractive qualities at all. Of course, there is some truth in this preconception. Tsarist and particularly Soviet authorities have sent criminals and political opponents to suffer cruelly in remote camps where they have been subjected to hard labour, many dying there without graves or the benefit of family funerals. The climate is severe, especially in the northeast, with Oimyakon registering some of the lowest temperatures outside Antarctica. Yet this is only part of the story. Perceptive visitors have waxed lyrical about beauty and freshness in the dry, still air, about seemingly limitless development possibilities and about the rugged, open qualities of the Sibiryaki – the Russian-speaking inhabitants of this 'land of the future'.

Administratively speaking the region is divided into three. West Siberia comprises the region between the Ural mountains and the Enisei drainage basin. It includes the flat, rather monotonous, marshy plain of the Ob–Irtysh river system which, like the other major river systems, drains into the Arctic Ocean. There is feverish activity in its inhospitable northern region because of the immense oil and gas deposits now being exploited there. To the south it includes the Altai region, an area of fertile steppeland providing much varied agricultural produce, which merges into mountainous country whose peaks contain some of the USSR's best climbing. Westerners are just beginning to be admitted to the Altai. As I write I have heard of a school party from Britain which has been allowed to climb in the Belukha alps.

Eastern Siberia comprises the whole of the Enisei drainage basin, Lake Baikal and the Transbaikaliya region beyond it, within which lies the Buryat-Mongol Autonomous Republic, the only Buddhist region of the USSR. Mineral extraction, forestry and electricity generation based on railways and an amazing hydro-power potential are the economic basis of this region's continuing growth.

The third section of 'Siberia' is the Soviet Far East, regarded as distinct fom Siberia proper by the Soviet authorities. Its north comprises the lower Lena basin, Chukotka and Kamchatka, a region with grim memories from the days of Stalin's Kolyma gold camps, but which is now sparsely populated, life being rather marginal in its extremely continental climate. In the centre lies the Yakut Autonomous Republic, whose Turkic-speaking inhabitants were diverted northwards centuries ago during one of the great tribal migrations, and still breed cattle in this northern land today. Diamond mining, some arable activity, reindeer herding and trapping for furs diversify the Yakut economy.

To the southeast lies a most interesting zone, the Maritime Region, absorbed into the Russian Empire from China only in the mid-nineteenth century. The haunt of many fauna, such as the Ussuri tiger, and a favoured location for exotic flora such as ginseng, this zone is heavily forested with broad-leaved species in contrast to the coniferous taiga forest prevalent elsewhere in Siberia. As well as being the USSR's Pacific military and naval bastion, the Soviet Far East is strategically situated to be involved in the emerging Pacific Rim economic community, a position acknowledged by Gorbachev not only in his Vladivostok speech of 1986 but also in the declaration of special economic areas here to attract foreign investment to a region urgently needing development, and with great economic potential. As is now known, the hopes placed by Leonid Brezhnev on the Baikal–Amur railway project for revitalizing the area to the east of Baikal have not been borne out in practice, despite the heroic efforts of many Soviet workers to build it in harsh conditions. Just as in the pre-revolutionary period Siberia and the Soviet Far East seem poised to accept an influx of foreign money and expertise to exploit resources of world importance.

This bibliography is by its very nature selective. For instance, the existence of the magnificent *Arctic bibliography* (q.v.) and of H. G. R. King's bibliography of Arctic and Subarctic regions (q.v.) has made the inclusion of items specifically Arctic in nature redundant. This does not mean that peoples inhabiting areas north of the Arctic Circle have been omitted, or that references to the lower reaches of the three great river systems have been eliminated. It does mean, however, that the selection of materials has concentrated on the swathe of land from the Urals eastwards to the Pacific, including the Altai, Minusinsk, Tuva, Amur and Ussuri regions in the south, but excluding Kazakhstan and Soviet Central Asia.

Since Siberia is only a region of a larger country, I have tended to exclude works on foreign policy, even when Siberia was involved, because they often deal with central policy decisions rather than matters of regional significance.

## Introduction

Selection of materials to include has often been a problem. The majority of publications in English are concentrated in certain areas, such as travel on the Trans-Siberian Railway or participation in the Allied Intervention of 1918-22. The works are of very varied quality and interest, and it is to be hoped that the major ones have been included. Publications of a very technical nature have been omitted. In certain cases I have deliberately excluded relatively well-known works. One example is *A journey into Siberia made by order of the King of France* by Chappe D'Auteroche (London: T. Jefferys, 1770; reprint New York: Arno Press & New York Times, 1970). This work was rejected owing to the controversy surrounding its quality when originally printed; details may be found in Nerhood (q.v.) and in remarks by A. G. Cross in item 32, p. 88. Naturally, the choices will not please everyone. I ask those who may have suggestions for additions or alterations to write to me.

There are gaps in English-language coverage of many areas such as medical and educational development, communications other than rail transport, literature, urban history, handicrafts, fortifications and rural customs. English historiography of Siberia, though improving, is still very thin. It is to be hoped that the publication of this bibliography will spur on researchers in the Western world to fill these gaps and others which I have perhaps not even noticed.

It is surprising how rapidly developments occur. Since I wrote the annotation to *Sibirskaya sovetskaya entsiklopediya* (Siberian Soviet encyclopaedia) (q.v.), lamenting the non-completion of this work, I have learned through issue no. 10 (Jan. 1991) of *SUPAR report* (q.v.) that a new Siberian encyclopaedia is being prepared by the Novosibirsk Scientific-Technical Library.

The sections into which the bibliography is divided should be self-explanatory. No cross-references have been provided in the text since it should be possible to locate all relevant material by use of the indexes.

The transliteration of Russian names and terms into English is a matter fraught with difficulties. The principle adopted here is set out below.


## Transliteration

The transliteration used in this work is a simplified version of the British Standard Transliteration (BS 2979: 1958). It is similar to the Library of Congress system without diacritics, but replaces the initial 'IU' and 'IA' by 'YU' and 'YA'.

| А | A | К | K | Х | KH |
|---|---|---|---|---|---|
| Б | B | Л | L | Ц | TS |
| В | V | М | M | Ч | CH |
| Г | G | Н | N | Ш | SH |
| Д | D | О | O | Щ | SHCH |
| Е | E | П | P | Ъ | – |
| Ё | Ë | Р | R | Ы | Y |
| Ж | ZH | С | S | Ь | – |
| З | Z | Т | T | Э | E |
| И | I | У | U | Ю | YU |
| Й | I | Ф | F | Я | YA |

Titles of items included in the bibliography are given as printed in the original whether or not that accords with the transliteration scheme. Authors' names are treated in one of two different ways. The names of authors living in the Soviet Union are transliterated according to the above system, even if the publication referred to was published in translation and the name was given a different form. The names of Slavic authors living outside the USSR are cited according to their preference, even when this clashes with the transliteration scheme. For instance, Vladimir Germanovich Bogoraz is cited as Waldemar Bogoras-Tan. Russian terms in the annotations are all transliterated according to BS 2979.

The names of the many indigenous peoples inhabiting Siberia and the Soviet Far East provide no end of problems. Tsarist, Soviet and Western usage has often differed. The system used is set out below.


## Ethnonyms

The names given to the minority peoples of Siberia and the Soviet Far East by outsiders have varied over the years. In order to avoid confusion the following table has been included. The names used are, with variations to coincide with my transliteration system, based on those in *The peoples of the USSR: an ethnographic handbook* by Ronald Wixman (London: Macmillan Press, 1984). More detailed information may be found on the pages indicated. (* = name not used, refer to item in brackets following it.)

## Introduction

| Name used | Self des. | Alternative names often encountered |
|---|---|---|
| Ainu | Ainu | Kuriltsy (Wixman p. 7) |
| Altai | Altai kizhi | Altaitsy, Altaians, Oirot (Wixman p. 7-8) |
| Beltir | | Abakan Tatars (Wixman p. 25; *see* Khakass) |
| Buryat Mongols | Buriat | (Wixman p. 33-4) |
| Chukchi | Lyg Oravetlian | Luoravetlantsy (Wixman p. 48) |
| Dolgan | Dulgaan | (Wixman p. 59) |
| Eskimo | Yupigut | Eskimosy (Wixman p. 63) |
| Even | Even | Eveny, Lamut, Orochen (Wixman p. 65) |
| Evenk | Evenk | Evenki, Tungusy (Wixman p. 65) |
| Gilyak* | | (*see* Nivkh) |
| Itelmen | Itelmen | Itelmentsy, Kamchadal (Wixman p. 84) |
| Karagas* | | (*see* Tofalar) |
| Kazakh | Qazaq | Kazakhi, Kirgiz, Kirgiz-Kaisak, (Wixman p. 98-9) |
| Ket | Ket | (Y)enisei Ostyak (Wixman p. 100) |
| Khakass | Khaas | Minusinsk, Abakan or (Y)enisei Tatars (Wixman p. 101) |
| Khant | Hant | Khanty, Ob or Surgut Ostyak (Wixman p. 102) |
| Koryak | | Koriaki, Nymlyan (Wixman p. 11-12) |
| Mansi | | Vogul (Wixman p. 131) |
| Nanai | Nani | Gold(y) (Wixman p. 141-2) |

xvi

| Name used | Self des. | Alternative names often encountered |
|-----------|-----------|-------------------------------------|
| Negidal | Elkan | Negidaltsy (Wixman p. 144) |
| Nenets | Nenets, Khasava | Nentsy, Yurak Samoyed (Wixman p. 144; 172) |
| Nganasan | Nya | Tavgi Samoyed (Wixman p. 145) |
| Nivkh | Nivkh | Nivhgu, Gilyak (Wixman p. 145-6) (*see* Evenk) |
| Oroch | Nani | Orochen (Wixman p. 149-50) |
| Orok | Nani, Ulta, Ulcha | Orochen [as Orochi] (Wixman p. 150) |
| Selkup | Selkup | Osytak- or Narym-Samoyed (Wixman p. 175-6) |
| Shor | Shor | Mrass, Kondoma or Kuznetsk Tatars (Wixman p. 178) |
| Soyot* | | (*see* Buryat Mongols) |
| Telengit | | Uryankhai Kalmyk (Wixman p. 189 and *see* Altai) |
| Teleut | | Belye Kalmyki (Wixman p. 189 and *see* Altai) |
| Tungus* | | (*see* Evenk) |
| Tuvinian | Tuva | Tuvans (Wixman p. 201) |
| Udegei | Udee, Udekhe | Udegeitsy (Wixman p. 203) |
| Ulchi | Nani | Olchi (Wixman p. 209-10) |
| West Siberian Tatar } | | Tatary, Barabantsy } (Wixman p. 186-7) |
| Yakut | Sakha | (Wixman p. 219-20) |
| Yukagir | Odul | (Wixman p. 224) |

**Introduction**

The items included in the bibliography are generally monographs, chapters from books and articles from periodicals. Entries are listed alphabetically within each section according to the authors, editors or compilers, or, in their absence, by title.

The few Western periodicals directly concerned with Siberia are listed. Several others, however, include substantial numbers of articles about Siberia, and many of these are referred to in the bibliography. They are mainly journals which specialize in translating Soviet articles and publishing them in English. They include: *Arctic Anthropology, Soviet Anthropology and Archeology, Soviet Economy, Soviet Geography, Soviet Literature* and *Soviet Sociology. Polar Record*, produced by the Scott Polar Research Institute in Cambridge, England, also has a considerable Siberian content, though it obviously concentrates on regions to the north of those stressed in this bibliography.

There are naturally many Soviet periodicals relating to Siberia. Especially useful are the bibliographical publications cited in item 726, which will include the contents of all the current items mentioned below plus many more.

All the periodicals up to the era of *glasnost* were sponsored by an official body. Some are published by the Siberian Section of the Soviet Academy of Sciences or one of its off-shoots *(filialy)*. Examples of these include *Izvestiya Sibirskogo otdeleniya Akademii nauk SSSR: seriya obshchestvennykh nauk* (News of the Siberian section of the Academy of Sciences of the USSR: Series on social sciences), published in Novosibirsk, and *Trudy Instituta yazyka, literatury i istorii* (Works of the Institute of Language, Literature and History) published by the Yakut filial in Yakutsk. Other periodicals are produced by universities. An example of this is *Voprosy istorii Sibiri* (Questions of Siberian history), an irregular series which appears as separate sections of the Tomsk University *Trudy: seriya istoricheskaya* (Works: Historical series).

Teacher-training colleges also produce a range of periodicals, among which are *Uchenye zapiski Eniseiskogo gosudarstvennogo pedagogicheskogo instituta* (Learned Notes of the Eniseisk State Pedagogical Institute) and *Voprosy istorii Dalnego Vostoka* (Questions of the history of the Far East), published by the Khabarovsk Pedagogical Institute. Museums too publish journals, such as *Kraevedcheskie zapiski* (Local history notes) produced by the Kamchatka Oblast Local History Museum in Petropavlovsk-Kamchatskii and *Ezhegodnik Tyumenskogo oblastnogo kraevedcheskogo muzeya* (Annual of the Tyumen Oblast Local History Museum).

Literary journals which contain interesting journalistic items and historical material include the long-standing Novosibirsk-published *Sibirskie ogni* (Siberian Fires), *Baikal* from Ulan-Ude and *Altai,* produced in Barnaul. They are usually connected with the Soviet Union of Writers.

There is a wealth of central and regional bibliographical work relating mainly to Russian-language materials. The pre-revolutionary era is represented by V. I. Mezhov's distinguished *Sibirskaya bibliografiya* (Siberian bibliography) (St. Petersburg, 1891-92. 3 vols) and its continuation *Materialy dlya bibliografii Sibiri* (Materials for the bibliography of Siberia) by S. N. Mameev (Tobolsk, 1892-94. 2 vols). The early post-revolutionary period is represented by works such as *Bibliografiya Prieniseiskogo kraya. Sistematicheskii ukazatel knig i statei na russkom i inostrannykh yazykakh, opublikovannykh s 1612 po 1923g. vklyuchitelno* (The bibliography of the Prienisei region. A systematic bibliography of books and articles in Russian and foreign languages published from 1612 to 1923 inclusively) by V. P. Kosovanov (Krasnoyarsk, 1923. 2 vols), *Obzor istochnikov po istorii Priamurya i Okhotsko-kamchatskogo kraya* (A review of sources on the history of Priamure and the Okhotsk-Kamchatka region) by V. A. Grachev, *Trudy Dalnevostochnogo universiteta,* seriya iii, no. 5 (1927) and 'Materialy dlya bibliografii Sibiri. Bibliograficheskii perechen statei po voprosam narodnogo khozyaistva Sibiri v periodicheskikh izdaniyakh 1891-1900gg.' (Materials for the bibliography of Siberia. A bibliographical survey of articles on Siberian economic questions in periodical publications, 1891-1900) by Mark K. Azadovskii in *Ocherki po zemledeliyu i ekonomike vostochnoi Sibiri* (Essays on the agriculture and economics of eastern Siberia) (Irkutsk, 1926), p. 153–67.

Later Soviet bibliographical work may be represented by works such as *Bibliografichekii ukazatel rabot po istorii, arkheologii i etnografii Dalnego Vostoka* (Bibliographical index of works on the history, archaeology and ethnography of the Far East) (Vladivostok, 1980) and *Novaya literatura o Kamchatskoi oblasti: tekushchii ukazatel literatury* (New literature about Kamchatka oblast: a continuing index of literature) which appears quarterly in Petropavlovsk-Kamchatskii.

Consequently, it is in theory easy to find out about publications on Siberia and the Soviet Far East in Russian. The problems with the post-revolutionary bibliographical materials mentioned above, however, are twofold. Firstly, they are produced in very small print runs, sufficient in general only for the official agencies and libraries in the USSR which subscribe to them, hence being difficult to obtain in the West. Secondly, they are often produced in a very primitive manner because the issuing agencies do not have decent technology available to them, and the paper employed is of low quality. They are sometimes bound with staples which restrict page opening, thus making the entries difficult to see, which rather defeats the object. Despite these problems I would like to thank the bibliographers of Siberia for their marvellous diligence in collecting and collating such a wide range of information.

*Acknowledgements*
I should like to thank the staff of many libraries, including the British Library in London, the British Library Document Supply Centre at Boston Spa, Yorkshire, the Scott Polar Research Institute and University Library in Cambridge, the Bodleian Library in Oxford, the Birmingham and Glasgow University Libraries, the Library of the School of Slavonic and East European Studies at London University, the City of Leeds Central Reference Library and Calgary University Library, whose Arctic Institute of North America collection was extremely useful. Above all, my heartfelt thanks to the Librarian of the Brotherton Library at Leeds University, Mr Reg Carr, to Mike Gollop, John Porter and the ever patient and helpful Inter Library Loans service, and in particular Mrs Pat Shute.

Some years ago the British Academy was kind enough to provide me with a grant towards the cost of travelling to conduct work in some of these libraries for another project which helped towards this one. My thanks to them. They provide one of the few lifelines available for researchers in the humanities who have so much difficulty in finding funds to pursue their relatively cheap projects. Had the University of Leeds Registrar not granted me periods of study leave the completion of this work would have been impossible. Thanks also to Dr Bob Neville of Clio Press at whose instigation I undertook this arduous but rewarding task.

Finally, I wish to express my gratitude to Chris, James and Rachel who have been very tolerant when much of my time has been spent hammering away at the word-processor in the study.

*David N. Collins*
*University of Leeds*
*April 1991*

# General Works

1 **Notes on the origin of the name Siberia.**
Anatole V. Baikalov. *Slavonic and East European Review*, vol. 29
(Dec. 1950), p. 287-9.
Having studied possible etymologies of the word 'Siberia', first encountered in a
written Chinese source in 1206 AD, the author concludes that it is composed of two
Turkic words: *su* (water) and *berr* or *birr* (a wild unpopulated land) both of which are
common in Turkic and Mongol languages.

2 **Soviet Asia.**
Raymond Arthur Davies, Andrew J. Steiger. London: Victor
Gollancz, 1943. 205p. maps. bibliog.
This account, by authors sympathetic to the Soviets, informs Americans about the
economic geography of lesser-known regions of their wartime ally's territory. Though
propagandistic, the detail it provides on agriculture, transport, social conditions and
industrial production is valuable. Cheerful accounts of conversations with locals and
poems honouring Stalin contrast the new 'democratic' Siberia with the misery of
Tsarist times. Relevant chapters cover Western Siberia, Yakutiya, Buryatiya, the Far
East, and Siberia's role in world affairs.

3 **Frozen Asia: a sketch of modern Siberia, together with an account of the
native tribes inhabiting that region.**
Charles H. Eden. London: Society for the Propagation of Christian
Knowledge, 1879. 320p. map.
Though dated, this account is valuable in showing us the extent of knowledge of
Siberia in Victorian Britain. It covers geography, natural and political history, the
economy and the indigenous peoples.

## General Works

### 4 Glimpses of Siberia.
Compiled by Nikolai Yanovskii. Moscow: Progress Publishers, 1972. 263p.

Provides translations of articles on the geography and economic development of Siberia by Soviet contributors to the journal *Sibirskie ogni* (Siberian Fires). Similar in its intent to give the Western reader an officially approved account of conditions under 'developed socialism' is *Siberia – land of great prospects* by Nikolai Alekseevich Meisak (Moscow: Novosti Press Agency, 1967). See also his *This warm Siberia* (Moscow: Novosti Press Agency, 1973. 63p.).

### 5 Handbook of Siberia and Arctic Russia.
Compiled by the Geographical Section of the Naval Intelligence Section, Naval Staff, Admiralty. London: Oxford University Press, 1918-20. 3 vols. maps.

Volume 1 presents a general survey of Siberian geography, flora and fauna, indigenous tribes, history, religion, diseases, agriculture, timber, minerals, industry, administration, transport and telegraph system. Volume 2 provides detailed information on West Siberia with road and rail routes and plans of the main towns. Volume 3 does the same for East Siberia and the Far East. It is illustrative of the level of development on the eve of revolution and civil war.

### 6 Siberia.
Pierre Rondière, adapted from a translation by Charles Duff. London: Constable, 1966. 205p. map.

A rapid sketch of historical events leads into glimpses of life in Novosibirsk, Akademgorodok, the Kuzbas, Irkutsk and Yakutiya. A visit to the Bratsk hydroelectric project and Lake Baikal and a section on advice to tourists complete this relatively lightweight eye-witness account of contrasts in the mid-sixties. An earlier but similar combination of travel book and historical introduction is provided in Emil Lengyel's *Secret Siberia* (London: Robert Hale, 1947, also published by the Travel Book Club, 1948. 285p.) which covers the geography, discovery and settlement of Siberia, railway construction, the Tsarist exile system, 1917 and the civil war, economic development under Stalin, and has vignettes on the Buryats, and Birobidzhan Jews.

### 7 Siberia: the new frontier.
George St. George. London: Hodder & Stoughton, 1970. 374p. maps.

Fond memories of life as a child in Irkutsk before the Revolution led the author back to Siberia in the 1960s. Personal impressions and conversations with local inhabitants make for a lively text. There are sections on geographical discovery, history and shamanism, women workers and education. Though wide-ranging and vivid the account tends to be overly sympathetic to the official Soviet view.

8    **The land beyond the mountains. Siberia and its people today.**
Leonid Iosifovich Shinkarëv, prepared by the Novosti Press Agency
Publishing House, Moscow.    London: Hart-Davis, MacGibbon, 1973.
246p. maps. bibliog.

A Soviet journalist with lengthy service in Siberia presents an illustrated account of its
discovery and settlement under the Tsars, and its subsequent industrial and social
development under the Soviets, projecting a glorious future by 2000 AD. This account
is enthusiastically written, with a wealth of circumstantial detail. In the same vein of
popular journalism is *Siberia and the Soviet Far East* by Abraham Resnick (Moscow:
Novosti Press Agency Publishing House, 1983; Hudson, Wisconsin: Gem Publications,
[*c.* 1985]).

9    **The Soviet north: present development and prospects.**
Samuil Venediktovich Slavin, translated from the Russian by Don
Danemaris.    Moscow: Progress Publishers, 1972. 194p. maps.

This book by a veteran Soviet Arctic specialist provides a semi-popular account of
recent developments. Kamchatka, Chukotka, the Enisei region and Yakutiya are
treated in detail. The state of the economy and transport are highlighted. The Russian
version from which the translation was made has been superseded by a second edition,
published by the Soviet Academy of Sciences in 1982.

10    **The new Siberia.**
Howard Sochurek, photographs by Howard Sochurek and John de
Visser.    St. Paul, Minnesota: EMC Corporation, [*c.* 1975]. 4 vols.

The unique set of colour illustrations in these four small-format volumes provides the
basis for an account of life in Siberia during the 1970s.

11    **Siberia and the Soviet Far East: strategic dimensions in multinational
perspective.**
Edited by Rodger Swearingen.    Stanford, California: Hoover
Institution Press, 1987. 298p. bibliog.

Contains nine essays among which are contributions on the communications
infrastructure by Victor L. Mote; on energy by Thane Gustafson; on trade and high
technology by Michael J. Bradshaw; and on military developments by Harry Gelman.
An important last chapter by Pat Polansky, a Slavic librarian at the University of
Hawaii, provides a profile of resources for research on the area.

12    **Siberia: problems and prospects for regional development.**
Edited by Alan Wood.    Beckenham, England: Croom Helm; New
York: Barnes & Noble, 1987. 233p. maps. bibliog.

The British Universities Siberian Studies Seminar (BUSSS) holds conferences on all
aspects of Siberian affairs. This series of essays by Anglo-American participants was its
first joint foray into print apart from the occasional reports of its conferences, entitled
*Sibirica* (q.v.). The book begins with geographical and historical overviews by Denis
Shaw and Alan Wood. It continues with detailed investigations of economic resources
by the late Theodore Shabad; transport and communications by Robert North; the
Baikal–Amur railway by the late Violet Conolly; military matters by John Erickson;

and papers on Siberia's role in the Pacific and world affairs by Stuart Kirby and John Stephan.

13  **The development of Siberia: people and resources.**
    Edited by Alan Wood, R. Anthony French.   London: Macmillan, in
    association with the School of Slavonic and East European Studies,
    1989. 266p. maps. bibliog.

Presents the papers of the 1986 BUSSS meeting. Three are historical (the seventeenth-century exile of the Old Believer priest Avvakum by Alan Wood; comparisons between J.-G. Gmelin and G.-F. Müller as reporters of scientific investigations by Larry Black; and the Orthodox Church's Mission to the Altai by David Collins [q.v.]). Four are about indigenous peoples: a general account of their status in the twentieth century by James Forsyth leads into a study of urbanization of the northern minorities by S. Savoskul, a Soviet ethnographer, to be followed by sections on the Oroks by Alfred Majewicz and the Buryat Mongols by Caroline Humphrey. The final five papers about current developments include a study of Siberian social problems by Tatyana Zaslavskaya, prominent in the critique of Soviet society which lay behind Gorbachev's reforms; a study of labour problems by John Sallnow; the role of water transport by Robert North; exploration for oil and gas by David Wilson; and a speculation by Theodore Shabad as to whether Gorbachev was turning away from Siberian development.

14  **Asiatic Russia.**
    George Frederick Wright.   New York: McClure, Phillips, 1902;
    London: Eveleigh Nash, 1903. maps. 2 vols.

Though much of the information on geography, geology, flora and fauna, climate, history, minority peoples, communications and the exile system which this book contains is obtainable elsewhere, it has some fascinating insights into the life of Old Believer settlers, the rural commune, Siberian homes and farming, the political structure of west and east Siberia and the Amur. The speculation about Siberia's capacity for development is lofty; the photographs taken by the author are unusual records in themselves.

# Travellers' Accounts

## Up to 1800

15 **Bering's expeditions.**
Terence Armstrong. In: *Studies in Russian Historical Geography*, no. 1, edited by James Bater, R. French. London: Academic Press, 1983, p. 175-95. maps. bibliog.
In the light of Soviet archival research the author presents a critical analysis of 'the scope and effectiveness' of Bering's First and Second Kamchatka Expeditions, from 1725 to 1743. Stress is laid on investigation of the Siberian landmass, which is often ignored in favour of the Pacific sea discoveries. More general accounts of travellers in Siberia appear in John Massey Stewart's 'Early travellers, explorers and naturalists in Siberia' (*Asian Affairs*, vol. 15 [OS vol. 71], part 1 [Feb. 1984], p. 55-64); 'The British in Siberia' (*Asian Affairs*, vol. 10 [OS vol. 66], part 2 [June 1979], p. 132-43) and 'Britain's Siberian connection' in *Siberia: two historical perspectives* by John Massey Stewart and Alan Wood (London: Great Britain–USSR Association/School of Slavonic and East European Studies, 1984, p. 1-21).

16 **The Life written by himself. With the study of V. V. Vinogradov.**
Archpriest Avvakum, translations, annotations, commentary, and a historical introduction by Kenneth N. Brostrom. Ann Arbor, Michigan: University of Michigan, 1979. 278p. bibliog. (Michigan Slavic Translations, no. 4).
Presents a richly illustrated and heavily annotated translation of the autobiography of the seventeenth-century Russian priest Avvakum Petrovich (1620/21-1682). In 1653 he was exiled to Siberia for schismatic activities, and from 1656 to 1662 acted as chaplain to Pashkov's Dauriya (Amur) expedition. His lyrical depiction of scenery and fauna contrasts markedly with his description of torment at the hand of his cruel master.

17 **A Journey from St. Petersburg to Pekin, 1719-22, by John Bell of Antermony.**
John Bell, edited with an introduction by J. L. Stevenson. Edinburgh: Edinburgh University Press, 1965. 248p. maps.

The Scottish physician John Bell, a keen observer of people and objects, made a valuable record of impressions on his journey through Siberia, via Tobolsk, Irkutsk and Selenginsk to China. This work, part of his *Travels from St. Petersburg in Russia to diverse parts of Asia* (2 vols. London, 1763), has been expertly edited and provided with suitable illustrations and maps. Roughly a hundred pages are relevant to Siberia.

18 **The memoirs and travels of Mauritius Augustus Count de Benyowsky in Siberia, Kamchatka, Japan, the Liukiu Islands and Formosa.**
Maurycy August Beniowski, translated from the original manuscript. London: G. G. J. & J. Robinson, 1790. 2 vols. Other English editions: Dublin, 1790; London, 1893, 1898 and 1904.

The unlikely adventures of a Hungarian nobleman (1741-86) who was captured by the Russians when serving in the Polish army. Exiled, he travelled through Siberia in the 1770s via Tobolsk, Tomsk, Krasnoyarsk, Yakutsk and Okhotsk to Kamchatka whence he escaped to Macao. The best edition is that edited by Pasfield Oliver (London: Fisher Unwin, 1893. 399p.) which has a lengthy introduction subjecting Benyowsky's claims to minute scrutiny.

19 **G.-F. Müller and the Imperial Russian Academy.**
J. Lawrence Black. Kingston, Montreal: McGill-Queen's University Press, 1986. 290p. map.

Chapter 3 of this scholarly biography of a noted eighteenth-century German historian of Siberia and avid collector of Siberiana is devoted to his exploits in that region. Other relevant publications include *G.-F. Müller and Siberia, 1733-43*, edited by J. Lawrence Black and D. K. Buse, translation of German materials by Victoria Joan Moessner (Kingston, Ontario; Fairbanks, Alaska: Limestone Press, 1989. 174p. [Russia and Asia, no. 1]). An introduction about Müller's Siberian career leads in to a publication of six lengthy contemporary documents. See also Black's 'G.-F. Müller and the Russian Academy of Sciences contingent in the Second Kamchatka Expedition' (*Canadian Slavonic Papers*, vol. 25, no. 2 [June 1983], p. 235-52) and pages 35-49 of the paper referred to in item 13.

20 **A journal of the embassy from their majesties John and Peter Alexievits, Emperors of Muscovy &c., over land into China, through the provinces of Ustiugha, Siberia, Dauri, and the Great Tartary to Peking, the capital city of the Chinese Empire, by Everard Isbrand, their ambassador, in the years 1693, 1694, and 1695.**
Adam Brand, translated from the German by H. W. Ludolf. London: D. Brown and T. Goodwin, 1698. 134p.

The German secretary to Ambassador Evert Ysbrantszoon Ides outlines the journey through Siberia to China. Though slight, the descriptions of native peoples, travel problems and Muscovite forts, such as Nerchinsk, have an air of interested authenticity. Pages 29-66 and 108-17 are relevant.

21  **The Transbaikalian routes to China as known to or explored by Nikolaie Milescu (Spathary), 1675.**
G. I. Constantin.  *Studia et Acta Orientalia* (Bucharest), no. 1 (1957), p. 83-119.
The author assesses the information available to the Moldavian, known to the Russians as Nikolai Spafarii, who was employed by the Muscovite state on an embassy to China in 1676.

22  **A Siberian journey: the journal of Hans Jakob Fries, 1774-1776.**
Hans Jakob Fries, translated from the German and edited with a bibliographical introduction by Walther Kirchner.  London: Frank Cass, 1974. 183p. maps. bibliog. (Russia Through European Eyes, no. 20).
The editor discovered this valuable first-hand account by a Swiss doctor in Zurich Central Library and published it in German in 1955. The English edition is to be welcomed for enabling a wider audience to read Fries, but in some ways the really valuable material may be found in the bibliographical introduction, which contains excellently annotated information on travel accounts relating to central Siberia from 1725 to 1825 – these are omitted from this present bibliography because they are not in English. One of these is *Reise durch Sibirien, von dem Jahr 1733 bis 1743* by Johann Georg Gmelin (Göttingen, 1751-2), an annotated English version of which is at present (1991) being prepared for publication in the Oregon Historical Society Press North Pacific Studies Series, edited by Peter A. McGraw.

23  **Three years travels from Moscow over-land to China thro' Great Ustiga, Siriania, Permia, Sibiria, Daour, Great Tartary etc. to Peking.**
Evert Ysbrantszoon Ides.  London: Printed for W. Freeman, 1706. 110p. map.
This volume consists of notes by the Ambassador sent to China by Peter the Great in 1693 – a Dutchman, E. Isbrants Ides – and is translated from the Dutch. Chapters 2-10 and 18-20 depict sights, towns and customs observed during travel to and from China, together with curiosities such as the remains of mammoths and data on the fur trade.

24  **The most remarkable year in the life of Augustus von Kotzebue; containing an account of his exile into Siberia, and of the other extraordinary events which happened to him in Russia.**
August Friedrich Ferdinand von Kotzebue, translated from the German by the Revd B. Beresford.  London: Richard Phillips, 1802. 3 vols.
Also published in *Sketch of the life and literary career of Augustus von Kotzebue*. London: Printed for Hunt & Clarke, 1827. 2 vols.
(Autobiography: a Collection of the most Instructive and Amusing Lives ever Published, vols 9-10).
The German poet and dramatist August von Kotzebue (1761-1819) was arrested and sent to Siberia during a visit to Russia in 1800. He was despatched to Tobolsk and Kurgan, but after several months was released. The book was a 'best-seller' in its day. A curiosity is his *Count Benyowsky, or the conspiracy of Kamtschatka, a tragi-comedy in five acts*, translated from the German by W. Render (Cambridge: printed for the author, 1798) and also translated by Benjamin Thompson (London, 1801).

7

25  **John Ledyard's journey through Russia and Siberia, 1787-1788.**
John Ledyard. The journal and selected letters edited with an
introduction by Stephen D. Watrous.  Madison, Wisconsin; Milwaukee,
Wisconsin; London: University of Wisconsin Press, 1966. 293p. maps.
bibliog.

John Ledyard (1751-89), an American, decided to travel across Eurasia to Kamchatka,
then across the Bering Straits to the USA. Having reached Yakutsk he was arrested
and sent back the way he had come. His journal was first published in *Travels and
adventures of John Ledyard*, edited by Jared Sparks (London: Richard Bentley, 1834).
The helpful introduction to this scholarly edition includes a biography, a study of
eighteenth-century Siberia, a discussion of editing problems and a critical investigation
of the journey's importance. Forty-eight letters and documents relating to the
expedition are included.

26  **Travels in Kamtschatka during the years 1787 and 1788.**
Jean Baptiste Barthélemey de Lesseps.  London: J. Johnson, 1790.
2 vols. Reprinted New York: Arno Press, 1970.

Baron de Lesseps (1766-1834), carrying despatches from La Pérouse's expedition
across Siberia to Paris, provides vivid and well-observed impressions of travel and life
in Kamchatka, Okhotsk, and across Siberia. This is a translation from the French
original.

27  **A naturalist in Russia: Letters from Peter Simon Pallas to Thomas
Pennant.**
Peter Simon Pallas, edited by Carol Urness.  Minneapolis, Minnesota:
University of Minnesota Press, 1967. 189p. map. bibliog.

Consists of a series of perceptive letters from the noted German explorer and naturalist
Peter Pallas (1741-1811) to Thomas Pennant (1726-98), published from the James Ford
Bell Collection in Minnesota University Library. Information about Pallas may be
found in 'Bering's successors: contributions of Peter Simon Pallas to the history of
Russian exploration towards Alaska' by James R. Masterson and Helen Brower
(*Pacific North West Quarterly*, vol. 38 [1947] p. 35-83 and 109-55), a heavily annotated
set of translations of material collected by Pallas, which relate to North Pacific voyages
rather than Siberia.

28  **An account of a geographical and astronomical expedition to the northern
parts of Russia performed by Commodore Joseph Billings, in the years
1785, &c. to 1794, the whole narrated from the original papers.**
Martin Sauer.  London: for T. Cadell and W. Davies, 1802. 332p.
maps. Reprinted with an introduction by Kenneth L. Holmes,
Richmond, England: Richmond Publishing Co., 1972.

The secretary to Catherine II's expedition sent out in response to voyages by Cook and
La Pérouse, writes a detailed account of travel to and from Russia through Siberia and
Kamchatka. He covers the native peoples, flora and fauna, and provisioning problems.
Some linguistic material is included in appendices. Also relating to the Billings
Expedition are *Account of a voyage of dicovery to the north-east of Siberia, the frozen
ocean and the north-east sea* by Gavriil Andreevich Sarychev (2 vols. London, 1806-7)
and *Siberia and northwestern America, 1788-1792: the journal of Carl Heinrich Merck,*

*naturalist with the Russian scientific expedition led by captains Joseph Billings and Gavriil Sarychev*, translated by Fritz Jaensch; edited, with an introduction, by Richard A. Pierce (Kingston, Ontario: Limestone Press, 1980. 215p. maps).

29  **An historico-geographical description of the north and eastern parts of Europe and Asia, but more particularly of Russia, Siberia and Great Tartary.**
Phillip Johann von Strahlenberg.   London: J. Brotherton, 1738. 463p. map. Reprinted New York: Arno Press & New York Times, 1970.
An account by a Swede (1676-93) who accompanied Daniel Messerschmidt (1685-1735) on a scientific investigation of western and central Siberia in the 1720s. The latter's account, sadly never translated into English, was of immense importance. Von Strahlenberg's book, translated from a German edition of 1730, contains much linguistic, ethnographic, geographical and military data. The German version was reprinted with an English introduction by John R. Krueger in *Studia Uralo-Altaica*, no. 8 (1975).

30  **Across Siberia in the dragon year of 1796.**
Tamai Kisaku, edited by Stewart Culin.   *Asia*, no. 20 (June 1920).
Though I have not been able to consult this work I have included it as the first Japanese account of Siberia translated into English. It concerns four shipwrecked Japanese who were sent to Irkutsk in 1796, and years later were allowed to return home via St Petersburg and a round-the-world voyage.

31  **The American expedition.**
Sven Waxell, with an introduction and note by M. A. Michael, translated from Johan Skalberg's Danish version 'Vitus Berings eventyrlige opdagefoerd 1733-1743' by M. A. Michael.   London: Hodge, 1952; New York: Collier, 1962. 236p. maps.
A thoughtful eye-witness account of the effects of the Second Kamchatka Expedition on the natives of Kamchatka, this book by a Swedish companion of Vitus Bering contains valuable information about the Itelmen in the 1730s.

# From 1800 to 1916

32 **The British in northern Siberia in the nineteenth century.**
Terence Armstrong. In Горски виЈенац *(Sylvan garland): a garland of essays offered to Professor Elizabeth Mary Hill*, edited by R. Auty, L. R. Lewitter, A. P. Vlasto. Cambridge: Modern Humanities Research Association, 1970, p. 12-23. (Publications of the Modern Humanities Research Association, no. 2).

A well-known investigator of the northern USSR employed by the Scott Polar Research Institute in Cambridge presents details of British travellers who entered 'his bit' of Siberia during the nineteenth century. This work is particularly useful, since it includes some items omitted from the present bibliography.

33 **Dersu the trapper.**
Vladimir Klavdievich Arsenev, translated from the Russian by Malcolm Burr. London: Martin Secker & Warburg, 1939. 351p. maps.

This is a very lively account by a renowned explorer and anthropologist (1872-1930) of three expeditions undertaken in the Russian Far East with Dersu Uzala, a guide from an indigenous tribe. Arsenev was fascinated by the character and lifestyle of the native, who had survived encounters with bears and trapped tigers. The tale inspired the Japanese film director Kurosawa to make an Oscar-winning film. A translation into English entitled *Dersu Uzala* has also been published in Moscow by the Foreign Languages Publishing House, [n.d.].

34 **Recollections of the Tartar steppes and their inhabitants.**
Lucy Atkinson. London: John Murray, 1863. 351p.

Consists of a vivid and honest set of recollections by the wife of a British traveller about her experiences in Siberia from 1848 to 1853. There is a good deal about political exiles, some of whom she met and with whom she sympathized. The book was reprinted, with an introduction by Professor Anthony Cross which provided revealing biographical details about Mrs Atkinson and her husband (London: Frank Cass, 1972 [Russia Through European Eyes, no. 14]).

35 **Oriental and western Siberia: a narrative of seven years' explorations and adventures in Siberia, Mongolia, the Kirghis steppes, Chinese Tartary, and part of Central Asia.**
Thomas Witlam Atkinson. London: Hurst and Blackett, 1858; Philadelphia: Bradley, 1859. 611p. map. Reprinted New York: Arno Press, 1970. 533p. maps.

Atkinson (1799-1861), an English architect and painter, travelled nearly 40,000 miles in the eastern regions of the Russian Empire leaving an impressive memorial of his trip in the form of this book. A considerable portion of it deals with his wanderings and meetings with native peoples in the mountainous Altai region of southwest Siberia and the steppes of present-day Kazakhstan. Coloured lithographs and monochrome wood-engravings of his paintings are included.

10

36  **Travels in the regions of the upper and lower Amoor and the Russian acquisitions on the confines of India and China, with adventures among the mountain Kirghis and the Manjours, Manyargs, Toungoutz, Goldi and Gelyaks: the hunting and pastoral tribes.**
Thomas Witlam Atkinson.  London: Hurst & Blackett; New York: Harper, 1860. 496p. map. 2nd ed., London, 1861. Reprinted New York: Arno Books & New York Times, 1971.
There are doubts as to whether Atkinson actually did travel along the lower Amur River (see the Introduction to the reprint of the previous entry – item 35). The book has little of the immediacy of his earlier account, or of his wife's. However, it does provide information about the geography and peoples of Transbaikalia and the sources of the Amur, which were little known in Europe. Some of his data were gleaned from Russian works.

37  **A visit to Karaginski Island, Kamchatka.**
Gerald Edwin Barrett-Hamilton, H. O. Jones.  *Geographical Journal*, vol. 12 (Sept. 1898), p. 280-99. map.
Notes taken during a brief visit to an island off the northeast coast of Kamchatka in 1897 enabled the authors to provide a surprisingly detailed account of the lifestyle of the local Itelmen population, and the island's flora and fauna. The photographs are a valuable historical document in themselves. See also the first author's more general article 'Kamchatka', *Magazine of the Royal Scottish Geographical Society*, vol. 15 (1889), p. 225-56.

38  **The Russian advance.**
Albert Jeremiah Beveridge.  New York: Harper, 1904. 485p.
Reprinted, with an introduction by Harry Schwartz, New York: Praeger, 1970.
One of many Americans who travelled on the Trans-Siberian Railway and reported about this 'highway of Russian advance', Indiana senator Beveridge was concerned about the international implications of Russia's penetration of Manchuria. Another American tourist who left a fine photographic record was Michael Myers Shoemaker, whose *The Great Siberian Railway from St. Petersburg to Pekin* was published in 1903 (New York; London: Putnam. 243p.).

39  **Siberia and central Asia.**
John Wesley Bookwalter.  New York: Frederick A. Stokes, 1899; London: C. Arthur Pearson, 1900. 548p. map.
In 1898, John Wesley Bookwalter, an Ohio businessman, had made a pilgrimage similar to Beveridge's, leaving an account replete with detail and his own photographs. There is much information on the hardships of rail and road travel and the need to improve transport in general. There are sections on Tomsk and on agriculture. Chapter twelve on peasant life is particularly illuminating, capturing the rural life of that epoch in an engaging manner.

40 **Among prisoners of war in Russia and Siberia.**
Elsa Brändström, translated from the German by C. Mabel Richmers.
London: Hutchinson, 1929. 284p.
Being a daughter of the Swedish ambassador to Russia, the authoress lived there from
1908 to 1920. She joined the Swedish/Danish Red Cross and helped prisoners of war
along the Trans-Siberian Railway. The book is now a bibliographical rarity as is her
biography, Maria Dehn's *Elsa Brandström, der Engel von Sibirien (1888-1948)*
(Stuttgart: Verlag Junge Gemeinde, 1955. 23p.).

41 **Russian life today.**
Herbert Bury.  London: Mowbrays, 1915. 270p.
An Anglican bishop with a vast diocese visits his flock in and around the Urals in a
Panhard car during 1912-13. Graphic descriptions are provided of the terrors of travel
in the unsprung Russian tarantass [four-wheeled vehicle] and the beauty of the steppes.
It is too complimentary to Nicholas II and the Tsarist exile system. John Sheepshanks,
a bishop in the same region earlier on, wrote *My life in Mongolia and Siberia, from the
great wall of China to the Ural mountains* (London: Christian Knowledge Society, 1903.
175p.).

42 **Reindeer, dogs and snow shoes. A journal of Siberian travel and
explorations made in the years 1865, 1866 and 1867.**
Richard J. Bush.  New York: Harper, 1871. 529p. map. Reprinted New
York: Arno Press & New York Times, 1970.
A member of an American expedition surveying the route for a trans-world telegraph
line (it reached no further than Telegraph Creek in British Columbia because a
transatlantic cable had rendered it redundant), Bush provides us with a very readable
account of wildlife, Russian and native settlements and travel conditions. He is critical
of Orthodox clergy who always seem drunk. Another account of the expedition was
left by Thomas W. Knox: *Overland through Asia: pictures of Siberian, Chinese and
Tartar life.* (Hartford, Connecticut: American Publishing Co., 1870. 608p. Reprinted
New York: Arno Press & New York Times, 1970). Like George Kennan (q.v.) Knox
mounts a severe critique of Tsarist treatment of exiles.

43 **The Island: a journey to Sakhalin.**
Anton Pavlovich Chekhov, translated by Luba and Michael Terpak,
introduction by Irina Ratushinskaya.  London: Century Hutchinson,
1987. 374p. map.
This translation of the Russian playwright's account of prison conditions on Sakhalin
Island, compiled after his visit there in 1890, is unfortunately somewhat stodgy. 'A
cross between a personal memoir and a lumbering sociological monograph', the book
reveals little of the real Chekhov. Happily Avraham Yarmolinsky has translated and
edited two other sources about the episode. The first, in *The unknown Chekhov:
stories and other writings* (London: Peter Owen, 1959), is a record of the journey
'Across Siberia' (p. 267-308) written for a St Petersburg newspaper. The second, in
*Letters of Anton Chekhov* (London: Jonathan Cape, 1974, p. 141-68), contains letters
written between May and October 1890. More detail may be gleaned from David
Magarshak's *Chekhov – a life* (London: Faber & Faber, 1952, p. 189-221) and Ernest
J. Simmons's *Chekhov – a biography* (London: Jonathan Cape, 1963), which also
includes a map of the journey. 'Chekhov's far eastern Scotsman' by Peter Barlow

(*Scottish Slavonic Review*, no. 8 [spring 1987], p. 7-15) identifies a Scot, Denbigh, living in Sakhalin whom Chekhov had known as 'Dembi'.

44 **Narrative of a pedestrian journey through Russia and Siberian Tartary to the frontiers of China and the Frozen Sea performed during the years 1820, 1821, and 1823.**
John Dundas Cochrane. London: John Murray, 1823. 560p. Several editions appeared in London and Philadelphia in 1824 and 1825, and Edinburgh, 1829. A reprint was published in New York by the Arno Press & New York Times in 1970. There was also an an abridged version, edited and with an introduction by Mervyn Horder (London: Folio Society, 1983. 217p.).

Chapters 5 onwards of this eccentric's account deal with western Siberia, Yakutiya, Chukotka, Okhotsk and the Kurils. There is some useful information on local customs, but he is not always well informed.

45 **Siberian journey down the Amur to the Pacific, 1856-1857. A new edition of *A voyage down the Amoor*.**
Perry McDonough Collins, edited with an introduction by Charles Vevier. Madison, Wisconsin: University of Wisconsin Press, 1962. 370p. maps. bibliog.

Acting for the United States government the author made a trip to Russia's newly acquired Amur river territory assessing its commercial possibilities. His proposal for a railway linking the town of Chita with the river was among the earliest rail schemes mooted for Siberia. The first edition of the book was published in New York by Appletons in 1860; a second edition came out in 1864. The 1962 publication contains a scholarly introduction which places Collins's trip in the context of Murav'ëv-Amurskii's forward policy with regard to China, and gives details of the transcontinental telegraph line in which Collins was involved. There is also a note on sources which explains how and why the original edition has been recast.

46 **Overland to China.**
Archibald Ross Colquhoun. New York, London: Harpers, 1900. 465p. maps.

A colonial administrator and special correspondent of *The Times* in the Far East who visited the region in 1898-99 discusses the revolutionary effects of the Trans-Siberian Railway. This is more historical geography than travelogue. The first third of the book surveys the settlement, government, and economic development of Siberia from the seventeenth century to 1900. See also his 'The Trans-Siberian–Manchurian Railway' (*Royal United Service Institution Journal*, vol. 44 [Dec. 1900], p. 1408-30).

47 **Recollections of Siberia in the years 1840 and 1841.**
Charles Herbert Cottrell. London: John W. Parker, 1842. 410p. map.

Consists of an account of a British businessman's tour to Irkutsk in 1840-41. There are references to Biisk in the Altai, Yakutiya, Kyakhta, and the expected sorry tales of travel and exiles. Though inferior to S. Hill's *Travels* (q.v.) it has been included because few Europeans travelled in Siberia at this time. Another traveller was Sir

George Simpson (1787-1860), manager in Canada of the Hudson's Bay Company from 1821, the second volume of whose *Narrative of a journey round the world during the years 1841 and 1842* (2 vols. London: Colburn, 1847) contains the perceptive comments of a man with years of experience in an area similar to Siberia.

48  **My Siberian year.**
Mary Antoinette Czaplicka.   London: Mills & Boon; New York, Oxford University Press, 1916. 315p. map.

Contains the personal record of a year's fieldwork carried out by an anthropologist from Oxford at Golchikha on the lower reaches of the Enisei river. There is a great deal of ethnographical information, including a section on the southern Enisei Ket and the Minusinsk Basin, written in a narrative form which finds its way in more formal style into her *Aboriginal Siberia* (q.v.). A photograph opposite page seven includes two of her companions, Dora Curtis and Maude Haviland. The former published a short account of her experiences in 'When ignorance was bliss: July and August in north central Siberia' (*The Nineteenth Century and After*, vol. 77 [March 1915], p. 609-30), whereas Maude Haviland, an ornithologist, produced a book, *A summer on the Yenesei*, in which her prose descriptions of the birds and flowers bring the tundra to life. This was published in London by Edward Arnold in 1915 (340p.), and reprinted in New York by the Arno Press and New York Times in 1971.

49  **A shooting trip to Kamchatka.**
Elim Pavlovich Demidov, Prince di San Donato.   London: Rowland Ward, 1904. 302p. maps.

A brief history of Kamchatka and a sketch of the transcontinental railway trip leads into a detailed record of hunting game in Kamchatka. There are effective descriptions of the wild scenery, and over a hundred clear photographs. The account of an earlier hunting trip may be found in his *After wild sheep in the Altai and Mongolia* (London: Rowland Ward, 1900. 324p. map) which concentrates on the Siberian argali (*Ovis ammon*) and is well illustrated.

50  **Siberia as it is.**
Harry de Windt.   London: Chapman & Hall, 1892. 504p.

An assiduous recorder of travel impressions, Harry de Windt (1856-1933) was requested by the Russian government to investigate Siberia's penal system (see his *From Pekin to Calais by land*. London: Chapman & Hall, 1889. 656p.). He travelled thither in 1890, coming to conclusions whose apparent whitewashing of the authorities sparked off a furious press controversy with George Kennan (q.v.). De Windt's *The new Siberia, being an account of a visit to the penal island of Sakhalin and political prisons and mines of the Transbaikal district, eastern Siberia, 1894* (London: Chapman & Hall, 1896) did nothing to cool the issue down. Details of a subsequent expedition 'Paris to New York overland' were published in serial form in *Wide World Magazine*, vol. 10, no. 56 (Nov. 1902) to no. 60 (March 1903) and as a book (London: George Newnes, 1904. 311p.). Further remarks may be found in *Russia as I know it* (London: Chapman & Hall, 1917), chapters 11-13.

51 **Travels in Kamtchatka and Siberia with a narrative of a residence in China.**
Peter Dobell.   London: Henry Colburn & Richard Bentley, 1830.
2 vols. Reprinted, in one volume, New York: Arno Press & New York Times, 1970.

This very detailed depiction of Kamchatka, the Okhotsk region, Yakutiya, Krasnoyarsk, Tomsk and Siberian native peoples describes the experiences of an Irishman working for the Russian government as he travelled westwards from the Far East in 1812.

52 **Travels in Siberia, including excursions northwards, down the Obi, to the polar circle, and southwards, to the Chinese frontier.**
Adolph Erman, translated from the German by William Desborough Cooley.   London: Longman, Brown, Green and Longmans, 1848;
Philadelphia: Lea & Blanchard, 1850. 2 vols. map. Reprinted New York: Arno Press & New York Times, 1970.

Chapters 13-19 of the first volume and the whole of volume two depict the travels and impressions of a German naturalist in 1828-29 who went from Tobolsk northwards along the Ob river and back, then via Tomsk to the Enisei to Irkutsk. From there he explored Buryatiya, giving information on Christian missions and Lamaism among the Buryats. He investigated the Lena, visiting Yakuts and Tungus, thence proceeding to Okhotsk. Useful for geology, climate, flora and fauna, trade, food, architecture and social customs, this is a fine work.

53 **The real Siberia. Together with an account of a dash through Manchuria.**
John Foster Fraser.   London: Cassell; New York: Appleton, 1902. 279p.
Several other editions appeared up to 1912.

Prejudices were swept away when this British traveller visited Siberia in 1901. The book's title is intended to stress that a new, vibrant economic area is being opened up. It bears close comparison with his *Canada as it is* (London: Cassell, 1905) which expresses even more enthusiasm for a similar geographical region which was, after all, in the British Empire.

54 **Greater Russia. The continental empire of the old world.**
Wirt Gerrare (pseudonym of William Oliver Greener).   London: Heinemann; New York: Macmillan, 1903. 310p. map.

Portrays another journey along the Trans-Siberian Railway in 1901. Photographs are again an important feature of this excited account. Annette M. B. Meakin's *A ribbon of iron* (Westminster, England: Constable; New York: Dutton, 1901. 320p. Reprinted New York: Arno Press & New York Times, 1970) is similar in its enthusiam about economic developments.

15

## 55 Wyna. Adventures in eastern Siberia.
D. Gourko, translated by Alexander Polovtsoff.   London: Methuen, 1938. 265p. maps.

A detailed travelogue, this work was written by a Russian general who had travelled in Transbaikalia around 1903-4. Details are given of people from various tribes. The Wyna of the title is a female sledge-driver with whom he formed a relationship, rescuing her from a cruel husband. Prejudice amongst 'civilized' Siberian society forced him to send her back.

## 56 Five thousand miles in a sledge: a midwinter journey across Siberia.
Lionel Francis Gowing.   London: Chatto & Windus, 1889; New York: Appleton, 1890. 257p. map.

Depicts a westward journey by an American in the late 1880s, along the old Siberian trail. Another pre-rail record of the horrors of journeys is Alexander Michie's *The Siberian overland route from Peking to Petersburg* (London: John Murray, 1864. 402p.). His steamship and land trip takes him from Kyakhta via Irkutsk to Tomsk and Omsk. There are helpful descriptions of the towns, and chapter twenty is an evocation of Siberian peasant life.

## 57 Through Russian Central Asia.
Stephen Graham.   London: Cassell, 1916. 279p.

Chapters 13-15 by this veteran russophile present details of a trip along the Irtysh river, then into the Altai mountains via the Russian settler village of Altaiskoe to Kosh-agach on the Mongolian border. The trade in Manchurian red deer horn (maral) is given some prominence. The trip was cut short by news of World War I. *The new Russia: from the White Sea to the Siberian steppe* by Alan Lethbridge (London: Mills & Boon, 1915. 314p. maps) is the result of a commercially minded visit to Russia by a Montreal banker who includes a whole chapter about British economic opportunities in Siberia. Lethbridge also depicts travel along the Ob–Irtysh river system. He proceeded through Verkhoture in the Urals and Tyumen, the starting point of Siberian navigation, to Omsk, which on his last visit in 1907 had suffered from 'horrible' hotels, but had by 1914 shot ahead to become 'a fine city' 'which might well be christened "the Winnipeg of Siberia" '. Books such as these deserve careful attention for the snippets of information they provide, not least in their photographs, about long-vanished customs and architectural monuments.

## 58 In the uttermost East, being an account of investigations among natives and Russian convicts of the island of Sakhalin, with notes of travel in Korea, Siberia and Manchuria.
Charles Henry Hawes.   London; New York: Harper, 1903. 478p. maps.

This detailed and very instructive illustrated travel account includes the first English survey of exiles and the native Nivkh in the northern interior of Sakhalin Island. There are also sketches of Vladivostok, and of rail and river travel to and from the island. See also his 'The island of murderers' (*Wide World Magazine*, vol. 10, no. 60 [March 1903], p. 573-80).

59 **Travels in Siberia.**

S. S. Hill. London: Longman, Brown, Green and Longmans, 1854. 2 vols. Reprinted, as one volume, New York: Arno Press & New York Times, 1970.

Includes extensive and very informative data culled during a trip from the Urals via Tyumen, Tomsk (to which seven chapters are devoted), Krasnoyarsk, Irkutsk (four chapters), Kyakhta, Buryatiya, the Lena to Yakutsk and Okhotsk, and on to Kamchatka. The author was a seasoned traveller who had written about emigration to the British colonies. Equals Erman (q.v.) as a really valuable source.

60 **Life with trans-siberian savages.**

Benjamin Douglas Howard. London: Longmans, Green, 1893. 237p.

A typical Victorian, this British doctor and anthropologist visited Sakhalin to gain knowledge and did not like what he found, either in the lives of the aboriginal population or in the prison régime. Yet there is some valuable information about the island and its population.

61 **Roughing it in Siberia, with some account of the Trans-Siberian Railway and the gold mining industry of asiatic Russia.**

Robert L. Jefferson. London: Sampson, Low, Marston, 1897. 249p. map.

Travelling by rail to Krasnoyarsk a group of businessmen visit the gold-mining region along the Enisei river.

62 **Tent life in Siberia and adventures among the Koraks and other tribes in Kamchatka and northern Asia.**

George Kennan. London; New York: Putnam's, 1871. 425p. map. Enlarged ed., London; New York: Putnam's, Knickerbocker Press, 1910. 482p. Reprinted New York: Arno Press & New York Times, 1970.

Employed on the same telegraph scheme as Bush (q.v.) Kennan learned a great deal about the local population in northeast Siberia, particularly the Koryak, Itelmen and Chukchi, of whom there are several illustrations. Note also his 'A dog sledge journey in Kamchatka and northeastern Siberia' (*Journal of the American Geographical Society of New York*, vol. 8 [1890], p. 96-130).

63 **Memoirs of a revolutionist.**

Pëtr Alekseevich Kropotkin, Prince. London: Smith, 1899. Enlarged ed., London: Sonnenschein, 1908. 468p. Reprinted New York: Dover Press, 1971.

Before his anarchist period Kropotkin volunteered to undertake army service in the Amur Cossacks. Chapter three of his memoirs recounts details of military life in the Far East from 1862 to 1867, when he requested transfer to European Russia because military units had been sent out against Polish insurgents. Further details may be found in *The anarchist prince* by George Woodcock and Ivan Avakumović (New York: Schocken Books, 1971, p. 49-82) and in *Kropotkin* by Martin A. Miller (Chicago, Illinois; London: University of Chicago Press, 1976, p. 53-71).

17

## 64  Through Siberia.

Henry Lansdell.   London: Low, Marston, Searle & Rington; Boston:
Houghton, Mifflin, 1882. 2 vols. 5th ed., London: Sampson, Low, 1883.
811p. map.

In 1879 the Reverend Lansdell travelled extensively in Siberia visiting prisons and
handing out Christian literature. His detailed travelogue is a very valuable account and
contains information on transport, local people, the Church in Siberia, gold mining,
Tobolsk, Tomsk, Krasnoyarsk, Irkutsk, Yakutsk, Vladivostok, the Enisei, Lena and
Amur, the Nerchinsk mines, Buryatiya, the maritime region, Kamchatka, Sakhalin,
the Nivkh, and the prison system. His attitude to the exile system being like de
Windt's, he was accused of being in the pay of the Russian government. Also urged to
spread the message of God's love in distant prisons an evangelical, Dr Frederick W.
Baedeker, made a trans-Siberian journey in 1890 by road and steamer, distributing
Bibles. He even reached Sakhalin. See Robert Sloan Latimer's *Dr. Baedeker and his
apostolic work in Russia* (London: Morgan & Scott, 1907, p. 109-63). There is a map
and a very clear selection of photographs.

## 65  Return to happiness.

Jonas Lied.   London: Macmillan, 1943. 317p. map. An American
edition entitled *Prospector in Siberia: the autobiography of Jonas Lied*
was published in New York: Oxford University Press, 1945. 307p.

This book was written by a Norwegian who was involved in trading into the Enisei via
the Kara Sea route from 1910 until 1931. Details are included of river traffic from the
Arctic to Krasnoyarsk under the Tsars, Provisional Government, Kolchak and the
Bolsheviks. See also his *Siberian Arctic: the story of the Siberian Company* (London:
Methuen, 1960. 214p. maps) which continues the company's story to the 1950s.

## 66  Through Siberia, the land of the future.

Fridtjof Nansen, translated by Arthur G. Chater.   London: William
Heinemann, 1914. 477p. maps.

Consists of a thorough and perceptive illustrated account of impressions gained during
this famous Norwegian explorer's Siberian trip in 1913. His conclusions are very
valuable because he was well acquainted with contemporary life in similar geographical
regions elsewhere in the world, and was able to assess Russia's attainments in Siberia
in that context.

## 67  Siberian days: an engineer's record of travel and adventure in the wilds of Siberia.

Algernon Noble.   London: H. F. & G. Witherby, 1928. 223p.

These valuable travel notes by an Englishman provide details about copper and gold
mining in present-day Kazakhstan, and gold prospecting in the Tomsk, Enisei and
Baikal regions from 1905 to 1914.

68    **All the Russias: travels and studies in contemporary European Russia, Finland, Siberia, the Caucasus and Central Asia.**
Sir Henry Norman.   London: Heinemann; New York: Scribner's, 1902.
3rd ed., 1904. 476p.

A British member of parliament long interested in Russian affairs, who travelled to Irkutsk and had earlier visited Vladivostok, included material on Siberia on pages 96-163 of this general study. More interesting than his sections on the railway and the exiles is his study of Siberian civilization from restaurant décor to agricultural techniques. The work is illustrated richly, the most impressive photograph being a shot of the bows of the train-ferry *Baikal* breaking ice.

69    **Man and mystery in Asia.**
Antoni Ferdynand Ossendowski, in collaboration with Lewis Stanton Palen.   London: Edward Arnold, 1924. 295p.

A Polish expert in coal and gold deposits in the Far East, who was adviser to General Kuropatkin about fuel resources during the Russo-Japanese War, and adviser to Sergei Witte, Russian Finance Minister on industrial matters, published these colourful memoirs in English with help. In 1905 he had headed an abortive Far Eastern Revolutionary Government and was sentenced to death, later commuted to two years' imprisonment through Witte's intervention. Details of these experiences, including sketches of the trial and prison life, are in his *From president to prison* (London: Allen & Unwin; New York: Dutton, 1925. 338p.).

70    **With the Russians in Mongolia.**
Henry George C. Perry-Ayscough, Robert Bruère Otter-Barry.
London: John Lane, 1914. 344p. map.

Chapters 15-17 recount a journey on the Chuya Trail from Mongolia through the Altai mountains to Novonikolaevsk (Novosibirsk). There are several photographs of this region, rarely travelled by Europeans. Another intrepid traveller was Harald G. C. Swayne. Parts of his *Through the highlands of Siberia* (London: Rowland Ward, 1904. 259p.) depict a trip up the Ob by ferry then overland to Mongolia searching for wild sheep to shoot. He is very lyrical in description of local flora, and compares conditions with those in British India (see also 'The future of Siberia', *Geographical Journal*, vol. 51, no. 3 [March 1918], p. 149-64, in which he relates experiences during two trips in 1903 and 1914 and speculates on the future development of this great land).

71    **From the Arctic Ocean to the Yellow Sea. The narrative of a journey in 1890 and 1891 across Siberia, Mongolia, the Gobi Desert, and northern China.**
Julius M. Price.   London: Sampson, Low, Marston; New York:
Scribner's, 1892. 384p. map.

A 'special artist of the *Illustrated London News*', he was attached to an expedition by the Anglo-Siberian Trading Syndicate, who agreed to drop him at Eniseisk. He recounts the river voyage up the Enisei, impressions of Eniseisk, Krasnoyarsk and Irkutsk, a settlement of religious sectarians called the Skoptsy, Turukhansk monastery and gold mining. Another artist, this time from the United States, was Marcus Lorenzo Taft who travelled on the railway in 1909, leaving an authentic pictorial record in

*Strange Siberia along the Trans-Siberian Railway: a journey from the great wall of China to the skyscrapers of Manhattan* (New York: Eaton & Mains, 1911. 260p.).

72  **Siberia.**
    Morgan Phillips Price.   London: Methuen, 1912. 308p. maps.
Another British traveller who goes by rail and post road to investigate life in a city (Krasnoyarsk), a small town (Minusinsk) and a village (Kushabar), Price includes a chapter on a backwoodsman and trader, discusses colonization and social relations, and then focuses on present and future economic prospects for western and central Siberia. Again the photographs add materially to the effectiveness of this account.

73  **Reminiscences of Russia. The Ural mountains and adjoining Siberian district in 1897.**
    James Cartmell Ridley.   Newcastle-upon-Tyne, England: Andrew Reid, 1899. 100p. map.
When attending a meeting of the International Geological Congress at St Petersburg in August 1897 the author travelled to the Urals to see mining and manufacturing operations there and in 'a small district of Siberia' near Myas and Kyshtym in the extreme west of Siberia. There are interesting (if brief) descriptions of the Siberian road, medical facilities for peasant emigrants, gold mines, peasant life and the beautiful views obtainable from the Urals over the vast plain to the east.

74  **In far north-east Siberia.**
    Isaak Vladimirovich Shklovskii (pseud. Dioneo), translated by
    L. Edwards and Z. Shklovsky.   London: Macmillan, 1916. 264p. map.
This is a picturesque report by a Russian journalist who travelled in Yakutiya along the Kolyma river, visited Yakutsk, Chukotka and ascended the Lena river towards Buryatiya in 1891. He is gloomy about the prospects for survival of small native tribes like the Yukagir and Koryak and gives details of their lifestyle and beliefs to preserve them for posterity.

75  **Side-lights on Siberia: some account of the great Siberian railroad, the prisons and exile system.**
    James Young Simpson.   London; Edinburgh: William Blackwood,
    1898. 383p.
More sympathetic than George Kennan to the exile system, this Scottish author did not go as far as de Windt in eulogizing it. There is a long section on the Aleksandrovskii Central Prison, seventy versts [a verst = about ⅔ of a mile] from Irkutsk, and briefer descriptions of penal institutions throughout Siberia, including the Nerchinsk mines and Sakhalin. His account of the railway is historical as well as impressionistic. He also depicts water and road travel and includes a cameo description of Tomsk. See also his 'The great Siberian iron road' (*Blackwood's Edinburgh Magazine*, vol. 161, no. 1 [1897], p. 1-20) which includes a sketch of early plans to build canals and railways through Siberia.

76 **Through Siberia.**
Jonas Jonsson Stadling, edited by F. H. H. Guillemand. Westminster,
England: A. Constable & Co., 1901. 315p. map.

This is a translation of an account by a Swede of a 15,000-mile journey in 1898 in
search of arctic explorers. Apart from the usual travel information, details are included
of the material and spiritual culture of the small religious sect called the Skoptsy and
the Yakut. Stadling is in favour of regional government for Siberia and is highly
critical of the Tsarist exile system.

77 **Siberia: a record of travel, climbing and exploration.**
Samuel Turner. London; Leipzig, Germany: T. Fisher Unwin, 1905.
320p.

This record of mountain climbing in the Altai range is by a British visitor whose main
brief was to inspect the West Siberian dairy industry. His report on this confirms the
belief that agriculture in Siberia was superior to that in European Russia. Further
details of his climbing experiences in the Altai may be found in book 2 of *My climbing
adventures in four continents* (London; Leipzig, Germany: T. Fisher Unwin, 1911).
Also keen on recreation in Siberia, 'a land of large, free, breezy sunlit spaces, beautiful
in summer with a glorious abundance of flowers', is James Bryce's 1913 travelogue
'Western Siberia and the Altai mountains, with some speculations on the future of
Siberia' (*National Geographic*, vol. 39, no. 5 [1921], p. 469-507). Despite the title this
article includes a section on eastern Siberia, including a rare photograph of the
Voznesenskii Monastery in Irkutsk. See also Bryce's *Memories of travel* (New York:
Macmillan, 1923), pages 254-97 of which repeat the above.

78 **Travels in the east of Nicholas II, Emperor of Russia, when Cesarewitch,
1890-91.**
Esper Esperevich Ukhtomskii, translated by R. Goodlet, edited by Sir
G. Birdwood. London: Constable, 1896-1900. 2 vols.

Beautifully produced, this is a luxurious large-format English version of the account of
Nicholas II's progression through the easterly sections of his future domain while he
was heir to the throne. There are 500 illustrations.

79 **In search of a Siberian klondike, as narrated by Washington B. Vanderlip
the chief actor and herein set forth by Homer B. Hulbert.**
Washington B. Vanderlip. New York: Century, 1903; London:
T. Fisher Unwin, 1906. 315p.

An American gold prospector describes his travels in eastern Siberia, Kamchatka and
Sakhalin (1898-1900) in search of ground worth working for ore. He refers to the
native population, alcohol abuse, the exile system and railway travel.

80 **On the island of Sakhalin.**
Mikhail Ivanovich Venyukov, translated from the Russian by Captain
Spalding. *Journal of the Royal Geographical Society,* vol. 42 (1872),
p. 373-88. map.
The article presents a brief survey by a well-known Russian military man and
geographer of the geography, topography, settlement and military significance of
Sakhalin which was little known in the West at this period. Another military account,
forming quite a contrast with this is 'Four weeks in Saghalien' by C. R. Woodroffe
(*Journal of the Royal Artillery,* vol. 35 [1908-9], p. 349-72) which records a camping
trip in southern Sakhalin in 1907 and provides information on changes brought about
as the Japanese took over after the Russo-Japanese War.

81 **Across Siberia on the great post road.**
Charles Wenyon. London: Charles H. Kelly, 1896. 240p. map.
Reprinted New York: Arno Press & New York Times, 1971.
Later editions were entitled *Four thousand miles across Siberia on the great post road*
(London: Cully, [1909]. 256p.). This doctor travelled during the summer of 1893 by
steamboat, tarantass and cart. It is easy to understand why the railway was so eagerly
welcomed.

82 **Through Siberia, an empire in the making.**
Richardson L. Wright, Bassett Digby. London: Hurst & Blackett; New
York: McBride, Nast, 1913. 260p. maps.
Two Americans provide a lively account, rather lurid in places, of a trip partly along
the Trans-Siberian Railway just before the First World War. Their sledge trip to the
Salair mountains, visit to a very rural village and journey via Stretensk, the Shilka river
(in a home-made boat as the ice was melting) and along the Amur towards Manchuria
are of interest.

# From 1917 onwards

83 **Beyond the Ural mountains: the adventures of a Siberian hunter.**
Ivan Aramilev, translated and adapted by Michael Heron. London:
George Allen & Unwin, 1961. 199p.
Rarely do we in the West obtain a flavour of life lived in the raw in Siberia. This
unsophisticated hunter's memoir has nothing of politics or the academic about it. It is
fresh with the tang of country air, a whiff of cordite, and the yelp of a favourite gun-
dog leaping after teal.

84 **Through Kamchatka by dog sled and skis. A vivid description of adventurous journeys among the interesting and almost unknown peoples of the most inaccessible parts of this remote Siberian peninsula.**
Sten Bergman, translated from the Swedish by Frederic Whyte.
London: Seeley, Service & Co., 1927. 284p. maps.

Sten Bergman was leader of a Swedish geographical expedition which went to Pacific Siberia in 1920-22 to study the region's zoology, botany and ethnology. The expedition's main findings were published in the *Transactions of the Royal Swedish Academy of Sciences.* This book is a popular depiction of two journeys: one on skis from northeast Kamchatka to Petropavlovsk, the other being a four-month dog-sled trip to the centre and north of Kamchatka. A companion volume is his *Sport and exploration in the Far East: a naturalist's experiences in and around the Kurile islands,* also translated by Frederic Whyte, and published in London by Methuen in 1933 (246p.).

85 **Soviet and Tsarist Siberia.**
George Borodin. London; New York: Rich & Cowan, [1944]. 168p.

The author (whose real name was either George Alexis Milkomanovich Milkomane or George Alexis Bankoff) had an uncle, Pavel Andreevich Borodin, who was governor of Irkutsk from 1910 to 1915. Bankoff, later an author of books on ballet and medicine, as well as a novelist, had lived in Irkutsk as a child and fought with the Whites in the civil war. Sadly, his travelogue is rather poorly researched and written, though it is oddly enthusiastic about post-revolutionary changes.

86 **One chilly Siberian morning.**
Douglas Botting. London: Hodder & Stoughton, 1965. Cheap edition, London: Travel Book Club, 1965. 192p.

Sent to the USSR to make a film for the BBC, Douglas Botting and John Bayliss were taken by a contact from the Novosti Press Agency to Irkutsk, Bratsk, Yakutiya and Chukotka. Though impressionistic this account is memorable in places, for instance when the travellers are taken to a service of ordination for an Orthodox priest at the Znamenskii Cathedral in Irkutsk.

87 **Siberia, sixty-five degrees east of Greenwich: oil and people.**
Compiled by Gennadii Budnikov, translated from the Russian by Valerii Krishkin. Moscow: Progress Publishers, 1985. 240p.

This book consists of accounts by several Soviet authors of developments in the rich oil and gas fields of western Siberia around Tymen and the Vasyugane. Industrial and social matters figure largely in the essays.

88 **The rim of mystery: a hunter's wanderings in unknown Siberian Asia.**
John Bird Burnham. New York; London: Putnam's, 1929. 281p. map.

An account of a hunting trip in 1921, this book by an American includes detailed observations of the Chukchi, as well as demonstrating the similarities between the Siberian and Alaskan mountain sheep. It is well illustrated.

89 **In bolshevik Siberia, the land of ice and exile.**
Malcolm Burr. London: H. E. and G. Witherby, 1931. 224p. map.

This is an atmospheric, rather chatty account by a British geologist who travelled down the Lena during the winter of 1930-31 searching for gold. He endured a thousand miles in a sledge. There are useful illustrations, as there are in a more serious early 1930s travelogue by a Frenchman, Pierre Dominique. His *Secrets of Siberia*, translated from the French by Warre B. Wells (London: Hutchinson, 1934. 288p.), has great immediacy, arresting the reader with stark accounts of poverty, snotty-nosed kids and peasants who 'chew the cud' rather than eating. He sees some hope in developments at Magnitogorsk and Kuznetsk and notes the beginning of mechanized agriculture.

90 **Wilderness survey: true story of a taiga tragedy.**
Vladimir Alekseevich Chivilikhin, translated from the Russian by Vic Schneierson. Moscow: Progress Publishers, [1966]. 159p.

Based on the diary of Aleksandr Koshurnikov, this is a dramatized tale of experiences by a Soviet scientist. The original Russian was entitled *Silver Rails* (Moscow: Molodaya gvardiya, 1960).

91 **Five times to Yakutsk.**
Dean Conger. *National Geographic*, vol. 152, no. 2 (Aug. 1977), p. 256-69. map.

A veteran photo-journalist, Dean Conger relates the frustrations and rewards experienced during the five journeys he had made to Yakutsk from 1961 onwards. A few of his atmospheric colour photographs are included. A contrasting report by a former head of the Soviet section of the British Foreign Office's Research Department, Violet Conolly, is 'The Soviet Far East and eastern Siberia: impressions of a recent visit' (*Asian Affairs*, vol. 12 [OS vol. 68], part 1 [Feb. 1981], p. 35-48. map).

92 **Letters home from the Far East and Russia, 1931.**
Paul Drennan Cravath. Garden City, New York: Country Life Press, 1931. 97p.

An American, well known for publications such as *Letters from India and Irak*, travels westwards on the Siberian Railway in the spring of 1931. Travellers were few in those days, and this is included here because the relevant portion (p. 78-97) contains local colour and information about the situation just before the purge era. Also from these years is Peter Fleming's *A forgotten journey* (London: Rupert Hart-Davis, 1952), the 'fourth stage' of which depicts a trip eastwards from the Turksib [Turkestan–Siberian] along the Trans-Siberian Railway in 1934, with a brief hunting excursion in the Far East. *Trans-Siberian* by Noel Barber (London: Harrap, 1942. 180p. map) consists of a rail journey from east to west in 1939 by a British writer and his wife. The timing is rather unusual, since Europe was on the verge of war. The travellers were impressed by the possibilities of this large country.

93 **Tigers, gold and witch doctors.**
Bassett Digby. London: Lane; New York: Harcourt, Brace, 1928.
341p.
Quite informative about the lives of aboriginal peoples in eastern Siberia including
Yakuts, Buryats, Oroch and Evenk (Tungus), and particularly fascinated by
shamanism, the author presents a colourful, if rather immaturely expressed travelogue,
punctured with historical titbits. Snide remarks about the Bolsheviks adorn the
conclusion. See also his other book, *The mammoth and mammoth hunting in northeast Siberia*.

94 **Siberia in from the cold.**
Mike Edwards, photographs by Steve Rayner. *National Geographic*,
vol. 177, no. 3 (March 1990), p. 2-39. map.
Fine photographs of everyday conditions in contemporary Siberia add spice to a
narrative full of concerns about the environmental damage being inflicted upon Siberia
in the name of progress. Valentin Rasputin's campaign to clean the region up is
highlighted, as are the gas and oil developments in the Yamal–Nenets area and the
BAM railway. This issue of the *National Geographic* contains a loose map of the USSR
which includes a colour-coded indication of Siberian ethnolinguistic groups.

95 **The incredible mile: Siberia, Mongolia, Uzbekistan.**
Harold Elvin. London: Heinemann, 1970. 263p. map.
A man with experience as the night-watchman in the British embassy in Moscow in
1941, a poet, fiction writer and traveller, provides glimpses of life in Nakhodka and
around Baikal. His eloquence is concentrated more on females than Siberia.

96 **Mountain trails.**
Grigorii Anisimovich Fedoseev, translated from the Russian by George
H. Hanna. Moscow: Foreign Languages Publishing House, [*c.* 1958].
494p.
A famous Soviet explorer and mountain climber provides graphic descriptions of his
exploits in the wilds of eastern Siberia, particularly the Dzhugdzhur mountains. See
also his *Death can wait*, translated by David Skvirskii (Moscow: Progress Publishers,
[1964]. 467p. map) which concerns travel adventures in the Okhotsk region and was
originally published by the Young Communist League publishing house, Molodaya
gvardiya, in 1963.

97 **Red road through Asia: a journey by the Arctic Ocean to Siberia,**
  **Central Asia and Armenia; with an account of the peoples now living in**
  **those countries under the hammer and sickle.**
Bosworth E. M. Goldman. London: Methuen, 1934. 270p. map.
bibliog.
The relevant portion of this account by a British traveller concerns a 1933 river trip up
the Enisei to Krasnoyarsk, then a rail journey via Novosibirsk to the Turksib Railway
and on into Central Asia. Pointed comments reveal that the author is not as naive as
some visitors in the thirties. He unfortunately failed to reach the Altai, despite all
efforts. The photographs are valuable. Another British account is *Eastern vistas* by

Audrey Harris (London: Collins, 1939. 392p.), parts of which refer to experiences on the Trans-Siberian Railway.

## 98 **Soviet frontiers of tomorrow.**
Harold Griffin. Moscow: Progress Publishers, 1982. 221p. map.

A writer on life in Alaska and British Columbia visits Siberia in the early 1980s, providing a kaleidoscope of impresssions about industrial, agricultural and social developments with some historical elements. For instance he quotes from documents of a British company which extracted gold in the Lena region before the Revolution. The work is illustrated.

## 99 **Argonauts of Siberia: the diary of a prospector.**
William Benjamin Jones. Philadelphia, Pennsylvania: Dorrance & Co., [1927]. 165p.

I have not been able to locate this account by an American prospector. It is mentioned (as item 3:225) in the bibliography by Roman Jakobson (q.v.).

## 100 **Red bear or yellow dragon.**
Marguerite Elton Harrison, née Baker. London: Brentano's; New York: George H. Doran, [1924]. 296p.

A correspondent of the *Baltimore Sun* visits eastern Siberia and the Far Eastern Republic. There are references to national minorities, the legal system and Sino-Russian relations. Her 'Red bear, yellow dragon, American lady' (*Literary Digest*, vol. 81 [April 1924], p. 38-44) provides a positive account of Japanese rule in Sakhalin.

## 101 **Trans-Siberia by rail and a month in Japan.**
Barbara Lamplugh. London: Roger Lascelles, 1979. 155p. maps.

A personal narrative from the 1970s, this account is half devoted to the trip across Siberia.

## 102 **Glimpses of Siberia, the Russian "Wild East".**
Cody Marsh. *National Geographic*, vol. 38, no. 6 (Dec. 1920), p. 513-36.

A captain of the United States Expeditionary Force waxes lyrical about wild flowers and local cookery. Soup kitchens for refugees, the pink politics of Siberia, faulty sanitation and night-life in Vladivostok are highlighted. He says that 500 of the 7,500-strong American force married Siberian girls. The text and photographs together form a unique panorama of the period. A more hostile American account is Frederick F. Moore's *Siberia today* (New York: Appleton, 1919. 333p.).

103   **Sibir: my discovery of Siberia.**
Farley Mowat.   Toronto, Canada: McClelland & Stewart, [1970].
313p. British edition, entitled *The Siberians*, London: Heinemann,
1972. 313p. maps.

A veteran Canadian traveller, writer and adopter of good causes visited northeast
Siberia in 1966 and 1969. He was accompanied by Yurii Rytkheu, the Chukchi writer.
There is a great deal of information in this account; comparisons between Canadian
and Siberian conditions are helpful, though the author is rather gullible.

104   **The big red train ride.**
Eric Newby.   Harmondsworth, England: Penguin Books, 1980. 267p.
map.

A seasoned British travel writer makes the trip from west to east over the Trans-
Siberian Railway in 1977. This is a diary, replete with snatches of irreverent and
irrelevant details which make it a delightful read. A less successful travel account is
Gaia Servadio's *A Siberian encounter* (London: Weidenfeld & Nicolson, [1971].
241p.), pages 3-106 of which give fleeting glimpses of the land and people.

105   **My Siberian life.**
Moise Abramovich Novomeysky, translated from the Russian by Alec
Brown.   London: Max Parrish, 1956. 352p. map.

A memoir rather than a travel account, this book was written by the grandson of
political exiles, who was born and bred in Barguzin near Lake Baikal, studied mining
and was involved in the extraction of Glauber's salt and in the use of the first gold-
dredger on the River Tsipikan in 1914. There is a section on the Revolution and the
civil war. A Zionist, he left Russia in 1920 to found the Palestine Potash Company.
The book also refers to Birobidzhan.

106   **I saw Siberia.**
Hugo Portisch, translated from the German by Henry Fox and Ewald
Osers.   London: Harrap, 1972. 210p. maps.

A richly illustrated account of Siberia by a German-speaking journalist, this work
contains travel notes, anecdotes about everyday life and excursions into history. It was
originally published in German (Vienna: Verlag Kremayr & Scherian, 1967, 1971). A
similar work, though politically far more leftist, is Peter Schütt's *Journey to Siberia*
(Moscow: Progress Publishers, 1982. 181p.). Of the latter only pages 123-73 refer to
Siberia, concentrating on the BAM [Baykal–Amur mainline] railway and its socio-
economic implications, with a thumbnail sketch of a Gilyak (Nivkh).

107   **The long walk.**
Slavomir Rawicz, as told to Ronald Downing.   London: Constable;
New York: Harper, 1956. 240p. Other editions, London: Pan Books,
1959; London: Longmans, 1960.

This is a remarkable escape story. The author walked from a north Siberian slave-
labour camp to Lake Baikal, and thence to India. A similar tale is *As far as my feet will
carry me* by Joseph Martin Bauer, translated from the German by Laurence Wilson
(London: André Deutsch, 1957. 253p.) whose hero walks from Chukotka via Chita to
the Caucasus between 1949 and 1952. Pseudonyms are used in both these books.

27

108 **Soviet Far East: a tour of Sakhalin.**
A. Ryzhkov. Moscow: Progress Publishers, 1966. 59p.

A brief Soviet account of life in Sakhalin in the mid-1960s. Other accounts of eastern parts of Siberia are Karl Staf's *Yakutiya as I saw it*, translated from the Russian by W. Perelman (Moscow: Foreign Languages Publishing House, 1958. 113p.) and A. Zlobin's *The Baikal meridian*, translated from the Russian by Ivanov-Mujiev (Moscow: Foreign Languages Publishing House, [c. 1960]. 190p.) both of which enthusiastically endorse Soviet developments in their respective regions.

109 **Sun and snow: a Siberian adventure.**
Doreen Napier Stanford. London: Longmans, 1963. 158p. American ed., entitled *Siberian Odyssey*, New York: Dutton, 1964. 157p.

The daughter of a British mining engineer based at Ulen, near Minusinsk, from 1916 to 1920 tells of her experiences during peacetime, revolution and civil war. They escaped by rail.

110 **One-arm Sutton.**
Francis Arthur Sutton. New York: Viking Press, 1933. 277p.

The autobiography of a major-general trading on the Russian–Manchurian border during the civil war. Grierson (q.v.) correctly calls it 'a racy account'.

111 **The winds of wanderlust: hiking and tourist trails in the Soviet Union.**
L. Tripolskii, translated from the Russian by I. Medow. Moscow: Progress Publishers, 1978. 229p.

Richly illustrated in colour, this book depicts in conversational style fishing, rambling and climbing in the Altai, Tien Shan and Sayan mountains. It also depicts the Enisei river route and Vladivostok.

112 **An adventurous journey (Russia – Siberia – China).**
Ethel Brilliana Alec-Tweedie. London: Hutchinson, [1926]. 397p. maps. Cheap ed., London: Thornton Butterworth, 1929. 285p.

Chapters four and five rapidly cover her Siberian journey, including a railway accident. She is fearful of harassment by the GPU [State Political Administration, an organization directed against espionage and counterrevolution]. More intrepid were a couple of American women working in the Kuzbas who travelled in the Altai region in 1925 in areas usually closed to Westerners: see *Vagabonding at fifty: from Siberia to Turkestan* by Helen Calista Wilson and Elsie Reed Mitchell (New York: Coward-McCann, 1929. 335p. map).

113 **Soviet Asia mission.**
Henry A. Wallace, with the collaboration of Andrew J. Steiger. New York: Reynal & Hitchcock, 1946. 254p.

The author, the Vice-President of the United States, accompanied by Owen Lattimore, visited Siberia and China at the end of World War II to investigate economic developments and the prospects for Sino-Soviet peace. The delegation was shown Yakutsk, gold mines in the northeast, Komsomolsk, Buryatiya, Krasnoyarsk and Novosibirsk. Their pre-Cold War hopefulness blinded them to deficiencies in the USSR. Chapter thirteen on agriculture is interesting, as are the photographs, one of which shows a local Communist Party headquarters festooned with portraits of leaders, Stalin in the centre. See also Lattimore's 'New road to Asia' (*National Geographic*, vol. 86, no. 6 [Dec, 1944], p. 649-76) whose colour illustrations are compelling. Both publications received a blast of condemnation from Robert Conquest in his *Kolyma*, pages 204-13 (q.v.) for being bamboozled by the Soviet authorities. *Through Russia's back door*, by Richard Edward Lauterbach (New York; London: Harper, 1946. 239p. map), also concerns the Allied war effort, this time concentrating on Vladivostok.

114 **From Siberia to Kuibyshev: reflections on Russia, 1919-43.**
Leolyn Dana Wilgress   *International Journal* (Toronto), vol. 22, no. 3 (1967), p. 364-75.
A participant in the Canadian Department of Trade and Commerce's mission to Vladivostok reflects on the Allied intervention in Siberia. See also the *Dana Wilgress Memoirs* (Toronto, Canada: Ryerson Press, 1967. 190p.).

115 **Incredible Siberia.**
Junius B. Wood.   New York: Lincoln MacKeagh, Dial Press; Toronto, Canada: Longmans, 1928. 261p. bibliog.
A European correspondent of the *Chicago Daily News*, Wood reports on his trip across Siberia in 1926. There are some very revealing photographs.

116 **Cossack girl.**
Marina Yurlova.   London: Cassell, 1934. 312p.
The memoir records how a young Cossack girl, caught up in the civil war, flees eastwards across the Urals out of Bolshevik-held areas. Only pages 243-81 are relevant. It is rather a flimsy personal account, yet with some pathos. The photographs of corpses are gruesome.

# Travel Guides

117 **Russia with Teheran, Port Arthur and Peking.**
   Karl Baedeker. Leipzig: Karl Baedeker, 1914. 590p. maps.
   Reprinted, entitled *Baedeker's Russia, 1914*. London: George Allen &
   Unwin; Newton Abbot: David & Charles, 1971.

Pages 528-42 include itineraries for trips along the Trans-Siberian Railway and
summary details and plans of many towns (Novonikolaevsk, Tomsk, Krasnoyarsk,
Irkutsk, Chita, Sretensk, Vladivostok, Blagoveshchensk and Khabarovsk). There are
timetables for rail travel and for trips by steamer down the Amur from Sretensk to
Khabarovsk.

118 **Russian gazetteer and guide, being an account of the territorial divisions**
   **and a description of over 300 of the principal towns and cities of Russia,**
   **Finland and Siberia.**
   William Henry Beable. London: Russian Outlook, [*c.* 1919]. 141p.
   map.

To be used in conjunction with his *Commercial Russia* (q.v.), this reference book has
descriptions of thirty Siberian towns and ten of its regions.

119 **Fodor's '91: Soviet Union.**
   New York; London: Fodor's Travel Publications, 1991. 420p. maps.

Details of trans-Siberian rail travel, short paragraphs about the main cities, and a brief
guide to entertainments are included on pages 388-401. Similar in its depth, but
stylistically very different, is *Soviet Union* by Martin Walker (London: Collins, 1989.
352p. maps [Collins Independent Travellers]). Apart from general information on
history, the USSR today and how to deport oneself as a tourist, this work contains a
section on Siberia and the Soviet Far East on pages 286-93.

120   **Novosibirsk.**
       Nikolai Alekseevich Meisak.   Moscow: Progress Publishers, 1971.
       [unpaginated].
A brief introduction to the city of Novosibirsk leads into a series of colour illustrations
of all aspects of the city's life. The introduction and captions are in five languages,
including English.

121   **Irkutsk: a guide.**
       M. Sergeev, translated from the Russian by Jan Butler.   Moscow:
       Raduga, 1986. 71p. maps.
Replete with excellent colour illustrations, this is a guide for the English-speaking
visitor to Irkutsk. A brief history of the city leads into four sightseeing tours, each
itinerary picking out important buildings and historical personalities. There is an
information section, brief notes on excursions from Irkutsk to Lake Baikal and Bratsk,
and finally a coloured schematic street-guide to Irkutsk.

122   **Trans-Siberian rail guide.**
       Robert Strauss.   Chalfont St. Peter, England: Bradt Publications,
       1987. 217p. maps.
Presenting a brief history of the railway and its rolling stock, the book includes
cautionary travellers' tales, route descriptions, timetables, details of open cities, in fact
everything of use to the tourist who wishes to travel by the Trans-Siberian route. The
guide was updated in 1988. It is distributed in the USA by Hunter Publications Inc. of
Edison, New Jersey. A Soviet attempt at a guide, written by a literary figure and
published in the Stalin era was *The Trans-Siberian express* by Vsevolod Vyacheslavovich Ivanov (Moscow: Intourist, [*c.* 1935]. 28p.).

123   **Trans-Siberia handbook.**
       Bryn Thomas.   Brentford, England: Roger Lascelles, 1988. Revised
       ed., 1989. 275p. maps. bibliog.
Similar to the previous entry this is a whole book describing travel along the Trans-
Siberian Railway. There is a kilometre-by-kilometre guide, with strip maps of each
section. Street plans and information on Novosibirsk, Irkutsk and Khabarovsk are
included. There are timetables, a section on fauna and cheerful colour illustrations. An
unpaginated appendix to the latest edition includes an update for 1991.

# Geography

## General

124 **The circumpolar north: a political and economic geography of the Arctic and sub-Arctic.**
Terence Armstrong, George Rodgers, Graham Rowley. London: Methuen, 1978. 303p. maps. bibliog.
This is a brief but well-structured comparison of all northern arctic and subarctic territories, including southern, western and eastern Siberia.

125 **Siberia 1. Siberian questions: economy, ecology, strategy.**
Edited by Boris Chichlo. Paris: Institut d'Etudes Slaves, 1985. 416p.
(Institut du monde soviétique et de l'Europe centrale et orientale, cultures et sociétés de l'est, no. 3).
The first of a projected three volumes of papers presented at the 1983 Paris Colloque internationale sur la Sibérie, this work contains valuable items in English. Robert North, Victor Mote and Marius J. Broekmeyer's papers all concentrate on transport. Leslie Dienes writes on economic strategy, Peter de Souza on territorial production complexes (TPCs), and J. A. Dellenbrant on Siberia in Soviet regional development policy. Richard A. Bridge contributes a paper on native labour resources for industry in Yakutiya. Terence Armstrong discusses climate as a limiting factor in Siberian development. Zeev Wolfson investigates the environmental risk of West Siberian oil and gas exploitation. Henry Ratnieks writes on Siberian pipelines, and David Wilson on new oil and gas technology. Philip Kelly and D. A. Campbell discuss the problems of large-scale water transfers. It is to be hoped that the remaining volumes will be published.

126 **Siberia: Russia's frozen frontier.**
Dean Conger. *National Geographic*, vol. 131, no. 3 (March 1967),
p. 297-345. maps.
Consists of a general geographical survey with eloquent colour illustrations by a noted
American traveller and staff member of the *National Geographic*.

127 **Russian land, Soviet people: a geographical approach to the USSR.**
James S. Gregory. London: Harrap, 1968. 947p. maps. bibliog.
This is a thorough physical, historical and economic geography of the territories now in
the USSR from preglacial times to the 1960s. It has excellent maps. Chapters 1-7 and
14-16 cover Siberia and the Soviet Far East. Other Western geographies with
substantial Siberian content include: *Geography of the Soviet Union* by John P. Cole
(London: Butterworths, 1984); *Geography of the USSR* by Paul E. Lydolph (5th ed.,
Elkhart Lake, Wisconsin: Misty Valley, 1990) and its associated *Topical analysis*
(Elkhart Lake, Wisconsin: Misty Valley, 1979); and *Geography of the USSR: a
regional survey* by Theodore Shabad (New York: Columbia University Press, 1951).

128 **Russian Siberia: an integrative approach.**
Gary Hausladen. *Soviet Geography*, vol. 30, no. 3 (March 1989),
p. 231-46.
Believing that the Russian conquest of Siberia was not an isolated phenomenon, but
part of a general European process related to mercantilist capitalism, the author
proposes using a three-tier system for studying Siberia: a world-systems analysis as
formulated by Wallerstein, a multidisciplinary approach, and a cross-cultural
comparison. This would enable a broad perspective to be obtained. He also laments
the undeveloped nature of Western social geography of Siberia. A commentary by
William Myckoff on pages 247-52 of the same issue of the journal agrees with some of
what Hausladen says, but notes that though intriguing questions have been raised, as
yet none have been answered.

129 **Soviet Union: a geographical survey.**
Edited by S. V. Kalesnik, V. F. Pavlenko, translation from the Russian
by Sergei Chulaki and Valerii Epstein. Moscow: Progress Publishers,
1976. 278p. maps.
Written by a collective of authors, this is a broad-ranging geographical survey, well
illustrated in colour and monochrome. Sections on Siberia and the Soviet Far East are
scattered through the text. A less luxurious publication is *Geography of the Soviet
Union: physical background, population, economy* by the well-known Vadim
Vyacheslavovich Pokshishevskii, translated into English by David Fidlon (Moscow:
Progress Publishers, 1974) which has its own loose map booklet.

130 **Siberia and the Soviet Far East.**
Edward Stuart Kirby. London: Economist Intelligence Unit, 1984.
52p. maps. bibliog. (Economist Intelligence Unit Special Reports,
no. 177).
Overpriced for the academic market, this pamphlet provides information suitable for
business concerns wishing to become involved in trade. Resources and prospects for
future economic development are highlighted. The Gorbachev revolution makes a
second edition desirable.

131 **Siberia 1971: a report on the visit of the Honourable Jean Chrétien,
Minister of Indian Affairs and Northern Development, and official
delegation, to the Soviet Union, July–August 1971.**
Walter Slipchenko. Ottawa: Indian and Northern Affairs, 1971. 124p.
maps.
This is a richly illustrated report with many technical diagrams about construction work
in permafrost conditions, forestry and mining, oil and gas extraction and the condition
of the indigenous peoples.

# Maps and atlases

132 **The first Russian maps of Siberia and their influence on West European
cartography of North East Asia.**
Leo Bagrow. *Imago Mundi*, vol. 9 (1952), p. 83-93. maps.
A facsimile of Semën Ulyanovich Remezov's 1667 map of Siberia is compared with
part of Antoine Thomas's map (q.v.), and those published in books by Ides (1687),
Delisle (1706) and Thornton (1700). For another early cartographer see 'Com-
memorating the three hundredth anniversary of the "Godunov map" of Siberia', by
Boris Petrovich Polevoi, translated from the Russian by James R. Gibson (*Canadian
Cartographer*, vol. 8, no. 1 [1971], p. 19-26).

133 **Semyon Remezov – a Siberian cartographer.**
Leo Bagrow. *Imago Mundi*, vol. 11 (1954), p. 111-25. maps.
The author outlines the career of Semën Ulyanovich Remezov (1642 to after 1720), the
foremost early cartographer of Siberia. Facsimiles of several maps are included, as is a
plan of the ruined fort which had been headquarters of the West Siberian Khan,
Kuchum, before the Russian invasion. A map by a Belgian, A. A. Winius, found in a
book by Remezov, is also published here.

134 **Sparwenfeld's map of Siberia.**
Leo Bagrow. *Imago Mundi*, vol. 4 (1947), p. 65-70. map.
This publication includes facsimiles of maps by Johan Gabriel Sparvenfeldt, a Swedish
historian and linguist (1655-1727) who studied Russian cartography while a member of
the Swedish Mission in Moscow. Hitherto unknown material is included. There are
also maps by Spathary (1682) and Remezov (1687).

135 **The USSR in maps.**
John Christopher Dewdney. London: Hodder & Stoughton, 1982.
117p. maps.

This is one of many convenient books of maps covering the whole Soviet Union which have a considerable Siberian interest. Another is *The Soviet Union in maps* by Harold Fullard (London: George Philip, 1972). Less specialized, but reliable, is *The Times atlas of the world: mid-century edition*, vol. 11 (London: Times Publishing, 1959) or its update *The comprehensive edition* (London: Times and J. Bartholomew, 1985).

136 **Maps of the Siberian route of the Belgian Jesuit A. Thomas, 1690.**
Anthony V. Florovsky. *Imago Mundi*, vol. 8 (1951), p. 103-8. maps.

Antoine Thomas, a Belgian Jesuit, left sketch-maps of the routes to China through territory partly belonging to the Muscovite state. His maps are published here, and show how he tried to define the southern borders of Muscovy in Asia.

137 **Russian history atlas.**
Martin Gilbert. London: Weidenfeld and Nicolson, 1972. 146p.

Much of this work, which has very clear maps from the Russian conquest of Siberia to the Soviet era, being particularly helpful on the civil war period, was later published as separate volumes on the Imperial and Soviet periods respectively (London: Routledge and Kegan Paul, 1978-79).

138 **The atlases of Siberia by S. U. Remezov as a source for old Russian urban history.**
Leonid Arkadevich Goldenberg. *Imago Mundi*, vol. 25 (1971),
p. 39-46. maps.

Semën Ulyanovich Remezov's Soviet biographer reveals that the graphic sketches of wooden dwellings on his maps are almost the only authentic sources for the study of seventeenth-century Siberian architecture. Sketches of buildings in numerous fortress towns are included, as are photographs of plaques in Tobolsk commemorating the great pioneer work by Remezov, who was born there.

139 **New map of Transbaikalia.**
Pëtr Alekseevich Kropotkin. *Geographical Journal*, vol. 24, no. 4
(Oct. 1904), p. 463-6.

Assessing a new geological map of the Transbaikal area drawn in the process of mapping for minerals along the line of the Trans-Siberian Railway, the author, an expert on orography, demonstrates that the map is in certain respects deficient.

140 **The atlas of Siberia. Facsimile edition with an introduction by Leo Bagrow.**
Semën Ulyanovich Remezov. The Hague: Mouton, 1958. 171p. maps.
bibliog. (Supplement 1 to *Imago Mundi*).

A costly full reproduction of Remezov's monumental *Sketch book of Siberia*, originally compiled in 1701, this work contains priceless information about conditions in Siberia in the late seventeenth century.

35

# Climate

141 **Climates of the USSR.**
A. A. Borisov, edited by Cyril A. Halstead, translated by
R. A. Ledward.   Edinburgh; London: Oliver and Boyd, 1965. 255p.
maps. bibliog.
A translation of a standard Soviet textbook on climates throughout the USSR, this
work contains quantities of material about Siberia and the Soviet Far East. The work is
divided into regions, with separate sections on the seas, plains and mountainous areas.
Tables are included for temperature ranges and precipitation. See the index for
relevant items.

142 **Cryospheric impacts of Soviet diversion schemes.**
T. Holt, P. M. Kelly, B. S. G. Cherry.   *Annals of Glaciology*, no. 5
(1984), p. 61-8.
The authors offer several hypotheses about the possible effects of proposed large-scale
river diversion plans on the climate of Siberia.

143 **Climates of the Soviet Union.**
Paul E. Lydolph.   Amsterdam: Elsevier, 1977. 443p. maps. bibliog.
(World Survey of Climatology, edited by H. E. Landsberg, vol. 7).
Richly provided with graphs, maps, and an extensive appendix of climatic tables this is
regarded as the standard English-language climatology of the USSR. The end of
chapter three and the whole of chapters four and five concern Siberia and the Soviet
Far East. Climatic tables for many Asiatic locations are included.

144 **Agricultural climatology of Siberia: natural belts and agro-climatic**
**analogues in North America.**
M. Y. Nuttonson.   Washington, DC: American Institute of Crop
Ecology, 1952. 64p. maps. bibliog. (International agro-climatological
series, no. 13).
This book surveys the effects of climate on agricultural possibilities in Siberia,
providing comparisons with similar regions in the USA and Canada to ease
comprehension for readers who are not experts in Soviet geography.

# Physical geography

### 145  Natural regions of the USSR.
Lev Semënovich Berg, translated from the Russian by Olga Adler Titelbaum, edited by John Morrison and C. C. Nikiforoff.  New York: Macmillan, 1950. 436p. maps. bibliog.

Written by the President of the USSR All-Union Geographical Society this valuable overview introduces all the country's geographical regions. Chapters thirteen to nineteen cover the Altai, the Sayans, Lake Baikal, the mountains in the east, Sakhalin and Kamchatka, including information on the relief, climate, soils, vegetation and fauna.

### 146  Large-scale water transfers in the USSR.
Philip Michael Kelly (et al.).  *Geo-Journal*, vol. 7, no. 3 (1983), p. 201-14.

This article examines the background of Siberian water diversion plans, the Soviet philosophy of the transformation of nature and the ecological and environmental impact of the proposed diversions. See also 'Soviet water diversion plans: implications for Kazakhstan and Central Asia' by Philip P. Micklin (*Central Asian Survey*, vol. 1, no. 4 [1982], p. 9-43) and 'The Siberian river diversion debate' in *The Soviet multinational state: readings and documents*, edited by M. Olcott (Armonk, NY; London: M. E. Sharpe, 1990), p. 143-63, which includes translations of several opposing Soviet views about water diversion. See also 'Environmentalism in the USSR: the opposition to the river diversion projects' by Robert G. Darst (*Soviet Economy*, vol. 4, no. 3 [July-Sept. 1988], p. 223-52. bibliog.) and the following article by Philip Micklin and Andrew Bond (p. 253-74).

### 147  The oil and gas potential of the Soviet Far East.
A. A. Meyerhoff.  Beaconsfield, England: Scientific Press, 1981. 176p. maps. bibliog.

Takes the form of a detailed investigation of the state of knowledge about petroleum reserves in the Soviet Far East in 1980. It is based on a working report prepared for the Canadian Department of Indian and Northern Affairs.

### 148  Geology of the USSR.
D. V. Nalivkin, translated from the Russian by N. Rast, edited by N. Rast, T. S. Westoll.  Edinburgh: Oliver and Boyd, 1973. 855p. maps. bibliog.

A sumptuously produced and very valuable publication, this is translated from a 1962 Soviet text. Considerable attention is paid to Siberia and the Soviet Far East. A shorter account is Nalivkin's *Geology of the USSR: a short outline*, translated from the Russian by S. I. Tomkeieff (Oxford: Pergamon Press, 1960).

149 **Ore deposits of the USSR.**
Edited by V. I. Smirnov.  London: Pitman, 1977. 352p.
Translated from a book published by a Soviet geological publishing house in 1974, this
work contains data on ore deposits from the whole of the USSR. References to Siberia
are scattered throughout the text.

150 **Agrochemistry of the soils of the USSR.**
A. V. Sokolov, R. V. Kovalëv and S. S. Trofimov, translated by
A. Gourevitch.  Jerusalem: Israel Program for Scientific Translations,
1971-72. 2 vols. bibliog.
In this translation of a standard Soviet textbook, volume 1 covers the soils of western
Siberia, volume 2 those of eastern Siberia. Companion volumes issued by the same
publishers and also translated by A. Gourevitch are: *The soils of southern Siberia from
the Urals to the Baikal* by K. P. Gorshenin, edited by I. V. Tyurin (1961. 758p. maps.
bibliog.); and *Soils of eastern Siberia* by E. N. Ivanova and *Genesis of the soils of
western Siberia* edited by R. V. Kovalëv, both published in 1969. They contain
numerous illustrations, diagrams and tables.

151 **Physical geography of Asiatic Russia.**
Sergei Petrovich Suslov, translated from the Russian by Noah
D. Gershevsky, edited by Joseph E. Williams.  San Francisco,
California; London: W. H. Freeman, 1961. 594p.
Reviewed in *Nature* (vol. 192, no. 4 [1961], p. 199-200) this work was found to be
flawed in geomorphology and structural geology, but good on hydrography, soils, flora
and fauna. Though dated in terms of mineral and energy resources, it contains valid
information in other fields. The first three sections deal with Siberia.

# Special features

152 **The fire came by: the riddle of the great Siberian explosion.**
John Baxter, Thomas Atkins.  London: Macdonald and Jane's, 1976.
165p. maps. bibliog.
A popular investigation of the Tunguska event, a devastating meteor strike which
caused a huge crater in a remote region of Siberia in 1908. This book was reviewed
critically in *Nature*, vol. 264, no. 5587 (16 Dec. 1976) because the authors speculated
that the event was caused by a spacecraft. Another study is *The Tungus event: the great
Siberian catastrophe of 1908* by Rupert Furneaux (Frogmore, England: Panther, 1977).

153 **The great Tolbachik Fissure eruption. Geological and geophysical data, 1975-1976.**
Edited by S. A. Fedotov, E. K. Markhinin, translated by J. E. Agrell (et al.). Cambridge: Cambridge University Press, 1978. 341p. maps.
Consists of a technical study by Soviet scientists about a massive eruption which took place in the Tolbachik volcano, part of Kamchatka's Mount Klyuchevskii range, in the mid-1970s.

154 **Catalogue of the active volcanoes of Kamchatka and the continental parts of Asia.**
Vladimir Ivanovich Vlodavetz, Boris Ivanovich Piip. Naples, Italy: International Volcanological Association, 1959. 110p. maps. (Catalogue of the Active Volcanoes of the World including Solfatara Fields, part 8).
Presents an exhaustive description of active volcanoes in the Soviet Far East with illustrations and tables. Other information may be found in 'Quaternary volcanism and tectonics in Kamchatka' by E. N. Erlich and Georgii S. Gorshkov, translated from the Russian by R. Sovkina and L. Tulynina (*Bulletin volcanologique*, vol. 42, nos 1-4 [1979], p. 1-298). A brief popular account is 'Russia's ring of fire' by John Massey Stewart (*Journal of Russian Studies*, no. 51 [1986], p. 21-32).

# Regions

## Birobidzhan

155 **People I know in Birobidzhan.**
E. I. Bugaenko. Moscow: Novosti Press Agency, 1975. 77p.
This Soviet view of life in the Jewish Autonomous Region of Birobidzhan, which was established in the Soviet Far East to combat Zionist tendencies among Jews in the USSR presents an idealized illustrated portrait of life there. A similar account may be found in *The people and land of Birobidzhan* by Vyacheslav Kostikov (Moscow, 1979). See also the luxurious publication to mark the 40th anniversary of the Region's founding: *Jewish Autonomous Region: photo album*, photographs by Anatolii Eshtokin, text by Naum Aizman (Khabarovsk: Khabarovskoe knizhnoe izdatel'stvo, 1980. 126p.). The captions are in Russian, English and Hebrew. A very broad spectrum of human activities and natural phenomena in Birobidzhan is covered.

# Chukotka

156 **Forbidden Kolyma.**
John Sallnow. *Geographical Magazine*, vol. 53, no. 4 (Jan. 1981),
p. 261-7. maps.
One of the first foreigners to be allowed into this closed region of the far northeast,
Sallnow presents a well-illustrated (if brief) survey of the history and present state of
the region. He was pleasantly struck by signs of improvement amidst the evident signs
of underdevelopment.

# Eastern Siberia

157 **Eastern Siberia.**
Handbook Prepared under the Direction of the Historical Section of
the Foreign Office. London: HM Stationery Office, 1920. 96p.
bibliog. (Peace Handbooks, Issued by the Historical Section of the
Foreign Office, vol. 9: The Russian Empire, no. 55).
This volume provides a general introduction to the geography, political history, social,
economic and financial conditions of the eastern half of Siberia, including the Maritime
region on the eve of civil war. A more limited purpose lay behind *Military monograph
on Siberia, containing information and route notes from Vladivostok to Irkutsk*
(Washington, DC: United States War Department General Staff, 1918. 2 vols). The
first volume describes seven possible routes for troops to reach Irkutsk from the east
and the conditions likely to be encountered; the second contains fascinating
photographs of each route. One error is a photograph of horses and carts on the Chuya
Trail in the Altai (southwest Siberia) whose caption announces that it is north of Lake
Baikal.

# Soviet Far East

158 **The Far Eastern Republic. Its natural resources, trade and industries.**
Washington, DC: Published by the Special Delegation of the FER to
the USA, 1922. 368p. maps.
Consists of a folder containing eight separately paginated sections covering: trade and
industry, furs, forests, fisheries, gold mining, coal mines, minerals, and the Far Eastern
Republic's (FER) constitution. A delegation from this short-lived, non-Bolshevik state
participated in the Washington Conference in 1922. The sections were also available as
separate pamphlets.

159 **The Soviet Far East.**
Edward Stuart Kirby. London: Macmillan, 1971. 268p. maps. bibliog.
Now ageing, this was a valuable economic geography of the whole Soviet Far East in
the late 1960s. It includes chapters on physical geography, population and livelihood,
economic development, and individual studies of Transbaikalia, the Amur region,
Khabarovsk, the Maritime Province, Yakutiya, Chukotka, Sakhalin, Kamchatka and
the Kurils. There are numerous tables and nine maps. It superseded *The Soviet Far
East: a survey of its physical and economic geography* by Erich Thiel, translated by
Annelie and Ralph Rookwood (London: Methuen, 1957).

160 **The Far Eastern Republic of Siberia.**
Henry Kittredge Norton. London: Allen and Unwin, 1923. 311p.

An eye-witness survey of the development and state of the Far Eastern Republic as it stood in the middle of 1922, this work includes contemporary documentary material difficult to locate elsewhere. Equally informative is Junius B. Wood's sometimes harrowing and richly illustrated 'The Far Eastern Republic' (*National Geographic*, vol. 41, no. 6 [June 1922], p. 565-92. map).

161 **The economic development of the Soviet Far East.**
E. Raikhman, B. Vvedenskii. New York, 1936. 50p. (Institute of Pacific Relations. USSR Council Papers, 1936, no. 2).

This paper was presented by members of the Soviet delegation at the 6th Conference of the Honolulu Institute of Pacific Relations in 1936. It provides an overview of the situation in the middle of the five-year plan period. It was reprinted with other materials in the conference's official proceedings *Problems of the Pacific, 1936*, edited by W. L. Holland and K. L. Mitchell (Chicago: University of Chicago Press, 1937).

162 **The Soviet Far East: questions and answers.**
Moscow: Novosti Press Agency, 1985. 63p. map.

Seventy-four of 'the most frequently asked' questions about the natural features, history, population, economy and culture of the Soviet Far East are answered by an official Soviet publishing house. There are colour and monochrome illustrations. An account of the region from a learned Western viewpoint is 'Economic and strategic position of the Soviet Far East' by Leslie Dienes (*Soviet Economy*, vol. 1, no. 2 [April-June 1985], p. 146-76. map. bibliog.) which stresses the region's continued economic weakness, owing to its remoteness and harsh climate, a weakness making it 'parasitically' dependent on the metropolis despite the military build-up there.

163 **Soviet Far East: a tour of Primorye Territory.**
V. Tkachëv, S Nikolaev. Moscow: Progress Publishers, 1966. 96p.

Though small in format, this book provides rare information on Vladivostok and its suburbs, and the settlements of Artëm, Ussurisk, Suchan and Nakhodka. Lyrical about the region's beauty, the work also includes information on the best coking coal deposits in the Far East. A later publication in similar vein is *The Soviet Far East* by P. Demidov (Moscow: Novosti Press Agency, 1972. 112p.).

# Kamchatka

164 **Explorations of Kamchatka, north Pacific scimitar.**
Stepan Petrovich Krasheninnikov, translated and introduced by E. A. P. Crownhart-Vaughan. Portland, Oregon: Oregon Historical Society, 1972. 375p. maps.

This recent rendering of Krasheninnikov's classic eighteenth-century observations on Kamchatka is very welcome. As may be seen from comparison with other accounts such as that of Sven Waxell (q.v.), Krasheninnikov's depiction of the geography, native population, flora and fauna constitute a unique source. All future knowledge of the peninsula has been based on his findings.

165 **Problems in the development of the Kamchatskaya Oblast.**
Ottawa, 1966. 141p. maps. (*Extracts from the Soviet Press*, Supplement 1 [1966]).

A translation by the Canadian Department of the Secretary of State Bureau of Translations, Foreign Language Division, of a work published by the Soviet Academy of Sciences in 1960. The work investigates the then current level of development of the region in and around Kamchatka, suggesting reasons for the slowness of that development.

# Sakhalin

166 **Pioneer economy of Sakhalin Island.**
Herman R. Friis. *Economic Geography*, vol. 15 (Jan. 1939), p. 55-79. maps.

This well-illustrated study with excellent maps provides details of the physical geography and natural resources of Sakhalin. A sharp contrast is drawn between the development of the northern section under Soviet rule and the southern part, Karafuto, in Japanese hands since 1905.

167 **Sakhalin.**
Handbook Prepared under the Direction of the Historical Section of the Foreign Office. London: HM Stationery Office, 1920. 46p. bibliog. (Peace Handbooks, Issued by the Historical Section of the Foreign Office, vol. 9: The Russian Empire, no. 56).

Prepared during the Allied intervention in Siberia this handbook briefly covers the physical and economic geography, history and social development of Sakhalin up to 1916.

168 **Soviet Sakhalin.**
Vladimir Yakovlevich Kantorovich. Moscow: Cooperative Publishing Society of Foreign Workers in the USSR, International Press, 1933. 96p.

This is a rare tract eulogizing Soviet achievements in Sakhalin. As John Stephan writes, it 'captured the rough, makeshift life of the first five-year plan' (*Sakhalin, a history* [q.v.]), thus despite its obvious shortcomings it is a valuable representation of Soviet views at the time. *Rediscovered country* by Gennadii Paderin (Moscow: Foreign Languages Publishing House, [c. 1962]) presents another enthusiastic view, but this time from the Khrushchëv era. The work is illustrated with maps.

# Tuva

169 **Republic in the heart of Asia. 40th anniversary of Soviet Tuva.**
Pëtr Zubkov, translated from the Russian by Sergei Chulaki,
translation edited by George Wood. Moscow: Novosti Press Agency,
1985. 62p.

This pamphlet briefly covers the history, geography and social development of the
Tuvan Autonomous Republic, providing colour and monochrome illustrations of past
and present life. It is noteworthy for the inclusion of an interview with Maksim
Munzuk who played the role of Dersu Uzala in Kurosawa's award-winning film of
Arsenev's tale (see item no. 33). Westerners have written little on Tuva, but a detailed
historical introduction may be found in 'The forgotten frontier: south Siberia (Tuva) in
Chinese and Russian history, 1600-1912' by Thomas E. Ewing (*Central Asiatic Journal*,
vol. 25, no. 3-4 [1981], p. 174-212).

# Western Siberia

170 **Siberia's empire road: the river Ob.**
Robert Paul Jordan, photographs by Dean Conger. *National
Geographic*, vol. 149, no. 2 (Feb. 1976), p. 144-81. map.

Richly illustrated in colour this typical *National Geographic* article provides a broad-
based introduction to the geography and human development of the Ob river region.

# Yakutiya

171 **Country life in northeast Siberia.**
Terence Armstrong. *Geographical Magazine*, vol. 46, no. 7 (April
1974), p. 344-9. maps.

Following a rare visit to the Yakut Autonomous Soviet Socialist Republic the author
presents a well-illustrated survey of life there in the early 1970s. Subjects covered
include agriculture, mining, housing development and the life of the Yakut.

# Flora and Fauna

172 **A selective index to Siberian, Far Eastern and Central Asian materia medica.**
John H. Appleby.    Oxford: Wellcome Unit for the History of Medicine, 1987. 48p. bibliog. (Research Publications of the WUHM, no. 8).

This large-format publication begins with a brief survey of expeditions to Siberia from the eighteenth century onwards which, among other things, were looking for new medicines. It lists plants, animals, organic and inorganic materials which are claimed to have medical properties. The author hopes that it will prove of therapeutic value in the West. It specifically excludes items referred to in 'Medicinal plants in Russia in the eighteenth and early nineteenth centuries' by Margery Rowell (PhD thesis, University of Kansas, 1977, available from University Microfilms, Ann Arbor, Michigan, order no. 77-28906).

173 **Freshwater fishes of the USSR and adjacent countries.**
Lev Semënovich Berg, translated from the Russian by Omry Ronen. Jerusalem: Israel Program for Scientific Translations, 1962-65. 3 vols.

This work was translated for the National Science Foundation in Washington from the fourth edition of a Soviet textbook published by the Academy of Sciences in 1948-49. Siberian species are scattered throughout the different volumes.

174 **Translations of Russian game reports.**
Ottawa: Canadian Department of Northern Affairs and National Resources, National Parks Branch, Canadian Wildlife Service, 1957-59. 6 vols.

These translations of reports about fur-bearing mammals in the USSR refer to the situation in the years 1951-55. The volumes cover several species of mammal, including beaver, muskrat, arctic and red foxes, sable and red squirrel. There is also a study of fur trapping and other aspects of the Soviet fur industry. A complementary survey is

'The problems of distribution and development of caged fur animals in the USSR' by A. A. Nazarov, translated by William Barr (*Musk-Ox*, no. 11 [1972], p. 33-8. maps. bibliog.) which, as its title indicates, concentrates on animals bred in captivity. Sections of both works refer to Siberia and the Soviet Far East.

## 175 The living tundra.

Yurii Ivanovich Chernov, translated by D. Löve. Cambridge: Cambridge University Press, 1985. 213p. maps.

Originally published by the Mysl (Thought) publishing house in the USSR in 1980, this volume surveys the flora, fauna and ecology of the tundra regions of the northern and eastern Soviet Union in connection with the exploitation of the area's resources. There are helpful diagrams and illustrations.

## 176 Birds of the Soviet Union.

General editors Georgii Petrovich Dementev, N. A. Gladkov (et al.), translated from the Russian by A. Birron, Z. S. Cole, edited by Z. S. Cole. Jerusalem: Israel Program for Scientific Translations, 1966-68. 6 vols.

An illustrated English version of a standard Soviet study of birds inhabiting the USSR, this work provides a compendium of information on the subject, including maps of population distribution. Descriptions of birds which inhabit or fly through Siberia and the Soviet Far East are scattered throughout the text.

## 177 The mammoth and mammoth hunting in north-east Siberia.

Bassett Digby. London: H. F. & G. Witherby; New York: Appleton, 1926. 216p. map.

The author surveys the history of the discovery of frozen mammoth carcasses in Siberia then sketches in details of his own trip to Yakutiya during which he searched for such beasts. Diagrams are included. A more recent investigation is 'The mammoth "cemetries" of north east Siberia' by N. K. Vereshchagin (*Polar Record*, vol. 17, no. 106 [1974], p. 3-12. map. bibliog.). This illustrated account includes the results of 1970-72 fieldwork. See also 'Baby mammoth discovered in Siberia' (*Polar Record*, vol. 19, no. 120 [Sept. 1978], p. 287), a report of the discovery of a complete carcass near Magadan in 1977.

## 178 Flora of Kamchatka and the adjacent islands.

Eric Hultén. Stockholm: Almqvist & Wiksells, 1927-30. 4 vols. maps. (Kungl. Svenska Vetenskaps Akademiens Handlingar, tredje serien, band 5, no. 1-2, plus band 8, no. 1-2.)

This is a systematic treatment of the flora of the Pacific littoral region prepared by a Swedish botanist who spent time in Kamchatka and the Kuril islands in the early 1920s. It was published in English by the Royal Swedish Academy of Sciences. There are coloured maps, diagrams and photographs. This may be compared with *Results of ornithological explorations in the Commander islands and Kamtschatka* by Leonard Stejneger (Washington, DC: Government Printing Office, 1885. 382p. Bulletin no. 29 of the US National Museum).

179 **The natural history of the USSR.**
Algirdas Knystautas, translated from the Russian by John S. Scott.
London: Century Hutchinson, 1987. 224p. maps. bibliog.

A beautifully produced coffee-table book with 275 colour illustrations of the flora and fauna of the USSR by a Lithuanian naturalist and freelance writer and photographer, this book demonstrates what good results may be obtained from collaboration between the Soviet Union and European organizations. Sections are included on the various regions of Siberia and the Soviet Far East.

180 **Mammals of eastern Europe and northern Asia.**
Sergei Ivanovich Ognëv (vol. 9 by A. G. Tomilin), translated from the Russian by A. Birron, Z. S. Cole. Jerusalem: Israel Program for Scientific Translations, 1962-67. 9 vols.

This translation of a monumental Soviet work published in the late 1920s has separate sections devoted to different species of mammal, for instance volumes 4-5 are concerned with rodents and volume 9 with Cetacea. See also *Carnivorous mammals of Siberia* by Sergei Ulyanovich Stroganov, translated from the Russian by Dr A. Birron (Jerusalem: Israel Program for Scientific Translations, 1969. 522p. maps. bibliog.).

181 **Siberian man and mammoth.**
Eugen Wilhelm Pfizenmayer, translated from the German by Muriel D. Simpson. London; Glasgow: Blackie, 1939. 256p. maps.

Provides an account of two expeditions by the Russian Imperial Academy of Sciences in 1901-2 and 1908 to northeast Siberia in search of mammoth remains. Details are provided of rhinoceros and mammoths, but in addition there are interesting remarks about the Skoptsy (a religious sect), *kumiss* (a drink made from fermented mare's milk), the Indigirka region, hunting, fishing and sledging. An American report based on data like Pfizenmayer's is 'The carcasses of the mammoth and rhinoceros found in the frozen ground of Siberia' by Innokentii P. Tolmachoff (*Transactions of the American Philosophical Society*, NS vol. 23, part 1 [1929], p. 1-74. bibliog.). See also Tolmachoff's *Siberian passage: an explorer's search into the Russian Arctic* (New Brunswick: Rutgers University Press, 1949. 238p.).

182 **The distribution of endangered fauna in the USSR.**
Philip R. Pryde. *Biological Conservation*, vol. 42, no. 1 (1987), p. 19-37.

Using materials in the Soviet Red Book for 1985 the author investigates the spatial distribution of the 70 endangered species of fauna in the USSR. Particular attention is devoted to a small area in the Maritime region between Lake Khanka and Vladivostok, where a large number of the species in question are concentrated.

183 **Nature and natural resources of the Soviet Far East.**
E. Raikhman, B. Vvedenskii. New York, 1936. 62p. (Institute of Pacific Relations. USSR Council Papers 1936, no. 2).

This is another paper presented by the Soviet delegation to the Sixth Conference of the Institute of Pacific Relations. Its title is self-explanatory, though the discussion is in the context of economic development rather than ecological considerations.

184   **The birds of Siberia.**
Henry Seebohm.   London: John Murray, 1901. 512p. map. Reprinted
in 2 vols, Gloucester, England: Alan Sutton, 1985; New York:
Hippocrene Books, 1986.

A steel manufacturer from Sheffield and amateur ornithologist, Henry Seebohm (1832-
95) visited the Pechora river region and then the Enisei looking for rare birds.
Accounts of the two trips were published separately in 1880 and 1882. Only the
second, originally entitled *Siberia in Asia: a visit to the valley of the Yenesay in east
Siberia* (London: John Murray, 1882. 298p.), is relevant to Siberia. Both were
combined for the 1901 edition, and they were separated again in the 1980s. The
account, while including detailed lists of birds seen in the field is also a travelogue, and
has sketches about the Skoptsy, the Dolgany and the Khanty and other traveller's
observations.

185   **Vascular plants of the Siberian north and the northern Far East.**
Edited by A. I. Tolmachëv, translated from the Russian by L. Philips.
Jerusalem: Israel Program for Scientific Translations (IPST), 1969.
340p. bibliog.

Like the other volumes published by IPST this botanical treatise is a translation of a
standard Soviet treatment of its subject published by the USSR Academy of Sciences
in 1966. There are many illustrations of the plants described.

# Environmental Problems and Protection

186  **The spoils of progress: environmental pollution in the Soviet Union.**
Marshall Irwin Goldman.   Cambridge, Massachusetts: MIT Press,
1972. 372p. maps. bibliog.
Dedicated to Lake Baikal this book includes devastating details about the degradation
of the environment in Siberia, with particular emphasis on this unique lake. The texts
of selected laws are included. Excellent colour photographs of the lake may be found
in *Baikal*, photographs by Aleksei Freidberg, introduction by Valentin Rasputin, text
by Mark Sergeev (Moscow: Planeta, 1985) and *Lake Baikal, Baikal nature reserve
areas* by Oleg Kirillovich Gusev (Moscow: Agropromizdat, 1986. 183p. map). Both of
these are large-format dual-language books, whose aim is to make the outside world
more intimately aware of the uniqueness of Baikal.

187  **Conservation in the Soviet Union.**
Philip R. Pryde.   Cambridge: Cambridge University Press, 1972. 301p.
bibliog.
This study takes the form of a detailed investigation of Soviet policies and legislation
on management of soils, national parks, fisheries and wildlife, timber and mineral
extraction and water resources. Scattered throughout it are references to situations in
Siberia including Lake Baikal and the ecological problems of local fauna. That the
situation had not improved by the late 1970s may be seen by reference to 'The
ecosystem of Lake Baikal and problems of environmental protection' by G. I. Galazii
(*Soviet Geography*, vol. 22, no. 4 [April 1981], p. 217-25). Galazii, the director of the
Limnological Institute on the shores of the lake, presents seven criteria for preserving
the water's purity and describes some of the more interesting fauna discovered by his
team.

188    **The destruction of nature in the Soviet Union.**
Boris Komarov, translated by Michael Vale, Joe Hollander.    White
Plains, New York: M. E. Sharpe; London: Pluto Press, 1980. 150p.
bibliog.

Written by a serving member of a Soviet government ministry and published
pseudonymously in the West this is a knowledgeable and severe critique of official
policies. Ecological problems caused by sewage, railway construction, mining and
industrial pollution in Siberia form a large part of the argument. *Environmental misuse
in the Soviet Union*, edited by Fred Singleton (New York: Praeger, 1976) adds a few
details on air pollution in the Kuzbas and the Angara–Baikal region.

189    **Problems of Lake Baykal in the current period.**
V. V. Vorobëv.    *Soviet Geography*, vol. 30, no. 1 (Jan. 1989),
p. 33-48. map.

Based on a talk given at the 5th Scientific Conference of Applied Geographers at
Irkutsk in 1987, the article depicts environmental problems around Lake Baikal and
suggests methods of tackling them. Plans to establish two small national parks in the
area, already agreed by the USSR Council of Ministers, are outlined. A colourful
account of these problems by John Massey Stewart, an English freelance writer, is
'Baikal's hidden depths' (*New Scientist*, no. 1722 [23 June 1990], p. 42-46, continued as
'The great lake is in peril' (*New Scientist*, no. 1723 [30 June 1990], p. 56-62.

190    **Protected areas of the Lake Baykal basin.**
V. V. Vorobëv, A. V. Martynov.    *Soviet Geography*, vol. 30, no. 5
(May 1989), p. 359-70.

Two Siberian geographers appeal for the establishment of a unified national park to
include the Selenga delta, the whole of Lake Baikal and the upper Angara. This would
involve the removal of industry and the establishment of luxury tourist accommodation.

# Prehistory and Archaeology

191 **Paleolithic art in the USSR.**

Z. A. Abramova. *Arctic Anthropology*, vol. 4, no. 2 (1967), p. 1-179.

Presents a detailed illustrated survey of traces of Old Stone Age art discovered in the territory now covered by the USSR. Another work devoted to indigenous art forms is *Ancient art of the Amur region* by Aleksei Pavlovich Okladnikov (Leningrad: Aurora Art Publishers, 1981).

192 **Ancient cemeteries of the Chukchi peninsula.**

S. A. Arutyunov. *Arctic Anthropology*, vol. 2, no. 1 (1964), p. 143-54.

Written by a Soviet expert, the article consists of a concentrated, illustrated description of early cemeteries excavated in Chukotka in far northeast Siberia.

193 **Northeast Asia in prehistory.**

Chester Stevens Chard. Madison, Wisconsin; London: University of Wisconsin Press, 1974. 214p. maps. bibliog.

A prolific writer on the prehistory of northeast Asia, Chard has here collated all the information available about the traces of early human settlement over an area far larger than present-day Siberia and the Soviet Far East. Chapter one deals with the Pleistocene era, and chapter two covers Neolithic Siberia.

194 **Prehistory of western Siberia.**
Valerii Nikolaevich Chernetsov, Wanda Moszynska, translated by
D. Kraus (et al.), edited by Henry N. Michael. Montreal, Canada:
McGill-Queen's University Press for the Arctic Institute of North
America, 1974. 377p. maps. (Anthropology of the North: Translations
from Russian Sources, no. 9).
Contains a selection of major articles by two Soviet scholars specializing in a
combination of physical and social anthropology and archaeology. The research work
dates from the 1950s. The findings, based on evidence from petroglyphs and
archaeological digs, concentrate on groups similar to the Khanty and Mansi, living in
the Ural–Ob region. There are many diagrams and photographs.

195 **The formation of the modern peoples of the Soviet north.**
Boris Osipovich Dolgikh. *Arctic Anthropology*, vol. 9, no. 1 (1972),
p. 17-26. bibliog.
Dolgikh (1904-71), a renowned Soviet student of ethnographic history, traces the
processes whereby the contemporary native peoples inhabiting the northern USSR
came into being. The article was originally published in the journal *Soviet Ethnography*
in 1967. See also *Ethnic origins of the peoples of northeast Asia* by Maksim Grigorevich
Levin (Toronto, Canada: University of Toronto Press, published for the Arctic
Institute of North America, 1963. 355p. bibliog. [Anthropology of the North,
Translations from Russian Sources, no. 3]) which covers similar ground for the peoples
of northeast Siberia.

196 **South Siberia.**
Mikhail Petrovich Gryaznov, translated from the Russian by James
Hogarth. London: Barrie & Rockliffe, Cresset Press; New York:
Cowles Book Co., 1969. 251p. maps.
This is a profusely illustrated study of the prehistory of the culturally diverse Altai and
Sayan areas of southwest Siberia and the intervening steppe zone from roughly 2500 BC
to 100 AD. The author is a well-known Soviet archaeologist and was personally
involved in excavating the famous Pazyryk burial site.

197 **The Bering land bridge.**
Edited by David Moody Hopkins. Stanford, California: Stanford
University Press, 1967. 405p.
A collection of papers presented to the Seventh Congress of the International
Association for Quaternary Research in 1965, this volume investigates the geology, Ice
Age environment and human migrations in the far northeast of Siberia and Alaska.

198 **Archaeological investigations in Kamchatka.**
Waldemar Jochelson. Washington, DC: Carnegie Institution, 1928.
88p. (Carnegie Institution Publications, no. 388).
The author (1855-1937), whose name is a preferred form of his original name Vladimir
Ilich Yokhelson, was an indefatigable investigator of the archaeology and ethnography
of northeast Siberia. This publication outlines the present-day life of the Itelmen
(Kamchadal) population of Kamchatka and lists artefacts excavated by the author.

## Prehistory and Archaeology

'The prehistory of Kamchatka' by George Irving Quimby (*American Antiquity*, vol. 12 [Jan. 1947], p. 173-9) is largely based on Jochelson's work.

199   **The Tom river petroglyphs of Siberia.**
      A. I. Martynov.   *Musk-Ox*, no. 31 (1982), p. 1-16. map. bibliog.
Describes three groups of early rock engravings (there are 300 items) on cliffs near Kemerovo in southwest Siberia dating from the Neolithic period to the first millennium AD. Illustrations are provided. See also another illustrated article 'The reindeer in the prehistoric art of Siberia' by I. Whitaker (*Antiquity*, vol. 58 [July 1984], p. 103-12. bibliog.). A very recent addition to literature in this field is the illustrated 'Images of bears in the neolithic art of northeast Asia' by R. S. Vasilevskii and Aleksei Pavlovich Okladnikov (*Soviet Anthropology and Archeology*, vol. 28, no. 4 [spring 1990], p. 81-90) – a translation of a short excerpt from a monograph published in Novosibirsk in 1980.

200   **A US – USSR symposium on the peopling of the new world.**
      Edited by Henry N. Michael.   *Arctic Anthropology*, vol. 16, no. 1 (1979), p. 1-165.
Publishes contributions by both Soviet and American researchers on the question of how man came to cross the Bering land-bridge and settle on the American continent during the last Ice Age. Interesting new material may be found in 'New data on the Bering sea route of the settlement of Siberia: the Maiorych site – first upper paleolithic remains in the valley of the Kolyma' by Yu. A. Mochanov (*Soviet Anthropology and Archeology*, vol. 28, no. 4 [spring 1990], p. 44-9. map). The find provides hard evidence for a theory long advocated without enough support.

201   **The archaeology and geomorphology of northern Asia: selected works.**
      Edited by Henry N. Michael.   Toronto, Canada: University of Toronto Press for the Arctic Institute of North America, 1964. 512p. map. (Anthropology of the North: Translations from Russian Sources, no. 5).
As well as investigating the geology of northeast Asia when man first appeared on the scene, these translations of learned Soviet articles include information about the Lena river in Palaeolithic times, the Enisei and Amur in the Neolithic era and the prehistory of Kamchatka and Chukotka. See also Henry Michael's article 'The neolithic age in eastern Siberia' (*Transactions of the American Philosophical Society*, NS vol. 48, part 2 [1958], p. 1-108. maps. bibliog.).

202   **Studies in Siberian ethnogenesis.**
      Edited by Henry N. Michael.   Toronto, Canada: University of Toronto Press for the Arctic Institute of North America, [1962]. 313p. maps. (Anthropology of the North: Translations from Russian Sources, no. 2).
Includes translations of seventeen papers by Soviet experts on the Yakut, Buryat Mongols, Kirghiz, Koybal, Altai, Nganasan, Ugrians and the Amur tribes. The articles were originally published in the 1950s and reveal the state of Soviet studies of Siberian ethnogenesis in the late Stalin period. Charts and photographs are included. A later contribution in the same field is 'The origin of the ancient Koryak culture on the

northern Okhotsk coast' by R. S. Vasilevskii (*Arctic Anthropology*, vol. 6, no. 1 [1969], p. 150-64).

203  **Ancient population of Siberia and its cultures.**
Aleksei Pavlovich Okladnikov, translated fom the Russian by Vladimir
M. Maurin.   Cambridge, Massachusetts: Peabody Museum, 1959. 96p.
maps. bibliog. (Translation series of the Peabody Museum of
Archaeology and Ethnology, vol. 1, no. 1).

The doyen of Soviet Siberian academics provides a compressed survey of the Neolithic and Bronze Ages in Siberia and proceeds to a regional study of events during the first millennium AD. Only the first sixty-five pages are text, the rest are illustrations. In a later publication, 'The riddle of Ulalinka' by Aleksei Pavlovich Okladnikov and L. A. Ragozin (*Soviet Anthropology and Archeology*, vol. 23, no. 1 [summer 1984], p. 3-20. bibliog.), a rather extraordinary claim is made: that a 1961 find on the Ulalinka river near Gorno-Altaisk in the Altai mountains demonstrates the existence of proto-tool makers 700,000 years ago. The editors of the original article in *Sovetskaya etnografiya* (Soviet Ethnography), no. 6 (1982) remark that the conclusions are 'very much disputed'.

204  **The Soviet Far East in antiquity: an archaeological and historical study of the maritime region of the USSR.**
Aleksei Pavlovich Okladnikov, edited by Henry N. Michael, translated
by Stephen P. Dunn (et al.).   Toronto, Canada: University of Toronto
Press for the Arctic Institute of North America, [1965]. 280p.
(Anthropology of the North: Translations from Russian Sources,
no. 6).

Okladnikov covers the Neolithic period and the beginning of the Bronze and Iron Ages in the Far East. The 'shell mound' culture, the Mo-Ho and P'o-hai states (5th–7th centuries AD) and the Jurchen state (12th–16th centuries AD) are included. See also his *Ancient art of the Amur region* (Leningrad: Aurora Art Publishers, 1981). Both works contain important illustrations.

205  **The royal hordes: nomad peoples of the steppes.**
Eustace Dockray Phillips.   London: Thames & Hudson, 1965. 144p.
maps. bibliog.

Accompanied by some gorgeous coloured illustrations of artefacts and a useful chronology but with a rather brief text, this book presents a general survey of the history of pastoral nomadism on the Eurasian steppes from the fourth millennium BC to the arrival of the Huns in the fifth century AD.

206  **Paleolithic man in northeast Asia.**
William Roger Powers.   *Arctic Anthropology*, vol. 10, no. 2 (1973),
p. 1-106. maps. bibliog.

Consists of an illustrated survey of such information as is available on man in northeast Asia in the Old Stone Age.

207  **Frozen tombs of Siberia: the Pazyryk burials of iron age horsemen.**
Sergei Ivanovich Rudenko, translated and with a preface by M. W.
Thompson.  London: J. M. Dent, 1970. 340p. bibliog.
This fine publication with colour plates describes the excavation of Iron Age burial
mounds in the Altai mountains in southwest Siberia dating from *c*. 400 BC. See also
*Frozen tombs: the culture and art of the ancient tribes of Siberia*, an illustrated catalogue
of an exhibition in the British Museum (London: British Museum, 1978. 102p.).

208  **Prehistoric culture in southern Sakhalin in the light of Japanese
research.**
Masakazu Yoshizaki.  *Arctic Anthropology*, vol. 1, no. 2 (1963),
p. 131-58.
During the period of Japanese rule in southern Sakhalin (Karafuto) archaeological
investigations were made which tended to emphasize the antiquity of Ainu settlement
and links with cultures in Hokkaido. This was later disputed by Soviet official sources
whose researchers claimed that the Ainu were late arrivals, preceded by a Tonchi
people.

# History

## General

209 **The library and archeography: acquisitions from the field in Siberia.**
V. N. Alekseev. *Library Review*, vol. 29 (1980), p. 247-55.
A noted archeographer from the Siberian Section of the USSR Academy of Sciences reports on recent finds of rare historical material in Siberia. This article is included because it is very rare for information of this type, freely available in the USSR, to be published in English in the West.

210 **Russia's conquest of Siberia: evolving Russian and Soviet historical interpretations.**
David Norman Collins. *European Studies Review*, vol. 12, no. 1 (1982), p. 17-44.
Studies the evolution of opinions in Imperial Russia and the USSR about the significance of Siberia's incorporation into the Russian state. Ideological considerations often influenced conclusions as to whether the incorporation was achieved by military subjugation or peaceful peasant incorporation. Another historiographical article, which presents an analysis of works by three fine present-day historians of Siberia is 'Contemporary Siberian historians: (i) B. P. Polevoi, P. N. Pavlov and A. P. Umanskii' by David Collins (*Sibirica*, no. 4 [1989], p. 44-9).

211 **Russian expansion in Siberia and America.**
James R. Gibson. *Geographical Review*, vol. 70, no. 2 (April 1980), p. 127-36.
Provides a compressed introduction to Tsarist Russia's colonial expansion into Siberia and Alaska from 1580 to 1867. An essay with a rather similar text is published in *Russia's American Colony*, edited by S. Frederick Starr (Durham, North Carolina: Duke University Press, 1987, p. 371-4.). Gibson's 'The significance of Siberia to tsarist Russia' (*Canadian Slavonic Papers*, vol. 14 [1972], p. 442-53) and 'Russia on the

Pacific: the role of the Amur' (*Canadian Geographer*, vol. 12, no. 1 [1968], p. 15-27) are interesting attempts to analyse Tsarist aims in the region.

212 **Russian imperialism from Ivan the Great to the Revolution.**
Edited by Taras Hunczak. New Brunswick, New Jersey: Rutgers University Press, 1974. 396p. maps. bibliog.
Sections of this wide-ranging introduction to the phenomenon of Russian imperialism refer to Siberia and the Russian Far East. They are best found by reference to the index. *Russia and Asia: essays on the influence of Russia on the Asian peoples*, edited by Wayne S. Vucinich (Stanford, California: Hoover Institution Press, 1972), has a usefully annotated chapter by Stephen and Ethel Dunn which continues the general historical introduction into the Soviet era.

213 **The urge to the sea. The course of Russian history. The role of rivers, portages, ostrogs, monasteries and furs.**
Robert Joseph Kerner. Berkeley, California: University of California Press, 1942. Reprinted New York: Russell, 1971. 212p. maps.
Part of this pioneering work investigates the methods by which the Muscovites penetrated Transuralia by river routes, forts and monasteries. The basic underlying theory is that the Russians needed to push outwards from their continental heartland to obtain sea outlets. The expansion across Siberia is seen in this light. Also still of interest is the author's 'The Russian eastward movement: some observations on its historical significance' (*Pacific Historical Review*, vol. 17, no. 5 [1948], p. 135-48).

214 **The geopolitical image of the fatherland: the case of Russia.**
Ladis K. D. Kristof. *Western Political Quarterly*, vol. 20, no. 4 (Dec. 1967), p. 941-54.
A study in imperialist ideology, this article sympathetically investigates the developing Russian consciousness of a Eurasian identity, and of a national messianic role in Siberia and the Far East, particularly in the late nineteenth century. The author posits the construction of a 'Eurasian Brasilia somewhere between Volga and Urals' to invigorate this concept. The article is incorporated as part of a broader essay, 'The Russian image of Russia: an applied study in geopolitical methodology', in *Essays in political geography*, edited by Charles A. Fisher (London: Methuen, 1968, p. 345-87). A recently published extensive treatment of this theme, and of the 'heartland' concept of Sir Halford John Mackinder (1861-1947) is *What is Asia to us? Russia's heartland yesterday and today* by Milan Hauner (Boston, Massachusetts; London: Unwin Hyman, 1990. 264p.). See also Hooson's book.

215 **Russia's eastward expansion.**
Edited by George Alexander Lensen. Englewood Cliffs, New Jersey: Prentice-Hall, 1964. 184p. maps.
Consisting of a series of brief excerpts from accounts by Russians and outsiders, this work seeks to encapsulate the experience of expansion across the continent and as far as Manchuria and Alaska. There is some material on Soviet developments in the region.

216 **Russian expansion in the Far East in the light of the Turner hypothesis.**
A. Lobanov-Rostovsky. In: *The frontier in perspective*, edited by W. D.
Wyman, C. B. Kroeger. Madison, Wisconsin: Madison University
Press, 1965, p. 79-94.

An ex-employee of the Tsarist Foreign Ministry discounts the possibility that Russian
society and institutions were influenced by frontier experiences in Siberia. He thus
maintains (in opposition to 'Russian expansion in the light of Turner's study of the
American frontier' by Donald Warren Treadgold [*Agricultural History*, vol. 26, no. 4
(1952), p. 147-52]) that Frederick Jackson Turner's frontier thesis was invalid for the
Russian Empire. Other factors connected with Russia's advance eastwards are stressed
in Lobanov's 'Russian imperialism in Asia: its origin, evolution and character'
(*Slavonic and East European Review*, vol. 8 [1929-30], p. 28-47); see also his book
*Russia and Asia* (New York: Macmillan, 1933. 334p.). Similar in tone is Benedict
Humphrey Sumner's 'Tsardom and imperialism in the Far East and Middle East, 1880-
1914' (*Proceedings of the British Academy*, vol. 27 [1940] and also issued as a separate
pamphlet [London: Oxford University Press, 1947. 43p.]).

217 **Siberia: its conquest and development.**
Yuri Semyonov, translated from the German by J. R. Foster.
London: Hollis & Carter, 1963. 414p. maps.

One of very few general histories of Siberia in English, this work is popular in tone and
rather superficial, but a great improvement on the author's garish *The conquest of
Siberia*, translated by E. W. Dicks (London: Routledge, 1944. 356p.). Another light
read is *From the Volga to the Yukon. The story of the Russian march to Alaska and
California* by Daniel Henderson (New York: Hasting House, 1944. 256p.). The latter
two are typical of the pro-Russian propaganda produced during World War II.

218 **The frontier in Central Asia.**
Ihor Stebelsky. In: *Studies in Russian Historical Geography*, no. 1,
edited by James Bater, R. French. London: Academic Press, 1983,
p. 144-73. maps. bibliog.

Demonstrates how the Russian conquest of Siberia and Central Asia necessitated the
construction of fortified lines to protect the newly ingested areas from nomad
incursions. Pages 144-53 refer to Siberia. The maps are very helpful.

219 **The Kuril Islands: Russo-Japanese frontier in the Pacific.**
John J. Stephan. Oxford: Clarendon Press, 1974. 279p. maps. bibliog.

This thoroughly researched study is the only serious treatment of its subject in English.
It covers the history of the islands from prehistoric times to the 1970s. Similarly
valuable is Stephan's *Sakhalin: a history* (Oxford: Clarendon Press, 1971. 240p. maps.
bibliog.). We eagerly await the publication of his *The Soviet Far East: a history*, which
is completed and should be published by 1992. It covers the geography, prehistory,
Chinese and Russian periods, development of the Tsarist and Soviet far eastern
empires, the civil war, the Kolyma death camps and reforms up to the Gorbachev
period.

220 **The Russian frontier: the impact of borderlands upon the course of early Russian history.**
Joseph L. Wieczynski. Charlottesville, Virginia: Virginia University Press, 1976. 108p.

Attempting to apply Frederick Jackson Turner's 'frontier thesis' to Siberia, the author comes to conclusions opposing those reached by Lobanov-Rostovsky (q.v.). Wiecynski's ideas, though stimulating for discussion, would not gain universal acceptance, based as they are on the predominance of free enterprise as a motive for exploring and exploiting Siberia.

221 **The history of Siberia from Russian conquest to revolution.**
Edited and introduced by Alan Wood. London; New York: Routledge, 1991. 192p.

The essays in this deceptively slim-looking volume investigate a variety of fascinating problems about Siberia's history. Basil Dmytryshyn looks at the seventeenth-century administrative apparatus, Collins (q.v.) studies aspects of colonial policy up to the eighteenth century, and Black returns to the theme of the great Siberian expeditions. Forsyth provides a glimpse into the contents of his forthcoming book on the native peoples by a survey of the consequences for them of Russia's conquest of the region (a previous essay in *The development of Siberia* [q.v.] surveyed the Soviet period). Wood investigates vagrancy and crime in the nineteenth century. The noted historian Leonid M. Goryushkin from the Siberian Section of the USSR Academy of Sciences distils some of his expertise about post-emancipation settlement of Siberia in a paper on migration, settlement and the rural economy. John Channon provides a rapid overview of events during the Revolution and civil war of 1917-21.

# From the earliest times to 1580

222 **The empire of the steppes. A history of Central Asia.**
René Grousset, translated from the French by Naomi Walford. New Brunswick, New Jersey: Rutgers University Press, 1970. 687p. maps.

A general history of the nomadic peoples of mediaeval Central Asia, this work includes information about the situation in Siberia prior to the Muscovite advance into the region.

223 **Russian eastward expansion before the Mongol invasion.**
George V. Lantzeff. *American Slavic and East European Review*, vol. 6, nos 18-19 (1947), p. 1-10.

Briefly recounts the exploits of mediaeval Novgorod on its northeastern frontier bordering Siberia and attempts by the Principality of Suzdal to oppose Novgorod's expansion there. A rather later period is covered in 'The Russian expansion towards Asia and the Arctic in the middle ages' by Charles Raymond Beazley (*American Historical Review*, vol. 13 [October 1907–July 1908], p. 731-41. (An excerpt from the latter is in *Russia's eastward expansion* by Lensen, p. 4-7 [q.v.]).

224 **Treasure of the land of darkness: the fur trade and its significance for mediaeval Russia.**
Janet Martin.   Cambridge: Cambridge University Press, 1986. 277p. maps. bibliog.
A thorough investigation of the significance of the fur trade in mediaeval Muscovy, this work sets the scene for the later penetration of Siberia which was motivated to a considerable extent by the search for furs. See also her article 'The land of darkness and the Golden Horde: the fur trade under the Mongols, XIII–XIV centuries' (*Cahiers du monde russe et soviétique*, vol. 19, no. 4 [1978], p. 401-21. bibliog.).

225 **Yakutiya before its incorporation into the Russian state.**
Aleksei Pavlovich Okladnikov, edited by Henry N. Michael.
Montreal, Canada; London: McGill-Queen's University Press for the Arctic Institute of North America. 499p. maps. bibliog. (Anthropology of the North: Translations from Russian Sources, no. 8).
Though marred by attempts to fit data into Marxist concepts, this pioneer volume, translated from a work published by the Soviet Academy of Sciences in Yakutsk in 1950, includes all the then known information on early Yakut history, from the Stone Age to the arrival of the Russians in the seventeenth century. Yakut traditions, culture and lifestyle are pieced together in the final chapters.

226 **The Cambridge history of early inner Asia.**
Edited by Denis Sinor.   Cambridge: Cambridge University Press, 1990. 518p. maps. bibliog.
A work of staggering breadth of scholarship, this book presents the first modern history of an area defined as 'inner Asia', which includes much of present-day Siberia. Particularly relevant are chapters by Academician Aleksei Pavlovich Okladnikov about early human habitation, and by Peter Golden on the peoples of the Russian forest belt.

# From Ermak's conquest to 1799

227 **The beginnings of the Irbit fair.**
V. A. Aleksandrov, translated from the Russian by James R. Gibson.
*Soviet Geography*, vol. 31, no. 3 (March 1990), p. 202-21. bibliog.
This highly detailed analysis of trade and traders at the West Siberian Irbit trade fair in the late seventeenth and early eighteenth centuries is based on data in the customs books for 1699-1700 and 1703-6. It is a good counterpoint to Drew's 'The Siberian fair' (q.v.).

228 **Samuel Bentham in Russia, 1779-1791.**
Matthew Smith Anderson. *American Slavic Review*, vol. 15, no. 2
(1956), p. 157-72.

Samuel Bentham (1757-1831), younger brother of Jeremy, spent a decade in the service of the Russian state. In 1781-82 he travelled extensively in Siberia, and in 1789 obtained command of a regiment there, leaving the country only in 1791. The article provides a summary of his energetic activities and critical reactions to shortcomings within a region which he believed destined for great developments. The account is based largely on letters to the family. Similar ground is covered in 'Samuel Bentham and Siberia' by Walther Kirchner (*Slavonic and East European Review*, vol. 36 [1957-58], p. 471-80). 'The regimental school established in Siberia by Samuel Bentham', by K. A. Papmehl (*Canadian Slavonic Papers*, vol. 8 [1966], p. 153-68) deals with the primary school for illiterate soldiers which he established at Kudarinskaya near Irkutsk between 1789 and 1791.

229 **Yermak's campaign in Siberia. A selection of documents.**
Edited by Terence Armstrong, translated from the Russian by Tatiana Minorsky and David Wileman. London: Hakluyt Society, 1975. 315p. maps. bibliog. (Works Issued by the Hakluyt Society, Second Series, no. 146).

Consists of a translation of several Russian sixteenth-century chronicles about the Ermak expedition which established a Muscovite presence on the eastern side of the Urals for the first time. Monochrome reproductions of illustrations from the original chronicles are included in abundance. The 33-page introduction successfully places Ermak and his expedition in their context, though further research has tended to show that the expedition's traditional departure date of 1 September 1581 is at least a year too early. See 'Ermak's Siberian expedition' by Ruslan Grigorevich Skrynnikov, edited and translated from the Russian by Hugh F. Graham (*Russian History/Histoire russe*, vol. 13, no. 1 [1986], p. 1-39). See also Skrynnikov's 'The early period in Russia's annexation of Siberia' (*Soviet Studies in History*, no. 1-2 [1985], p. 113-36) and also the 2nd edition of his monograph *Sibirskaia ekspeditsiia Ermaka* (Moscow: Nauka, 1986).

230 **The conquest and colonisation of Siberia.**
Anatole V. Baikalov. *Slavonic and East European Review*, vol. 10
(1932), p. 555-71.

Briefly but valuably surveys Siberian geography and Russia's conquest and colonization of the region during the seventeenth and eighteenth centuries.

231 **Expansion and colonization on the frontier: views of Siberia and the Far East in pre-Petrine Russia.**
Mark Bassin. *Journal of Historical Geography*, vol. 14, no. 1 (Jan. 1988), p. 3-21. map. bibliog.

The author maintains that Russian colonial expansion in the seventeenth century was essentially mercantile in nature. The Far East is assumed to have been important solely as a provider of colonial commodities. The argument counters recent Soviet assertions that the Muscovites had an overriding territorial interest in the region.

232    Russia's 'Age of silver': precious metal production and economic growth
       in the eighteenth century.
       Ian Blanchard.    London; New York: Routledge, 1989. 431p. maps.
       bibliog.
Has a considerable amount of space devoted to the Demidov mines and smelting works
in the Altai mountains and other Siberian material. For details of the coins minted in
the Altai, see *The Russian monetary system: a historico-numismatic survey* by I. G.
Spasskii, translated from the Russian by Z. I. Gorishina and revised by L. S. Forrer
(Amsterdam: Jacques Schulman, 1967, p. 202-5).

233    Bukharans in trade and diplomacy, 1558-1702.
       Audrey Burton.    PhD thesis, University of Manchester, 1986.
Chapter eleven of this abstruse but competently researched thesis consists of an
analysis of Bukharan trade with Siberia in the sixteenth century. This is a considerable
addition to Western historiography of the subject, especially since it employs sources in
several oriental languages.

234    An account of the Russian discoveries between Asia and America. To
       which are added the conquest of Siberia and the history of the
       transactions and commerce between Russia and China.
       William Coxe.    London: T. Cadell, 1780. 344p. maps.
This very early documentary account by an Englishman (1747-1828) who had travelled
in Russia contained a good deal of information on Siberian exploration. It became a
standard work, and by 1803 was into its fourth, 'considerably enlarged' and revised
edition (London: Cadell & Davies, 1804. 492p.).

235    Russian expansion to the Pacific 1580-1700: a historiographical review.
       Basil Dmytryshyn.    *Slavic Studies* (Sapporo), no. 25 (1980), p. 1-26.
This brief, though informative overview of Russian, Soviet and Western writing about
early Russian exploits in Siberia was presented at the first annual meeting of the Slavic
Research Center, Hokkaido University. It has been reprinted with minor amendments
and a short epilogue in the first issue of the Oregon Historical Society's journal
devoted to Siberian affairs (*Siberica*, vol. 1, no. 1 [summer 1990], p. 4-37, bibliog.).

236    To Siberia and Russian America. Three centuries of Russian eastward
       expansion, 1558-1867. Vol. 1: Russia's conquest of Siberia, 1558-1700,
       a documentary record.
       Edited and translated by Basil Dmytryshyn, E. A. P. Crownhart-
       Vaughan, Thomas Vaughan.    Portland, Oregon: Western Imprints,
       1985. 540p. maps. bibliog.
This superb translation of 133 original Russian documents about the Muscovite
expansion through Siberia is excellently produced, with a long introduction, a glossary
and numerous illustrations. It will remain an indispensable source for any English-
speaking person wishing to learn about the region in this era. Its two companion
volumes, which cover Russian expansion across the Pacific and the colonial presence in
Alaska and California (published in 1988 and 1989 respectively), both contain some

material relevant to Siberia and the Far East, as reference to their indexes will demonstrate.

237 **Siberia: an experiment in colonialism. A study of economic growth under Peter I.**
Ronald Farinton Drew. PhD thesis, Stanford University, Stanford, California, 1958. (Available from University Microfilms, Ann Arbor, Michigan, order no. 58-1283).

A valuable study of economic developments under Peter the Great, this work covers agriculture, industry, commerce and finance. The most notable growth was found in manufacturing, but the Russo-Chinese trade and fairs were also important. Attention is paid to the growth and activities of the urban population. Offshoots from the thesis are: 'The emergence of an agricultural policy for Siberia in the seventeenth and eighteenth centuries' (*Agricultural History* [Urbana, Illinois], vol. 33, no. 1 [1959], p. 29-39) and 'The Siberian fair, 1600-1750' (*Slavonic and East European Review*, vol. 39, no. 93 [1961], p. 423-39).

238 **Managazeia: a boom town of seventeenth century Siberia.**
Raymond H. Fisher. *Russian Review*, vol. 4, no. 1 (1944-45), p. 89-99.

Studies the rapid rise of an obscure *ostrog* [fort] on the Taz Gulf, part of the northern Enisei basin, during the seventeenth century. Furs made the merchants rich, until conditions changed and fire destroyed much of the settlement. The remains have been subjected to minute archaeological investigation by a Soviet team including Mikhail Ivanovich Belov since Fisher wrote his article. See *Mangazeya*, 2 vols (Leningrad: Gidrometeoizdat, 1980; Moscow: Nauka, 1981).

239 **The Russian fur trade, 1550-1700.**
Raymond H. Fisher. Berkeley, California: University of California Press, 1943. 275p. map. bibliog.

Derived from a PhD based on materials available at the time, this study provides a quantitative insight into the operations of the fur trade in Siberia and gives many details about the general situation in the pre-Petrine era. Subsequent Soviet research, not least by Pavel Nikolaveich Pavlov (1921-74), has rendered some of it dated, though it retains significance as a pioneering Western study. See Pavlov's 'Fur trade in the economy of Siberia in the 17th century' (*Soviet Geography*, vol. 17, no. 8 [1986], p. 567-90) and 'The trail of the sable: new evidence on the fur hunters of Siberia in the seventeenth century' by Stuart Kirby (*Slavic Studies* [Sapporo], no. 25 [1981], p. 105-18) which brings to non-Russian attention Pavlov's conviction that fur trappers were the predominant element in exploring and opening up Siberia.

240 **Muscovite and mandarin: Russia's trade with China and its setting, 1727-1805.**
Clifford M. Foust. Chapel Hill, North Carolina: University of North Carolina Press, 1969. 424p. bibliog.

A fascinating investigation into the vagaries of eighteenth-century overland trade with China, this work also concerns the economic development of Siberia. A great deal of work was done in the Irkutsk *oblast* [region] archive. His article 'Russia's Peking caravan, 1689-1762' (*South Atlantic Quarterly*, vol. 67, no. 1 [winter 1968], p. 108-24) is a history of Russian state control of caravans trading into China from the Treaty of Nerchinsk to the abolition of trade monopolies by Peter III.

241 **Russian expansion to the east through the eighteenth century.**
Clifford M. Foust. *Journal of Economic History*, vol. 21 (1961),
p. 469-82.

A brief overview, this article covers the administrative and economic development of Siberia as the Russians spread across it up to the late eighteenth century. The author stresses the weakness of Russian trade, especially their problems with using money as a medium of exchange.

242 **Russian expansion on the Amur.**
J. J. Gapanovich. *China Journal*, vol. 15 (1931), p. 173-82.

This rapid survey of Russian experiences in the Amur region from the seventeenth to twentieth centuries is notable for a gushing approval of Russians, whose colonization, unlike that of the Europeans, 'without being brilliant is opulent and fecund'.

243 **Russian occupance of the Far East, 1639-1750.**
James R. Gibson. *Canadian Slavonic Papers*, vol. 12, no. 1 (1970),
p. 60-77. maps.

A historical geographer's approach characterizes this study of Russian exploration, settlement and exploitation of the Okhotsk seaboard and Kamchatka to the mid-eighteenth century. The area was of little significance to the state until the great Kamchatka expeditions headed by Vitus Bering.

244 **From the history of the construction of forts in the south of western Siberia: the New Ishim Fortified Line.**
N. V. Gorban, translated from the Russian by James R. Gibson.
*Soviet Geography*, vol. 25, no. 3 (1984), p. 177-94.

Translated from the Soviet journal *Voprosy geografii* (Questions of Geography), no. 31 (1953), this article provides the only detailed study in English of the fortified line constructed in the 1750s to protect the Tobol–Irtysh region from incursions by nomadic tribesmen under Dzhungar influence. It was called the 'cruel line' because of the harsh conditions, diseases and raids suffered by the Cossack defenders.

245 **The founding of the Russian empire in Asia and America.**
John Armstrong Harrison. Coral Gables, Florida: University of
Miami Press, 1971. 156p. maps. bibliog.

Published almost as a tribute to Robert J. Kerner and George Lantzeff, this general study of Russia's eastwards expansion paints developments in Siberia with a broad brush, without which, it is claimed, the significance of the 'moving frontier' is lost. There are some interesting entries in the bibliography.

246 **Russian statecraft: the *Politika* of Iurii Krizhanich.**
Juraj Križanić, analysis and translation by John M. Letiche, Basyl
Dmytryshyn. Oxford: Blackwell, 1985. 283p. maps.

One of the first people to write about Siberian trade possibilities, the Croat Križanić
was exiled to Tobolsk from 1661 to 1676. Much of his material was collected during the
exile. His pamphlet on the history of Siberia does not seem to have been published in
English. A related study is 'Iurii Krizhanich: the first sibirologist' by Basil Dmytryshyn
(*Sino-Soviet Affairs*, vol. 10, no. 4 [1986-87], p. 195-211).

247 **Siberia in the seventeenth century: a study of colonial administration.**
George V. Lantzeff. Berkeley, California: University of California
Press, 1943. 231p. (University of California Publications in History
Series, vol. 30). Reprinted New York: Octagon Books, 1972.

Despite its age this study of Muscovite colonial administration in Siberia remains the
only detailed Western account for the seventeenth century. Since much archival
research has been done in the USSR since its publication, a new work on the subject is
needed. It investigates fortifications, fur trade, the imposition of *yasak* [fur tribute] on
the natives and their subsequent abortive rebellions, the endemic maladministration in
local areas and the long chain of command from the Siberian Office in Moscow. There
is little information on the Orthodox Church's presence.

248 **Eastwards to empire. Exploration and conquest on the Russian open
frontier to 1750.**
George V. Lantzeff, Richard A. Pierce. Montreal, Canada;
London: McGill-Queen's University Press, 1973. 273p. maps.
bibliog.

A survey of Russian penetration into Siberia from mediaeval times to the mid-
eighteenth century, this book includes chapters on Kievan and Mongol times, the
Cossacks, the Stroganovs, Ermak, Ivan III and IV, Boris Godunov, the race to the
Pacific, Buryatiya, Transbaikaliya, the Amur, Kamchatka and Chukotka. There is
some truth in the contention of a reviewer in *Queen's Quarterly* [Kingston, Ontario],
vol. 81 [1974], p. 30-2) that it is really a military history, and is one-sided, lacking a
thorough study of the effects of the Russian presence on aboriginal peoples. Yet it
remains the best English-language study of the subject and is based on a wide range of
published sources. A short chapter covering similar ground in *Russian colonial
expansion to 1917*, edited by Michael Rywkin (London; New York: Mansell, 1988,
p. 70-102), unfortunately contains several errors in the text and the map. It is a pity
that the author did not benefit from the use of Lantzeff and Pierce, Skrynnikov (q.v.)
and other recent Soviet work.

249 **The territorial reform of the Russian Empire, 1775-1796. (II) the
borderlands, 1771-1796.**
John P. Le Donne. *Cahiers du monde russe et soviétique*, vol. 24,
no. 4 (1983), p. 411-57.

Pages 428-31 and 451-4 of this study deal with changes in the administraion of Siberia
during the reign of Catherine the Great. See also his 'The evolution of the governor's
office, 1727-1764' (*Canadian–American Slavic Papers*, vol. 12, no. 1 [spring 1978],

p. 86-115.) and *Ruling Russia: politics and administration in the age of absolutism, 1762-1796* (Princeton, New Jersey: Princeton University Press, 1984).

250 **The conquest of Siberia and the history of the transactions, wars, commerce etc. carried on between Russia and China, from the earliest period.**
Gerhard Friedrich Müller, Peter Simon Pallas. London: [n.p.], 1842. [n.p].
I have been unable to consult this work, which appears to be a translation of Russian eighteenth-century sources.

251 **The Russian conquest of Kamchatka, 1697-1731.**
Isaac Morris Schottenstein. PhD thesis, University of Wisconsin, Madison, 1969. (Available from University Microfilms, Ann Arbor, Michigan, order no. 69-12,413).
Though in some ways the summary of Muscovite advance to Kamchatka is not much more detailed in this thesis than in Lantzeff and Pierce (q.v.), the coverage of Cossack rebellions and the Itelmen anti-Russian rising of 1731 is still of some value. The fur trade and Orthodox missions are touched on too.

# From 1800 to 1916

252 **Siberia since 1894.**
Anatole V. Baikalov. *Slavonic and East European Review*, vol. 11, no. 32 (1933), p. 328-40.
Positively assesses developments in Siberian transport, agriculture, industry and trade in the decades leading up to the 1917 Russian Revolution. The character of Siberians is held to be more adventurous than that of European Russians, despite a neglect of education. A more recent but essentially similar survey is to be found in 'The economic and cultural development of Siberia', by Nikolaus Poppe, in *Russia enters the twentieth century*, edited by George Katkov (et al.) (London: Methuen, 1970, p. 138-51, 321-33).

253 **The Russian Geographical Society, the 'Amur Epoch' and the Great Siberian Expedition, 1855-1863.**
Mark Bassin. *Annals of the Association of American Geographers*, vol. 73, no. 2 (1983), p. 240-56.
Investigates the interrelationship between rising Russian nationalism in the 1840s, the founding of the Russian Geographical Society (1845) and expansion into the Amur region a decade later. A sense of Russia's mission towards the east lay behind the forward policy in the Amur and Central Asia. A revised version of '"A Russian Mississippi"? A political-geographical enquiry into the vision of Russia on the Pacific, 1845-1865' by Mark Bassin (PhD thesis, University of California, Berkeley, 1983) is to be published by Cambridge University Press in 1991-92.

254 **Agricultural development on the frontier: the case of Siberia under Nicholas II.**
Daniel R. Kazmer. *American Economic Review*, vol. 67, no. 1 (1977), p. 429-32.

This paper is in a separate section of the journal entitled *Papers and Proceedings of the Eighty-Ninth Annual Meeting of the American Economic Association.* It is a complex theoretical formulation, presenting a theory of the economic interactions which determined the nature and extent of Siberian agricultural development after the opening of the West Siberian section of the railway in 1896, and derived from 'The agricultural development of Siberia, 1890-1917' (PhD thesis, MIT, 1973).

255 **Siberian industry before 1917: the example of Tomsk guberniya.**
Richard E. Lonsdale. *Annals of the Association of American Geographers*, vol. 53 (1963), p. 479-93. maps.

A rare and valuable foray into the industrial geography of pre-revolutionary southwestern Siberia, this article covers three phases of development: pre-emancipation, pre-railway but after the emancipation, and the railway era. The dominant form of industry before 1861 was mining and smelting of precious ores. The second period was characterized by local craft industries, and the third by competition from outside causing decline of inefficient plants and the opening of new ones relevant to the conditions attendant upon rapid transport.

256 **The Cheliabinsk grain tariff and the rise of the Siberian butter industry.**
Victor L. Mote. *Slavic Review*, vol. 35, no. 2 (June 1976), p. 304-17. map.

More down to earth and accessible to the non-mathematician than Kazmer's study (q.v.), Mote's article assesses all the factors, including the 1896-1913 Chelyabinsk tariff which might have contributed to the spectacular development of the butter trade in Siberia before World War I.

257 **The southern Ussurian district at the present time.**
I. P. Nadarov, translated from the Russian by J. C. Dalton. London: Harrison & Sons, 1890. 19p.

This pamphlet, translated from an article in *Izvestiya Imperatorskogo Russkogo Geograficheskogo Obshchestva* (*Proceedings of the Imperial Russian Geographical Society*), vol. 25 (1888), provides details of Vladivostok's hinterland in the mid-1880s, an area about which there is very little in English for any period.

258 **Siberia and the reforms of 1822.**
Marc Raeff. Seattle, Washington: University of Washington Press, 1956. 210p. maps. bibliog.

Raeff's pioneering Western study of maladministration in Siberia under Alexander I and Speranskii's attempts to improve the situation with his 1822 reforms remains a key book for students of the era. The new system of administration, intended to invest institutions rather than individuals with power to prevent corruption and to give a new deal to the native inhabitants was bold, but flawed in the execution. See also the Siberian section of his *Michael Speransky: statesman of imperial Russia, 1772-1839* (The Hague: Nijhoff, 1957).

259 **The Russians on the Amur: its discovery, conquest and colonization, with a description of the country, its inhabitants, productions, and commercial capabilities, and personal accounts of Russian travellers.**
Ernest George Ravenstein. London: Trubner, 1861. 467p. maps.
Published very soon after the Russian annexation of the Amur region in 1855-60 this study includes geographical, economic, political and ethnographic details about the aboriginal inhabitants, the Nivkh, and the early Russian settlements. See also 'Notes on the River Amur and the adjacent districts' by M. M. Peshchurov (et al.) (*Journal of the Royal Geographical Society*, vol. 28 [1858], p. 376-446).

260 **The 1905 revolution on the Siberian railroad.**
Henry Reichman. *Russian Review*, vol. 47, no. 1 (Jan. 1988), p. 25-48.
Based on extensive work in the Central State Historical Archive in Leningrad this article examines the progress of events along the Trans-Siberian Railway in 1905 and assesses the reasons for the workers' varying militancy. Comparison of this work with 'The Trans-Siberian railroad and the Russian revolution of 1905' by Patrick Robinson Taylor (PhD thesis, University of Tennessee, 1969 [available from University Microfilms, Ann Arbor, Michigan, order no. 70-07004]) reveals how far Western historiography of Siberia has developed in two decades.

261 **An American's Siberian dream.**
Norman Saul. *Russian Review*, vol. 37, no. 4 (Oct. 1978), p. 405-20.
A study of attempts by an American, Bernard Peyton, to obtain a monopoly of foreign trade on the Amur river in the 1850s, this article is based partly on Peyton's unpublished correspondence. It is evident that the Russians were correct in fearing foreign penetration of the area if they did not establish firm control over it.

262 **Count N. N. Muraviev-Amursky.**
Joseph L. Sullivan. PhD thesis, Harvard University, Cambridge, Massachusetts, 1955.
I have been unable to consult this political biography. Muravëv, as an energetic and far-sighted governor-general of East Siberia presided over the Russian annexation of Chinese territory in the Amur–Ussuri region, and the consolidation of Russia's Far Eastern possessions on the mainland from the mid-1850s.

263 **Russia's tea traders: a neglected segment of a still neglected entrepreneurial class.**
S. Thompstone. *Renaissance and Modern Studies*, vol. 24 (1980), p. 131-63.
This unique investigation concentrating at least to some extent on the Kyakhta tea-merchants is an important contribution to filling one of the many gaps in Western studies of Siberia, namely an investigation of the contribution of trade and traders to the region's development.

264 **Notes on the late expedition against the Russian settlements in Eastern Siberia, and of a visit to Japan and to the shores of Tartary, and of the Sea of Okhotsk.**
Bernard Whittingham. London: Longman, Brown, Green & Longmans, 1856. 300p. map.

A participant in the Anglo-French naval attack on Kamchatka during the Crimean War (1854-55) relates the problems suffered by the largely unsuccessful campaign, and makes suggestions for the future. A brief overview of the events is provided in 'The Crimean War in the Far East' by John Stephan (*Modern Asian Studies*, vol. 3 [1969], p. 257-77).

# During the Revolution and civil war, 1917 to 1922

265 **Trailing the Bolsheviks. 12,000 miles with the allies in Siberia.**
Carl W. Ackerman. New York: Scribner's, 1919. 308p.

The author, a reporter from the *New York Times*, travelled with the Czechoslovak Legion in Siberia over the winter of 1918-19. His graphic descriptions of events are clearly anti-Bolshevik. See also *The lost legion: a Czech epic* by Gustav Bečvar (London: Stanley Paul, 1939. 256p.) by a member of the Legion, who relays his personal impressions with clarity. A lively secondary account by a prolific writer of travel books and novels is *The march of the 70,000* by Henry Philip Bernard Baerlein (London: Leonard Parsons, 1926. 287p. map. Reprinted New York: Arno Press, 1971). The sources for this book, which include Czech newspapers and rare pamphlets of the period, are alluded to in passing.

266 **Commercial Russia.**
William Henry Beable. London: Constable, 1918. 278p.

Author of a *Russian gazettee and guide* published in 1919 (q.v.), Beable here provides masses of information about the possibilities for investment in and trade with Russia and Siberia. Though the Bolshevik success in the civil war rendered his optimism null and void, the information is very important for students of Siberian trade and industry at the period.

267 **Sidelights on the Siberian campaign.**
James Mackintosh Bell. Toronto, Canada: Ryerson Press, 1923. 132p. (Available from University Microfilms, Ann Arbor, Michigan, order no. OP 51121/AS).

These memoirs of a Canadian member of the British intervention forces provide valuable cameos of Siberia's internal situation during the civil war. His reaction to the lack of sanitation is similar to that of Raymond Massey who refers to the 'olfactory catastrophe' of barracks latrines. Massey, later a Hollywood film star, participated in theatricals for the Allied troops in Vladivostok. See chapters 24-25 of his *When I was young* (London: Robson, 1977).

268 **The coup d'etat of Admiral Kolchak: the counterrevolution in Siberia and east Russia, 1917-1918.**
Stephen Michael Berk. PhD thesis, Columbia University, New York, 1971. (Available from University Microfilms, Ann Arbor, Michigan, order no. 74-29,564).
Concentrates on conflicts within the anti-Bolshevik camp up to the seizure of power by Kolchak in November 1918. Valuable on the cooperative and regionalist movements, but it does not refer to events in East Siberia or the Far East.

269 **Left behind: fourteen months in Siberia during the Revolution, December 1917 – February 1919.**
Sophie Buxhoeveden. London: Longmans, Green, 1929. 182p. map.
A lady-in-waiting to the Russian royal family caught up in revolution attempts to rejoin her employers in their Tobolsk exile, accompanied by her Scottish governess, Miss Mather, but owing to their deaths has to leave Siberia via the Pacific. Her account is naive in places, but expressive of the reactions of a certain sector of society to the Revolution. Her remarks about Tobolsk convincingly convey the atmosphere of a provincial town.

270 **Report of the Canadian Economic Commission (Siberia).**
Canadian Department of Trade and Commerce. Ottawa: King's Printer, 1919. 79p. maps.
Published as a supplement to the *Weekly Bulletin of the Canadian Department of Trade and Commerce*, this report presents a very revealing account of the state of the Siberian economy during the civil war. At the same time it reveals a great deal about the mentality of the interventionist forces.

271 **Japan moves north: the inside story of the struggle for Siberia.**
Frederic Abernethy Coleman. London; New York: Cassell, 1918. 177p.
Ardently supports Japanese intervention against the Bolsheviks in the Russian Far East. More objective in its treatment is *The Japanese thrust against Siberia, 1918* by James William Morley (New York: Columbia University Press, 1957. 395p. map. Reprinted Freeport, New York: Books for Libraries Press, 1972), derived from a Columbia University PhD. See also *Japanese intervention in the Russian Far East* (Washington, DC, 1922. 165p.) and *A short outline history of the Far Eastern Republic* (Washington, DC, 1922. 69p.) which were issued by a special delegation of the Far Eastern Republic's government to the United States.

272 **Kolchak i Sibir: dokumenty i issledovaniia, 1919-1926. (Kolchak and Siberia: documents and studies, 1919-1926.)**
Edited with introduction, notes and indexes by David Norman Collins, Jon Smele. White Plains, New York: Kraus International Publishers, 1988. 2 vols. (Publications of the Study Group on the Russian Revolution, no. 11).
The introduction by Jon Smele, the bibliographical essay, two declarations by Kolchak and the notes are in English. They provide otherwise unavailable details about the civil war in Siberia. 'Labour conditions and the collapse of the Siberian economy under Kolchak, 1918-1919' by Jon Smele (*Sbornik* [Durham, England], no. 13 [1987], p. 31-59. bibliog.) is derived from his PhD thesis and probes into the economy under Kolchak with a depth hitherto unattained.

273 **The republic of Ushakovka. Admiral Kolchak and the Allied intervention in Siberia, 1918-1920.**
Richard Michael Connaughton. London; New York: Routledge, 1990. 193p. maps. bibliog.
Rambling through the Russo-Japanese rivalry in the Far East, the 1917 Revolution and civil war, this book by a colonel in the British army uses no sources in Russian. It provides an unremarkable popular biography of Aleksandr Vasilevich Kolchak.

274 **The struggle for a democracy in Siberia, 1917-1920: eyewitness account of a contemporary.**
Paul Serge Dotsenko. Stanford, California: Hoover Institution Press, Stanford University, 1983. 178p. maps. bibliog.
Paul Dotsenko (1894-1988), a Socialist revolutionary in exile in Siberia in 1917, became governor of Eniseisk Province for a while after the Bolsheviks were thrown out, then saw active service in the anti-Bolshevik Siberian army. His part-memoir, part-history provides a great deal of insight into the failures of the 'democratic counterrevolution', hounded as they were by Red and White forces antipathetic towards democracy.

275 **The army behind barbed wire: a Siberian diary.**
Edwin Erich Dwinger, translated from the German by Ian F. D. Morrow. London: George Allen & Unwin, 1930. 341p.
Contains the text of the diary of a German military prisoner kept in Siberia from 1915 to 1918. The second volume of an American publication *Between White and Red*, translated from the German by M. Saunders (New York: Scribner's, 1932. 2 vols) continues with his experiences in Kolchak's army, and the eventual retreat eastwards. *Secret service on the Russian front* by Max Wild, translated from the German by Anthony Haigh (London: Geoffrey Bles, 1932. 324p.) also concerns the experiences of a German, this time a spy, who was imprisoned in Siberia until May 1918.

276   **The Bolsheviks and the Czechoslovak Legion: the origin of their armed conflict, March–May 1918.**
Victor M. Fic.   New Delhi: Abhinar Publishers, 1978. 495p. maps. bibliog.

A detailed investigation of the circumstances leading to the break between the Bolsheviks and the Czech Legion which precipitated civil war in Siberia, this work is based on sources in Czech, Russian and English. It contains a valuable chapter on conflicting Soviet interpretations, and a series of rare documents in English.

277   **The fate of Admiral Kolchak.**
Peter Fleming.   London: Rupert Hart-Davis, 1963. 253p. maps. bibliog.

Popularly written, this book of many photographs is by a traveller (see his *A forgotten journey*) who had heard survivors of the events relating their tales, and interviewed Kolchak's son. Fleming picks his way over 'a sort of bog of history' where facts immediately cease to be valid and sink under'. The attempt to establish accurately the circumstances of Kolchak's failure, betrayal and death is relatively successful, given the total lack of use of Russian sources.

278   **Siberian partisans in the Civil War.**
David Footman.   *St. Antony's Papers*, no. 1: *Soviet Affairs*, no. 1 (1956), p. 24-53.

An informed critique of the accepted Marxist analysis of the Siberian partisan movement in the Russian civil war, this essay claims that the old established settlers (*starozhily*) were as involved as the newcomers (*novosely*). Clothing, medical supplies, finance and the democratic structure of partisan bands are discussed. Compare with chapter 5 of his *Civil war in Russia* (London: Faber & Faber, 1961) which presents a broader account.

279   **Letters from Vladivostok, 1918-1923.**
Edited by Dorothy Galton, John Keep.   *Slavonic and East European Review*, vol. 45, no. 105 (1967), p. 497-530.

John Findlay (1885-1964) represented the Becos Traders in the Far East from 1913 to 1932, spending much of his time in Vladivostok. These informative letters, written by himself and his wife, Dorothy, concern events in the region during the Russian civil war and the final establishment of Bolshevik rule.

280   **Some observations of eastern Siberia, 1922.**
Edited by James Thomas Gay.   *Slavonic and East European Review*, vol. 54, no. 2 (April 1976), p. 248-61. map.

US Naval Intelligence lieutenant John Marie Creighton visited the Anadyr and Petropavlovsk regions in the summer of 1922. His reports, made three months before the Bolshevik takeover, are reprinted from State Department records.

281 **America's Siberian adventure, 1919-1920.**
William S. Graves.   New York: Cape & Smith, 1931. 363p. map.
Reprinted New York: Arno Press/New York Times, 1971.

General Graves, in command of the American Expeditionary Force to Siberia during the civil war, published this extremely anti-interventionist, anti-White and anti-Japanese account of events. One wonders whether the US government deliberately chose him to command the detachment because his views would ensure their remaining on the sidelines, or whether these views developed only with hindsight.

282 **Britmis. A great adventure of the war, being an account of Allied intervention in Siberia and of an escape across the Gobi to Peking.**
Alexander Phelps Hodges.   London: Jonathan Cape, 1931. 364p.
maps.

A member of the British Expeditionary Force in Siberia recounts his exploits from January 1919 to May 1920.

283 **American soldiers in Siberia.**
Sylvian G. Kindall.   New York: Richard R. Smith, 1945. 251p.

Another critical account by an American soldier, this book criticizes the Japanese and also the Bolsheviks. 'I capture Vladivostok' by Frazier Hunt, in *We cover the world*, edited by Eugene Lyons (New York: Harcourt, Brace, 1937, p. 77-89) vividly depicts guerrilla activities around Vladivostok over the winter of 1919-20. Another aspect of the American intervention is covered in 'American railroaders in Siberia, 1917-1920' by Carolyn B. Grubbs (*Railroad History Bulletin*, no. 150 [spring 1984], p. 107-14).

284 **General Janin's Siberian diary.**
Alfred W. F. Knox.   *Slavonic and East European Review*, vol. 3
(March 1925), p. 724.

General Maurice Janin of the French delegation first published fragments from the diary which he had kept while in Siberia during the civil war in *Le monde slave* during 1924 and 1925. General Knox, who was politically active in pro-Kolchak circles at the same time, published this riposte, but unfortunately no more. See 'General Sir Alfred Knox and the Russian Civil War: a brief commentary' by John Long (*Sbornik* [Leeds], no. 9 [1983], p. 54-64).

285 **British economic interests in Siberia during the Russian Civil War, 1918-1920.**
Arno W. F. Kolz.   *Journal of Modern History*, vol. 48, no. 3 (Sept.
1976), p. 483-91.

This note is included not so much because of its heavily documented contention that Britain wished to separate Siberia from Russia proper to obtain the maximum economic advantage from it, but because of its information about British involvement in Siberia's economy. One aspect of this is highlighted in 'An attempt to utilize the northern sea route to Siberia in 1919' by Jon Smele (*Sibirica* [Lancaster], no. 4 [1988], p. 28-39).

286    **A prisoner of the Reds: the story of a British officer captured in Siberia.**
Francis McCullah.   London: Murray, 1921. 346p.
Relates the story of a British intelligence officer captured by the Bolsheviks at Krasnoyarsk early in 1920, who was convinced that Bolshevism would not survive. See also *Held by the Bolsheviks: the diary of a British officer in Russia*, 1919-1920 by L. E. Vining (London: St. Catherine's Press, 1924. 281p.).

287    **Canadians in Russia, 1918-1919.**
Roy Maclaren.   Toronto, Canada: Macmillan of Canada, 1975. 301p. maps.
This thorough investigation of the part played by Canadian troops in the British contingents sent to north Russia and eastern Siberia during the civil war was written by a Canadian member of parliament. See also *A Canadian's road to Russia: letters from the Great War decade* by Stuart Ramsay Tompkins, edited by Doris H. Pieroth (Edmonton, Canada: University of Alberta Press, 1989). Chapters ten to thirteen refer to a period spent in Vladivostok by a man who later wrote several well-known books on Russian intellectual and colonial history.

288    **The Russian civil war.**
Evan Mawdsley.   Boston, Massachusetts; London: Allen & Unwin, 1987. 351p. maps. bibliog.
Chapters eight, ten, eleven and sixteen of this refreshing history of the civil war in Russia refer to Siberia and the Far East. Soviet and Western works published up to the early 1980s, and documents in the British Public Records Office, form its source base. This is the best general history so far.

289    **The Russian Revolution in the Amur basin.**
James William Morley.   *Slavic Review*, vol. 16, no. 4 (1957), p. 450-72.
That this rather thin effort remains one of the most significant investigations of events in the Amur region in the English language, despite the fact that Soviet historiography of the area had progressed even before the era of *glasnost* [openness], shows what lacunae are present in contemporary Western studies of Siberia.

290    **The Canadian economic commission to Siberia, 1918-1919.**
Robert N. Murby.   *Canadian Slavonic Papers*, vol. 11, no. 3 (1969), p. 374-93.
Depicts the work of a Canadian Economic Commission (q.v.) sent to investigate the trade prospects in Siberia and the Far East. See also 'Siberia 1919: a Canadian banker's impressions' by William Rodney (*Queen's Quarterly* [Kingston, Ontario], vol. 79, no. 3 [autumn 1972], p. 324-35) which presents an account by A. D. Braithwaite of the Commission's labours.

291   **The fate of the Russian gold reserve.**
V. I. Novitskii.   *Russian Economist*, vol. 1, no. 2 (Jan. 1921),
p. 346-57.

Reports how the Tsarist gold reserve, stored in Samara during World War I, was seized by the Czechs and later anti-Bolshevik Russian forces. Kolchak attempted to evacuate it to the east, but the train was captured by the Bolsheviks. Details of gold production from 1910 to 1919 are included.

292   **Beasts, men and gods.**
Ferdinand Ossendowski.   London: Edward Arnold, 1923. 325p.

A Polish mining engineer, Ossendowski (q.v.) was about to be arrested by Bolsheviks in Krasnoyarsk in 1920. This volume of his memoirs describes his escape via the Sayan mountains with the help of anti-Bolshevik Soyot (Tuvans who had adopted a Buryat mode of life) to Tuva and Mongolia. During these exploits he met Baron Ungern-Sternberg whose biography is included in the book.

293   **White power during the Civil War in Siberia (1918-1920): dilemmas of Kolchak's 'war anti-communism'.**
Norman G. O. Pereira.   *Canadian Slavonic Papers*, vol. 29, no. 1
(March 1987), p. 45-62.

Part of the new wave of Western studies of Siberia, this article analyses five reasons why Kolchak's internal policies were bankrupt: his government's legitimacy was not recognized in Siberia; its identity as distinct from Tsarism was not clear; it did not develop a progressive alternative to Bolshevism; it was not organically tied to the region; and it was too dependent on foreign aid. See also his 'The "democratic counterrevolution" of 1918 in Siberia' (*Nationalities Papers* [New York], vol. 16, no. 1 [spring 1988], p. 71-93) which investigates the deficiencies of the democratic alternative to Bolshevism in Siberia.

294   **Boche and Bolshevik. Experiences of an Englishmen in the German army and in Russian prisons.**
Hereward Thimbleby Price.   London: Murray, 1919. 247p.

This memoir depicts life as a prisoner-of-war in Irkutsk, followed by a narrative of a successful escape from the revolution-torn region via the Far East in 1918.

295   **Liberals in the Russian Revolution.**
William G. Rosenberg.   Princeton, New Jersey: Princeton University
Press, 1974. 534p. map. bibliog.

This general study of the Russian Constitutional Democratic Party during the years of war and revolution has a good deal of material, particularly in chapters thirteen and fourteen, on the Kadets' experiences in Siberia. The regionalist movement is also discussed in relation to the Kadets.

296 **Admiral Kolchak.**
M. I. Smirnov. *Slavonic Review*, vol. 11 (1932-33), p. 373-87.
A former chief-of-staff of the Siberian dictator provides a concentrated, very sympathetic biography, only the latter part of which refers to events in Siberia from 1918 to 1920.

297 **Vladivostok under Red and White rule. Revolution and counterrevolution in the Russian Far East, 1920-1922.**
Canfield F. Smith. Seattle, Washington; London: Washington University Press, 1975. 304p. map. bibliog.
The author attempts to unravel the complex chain of events during the civil war in the city of Vladivostok. Given the sources available this is a useful work, but cannot be considered definitive. His 'The Ungernovščina – how and why?' (*Jahrbücher für Geschichte Osteuropas*, vol. 28 [1980], p. 590-5) presents a neat survey of the brief but bloody career of Baron Ungern-Sternberg, a White leader operating from Mongolia into eastern Siberia.

298 **The Bolsheviks in Siberia, 1917-1918.**
Russell E. Snow. Rutherford, New Jersey: Fairleigh Dickinson University Press; London: Associated University Presses, 1977. 269p. bibliog.
Based on a New York University PhD of 1972 this work is unfortunately poorly written and somewhat shallow in its research. Its reliance on published Soviet sources renders the conclusions suspect. His 'The Russian Revolution of 1917-1918 in Transbaikalia' (*Soviet Studies*, vol. 23, no. 2 [Oct. 1971], p. 201-15) provides a rare English-language insight into revolutionary developments in Buryat Mongolia.

299 **The White armies of Russia: a chronicle of counter-revolution and allied intervention.**
George Stewart. New York: Macmillan, 1933. 469p. maps. bibliog.
Reprinted New York: Russell & Russell, 1970.
The sections on the White armies in Siberia have still not lost their usefulness, despite the age of this work. Less successful is the section on Kolchak in *The White generals: the White movements and the Russian Civil War* by Richard Luckett (London: Longman; New York: Viking Press, 1971. 413p. rev. ed., London: Routledge & Kegan Paul, 1987. 428p.).

300 **Civil war in the taiga: a story of guerilla warfare in the forests of eastern Siberia.**
Ivan Jakov Strod. Moscow: Cooperative Publishing Society of Foreign Workers in the USSR; New York: International Publishers, 1933; London: Modern Books, 1935. 152p. map.
Written by a Latvian who became a Red partisan leader, this account is naturally very pro-Bolshevik. It deals with the late civil war period in Yakutiya. The 'Strod epic' has been commemorated in print in *Strod* by Vasilii Nazarovich Chemezov (Yakutsk: Yakutskoe knizhnoe izdatelstvo, 1972. 228p. [in Russian]).

301 **The testimony of Kolchak and other materials.**
Edited by Elena Varneck and H. H. Fisher, translated by Elena
Varneck. Stanford, California: Stanford University Press; London:
Oxford University Press, 1935. 466p. maps. bibliog. (Hoover War
Library Publications, no. 10).
Contains the text of Kolchak's interrogation by the Bolsheviks, *Memoirs of the Red
partisan movement in the Russian Far East* by Anton Zakharovich Ovchinnikov;
accounts of the massacre of citizens in Nikolaevsk by Reds during a Japanese advance;
and accounts of the Japanese seizure of Vladivostok in April 1920. Each section is
translated into English and provided with copious explanatory notes. This is a very
important primary source on the era.

302 **With the 'die-hards' in Siberia.**
John Ward. London: Cassell, 1920. 278p.
This rather self-congratulatory memoir by a colonel in the British Expeditionary Force
provides insights into the atmosphere surrounding Kolchak, but ends in June 1919.
Though of limited value, it was translated into Russian and published by the Soviet
authorities in 1923.

# Since the end of the civil war, 1923-

303 **Siberia: its resources and possibilities.**
Boris Baievsky. Washington, DC: Government Printing Office, 1926.
69p. (Department of Commerce Trade Promotion Series, no. 36).
Attempting to stimulate American trade with the Soviet Union in the era before
*de jure* recognition of the USSR by the United States, this pamphlet outlines the
possibilities for trade east of the Urals.

304 **The Bolsheviks discover Siberia.**
Sergei Konstantinovich Bezborodov, translated by Falkov. Moscow:
Cooperative Publishing Society of Foreign Workers in the USSR, 1933.
131p.
A very pro-Stalin work translated into quaint English, this breathlessly rushed book is
a committed account of industrial developments in the Kuzbas, transport improvements, electrification and collectivizing agriculture. Though poorly reproduced the
photographs present a unique record of the era.

305 **Siberia's untouched treasure: its future role in the world.**
C. G. Fairfax Channing [pseudonym of Christian Channing Gross].
New York; London: G. P. Putnam's Sons, 1923. 475p. 15 maps.
A member of the American Expeditionary Force in the Far East, the author presents a
full, illustrated account of his experiences in eastern Siberia and speculates about the
region's industrial future. A good deal of detail about mineral resources is included.

306   **The nation killers.**
Robert Conquest.   London: Macmillan, 1970. 239p. maps. 2nd. ed.
London: Sphere Books, 1972.
A largely reworked version of the author's *The Soviet deportation of nationalities*
(London: Macmillan, 1960), this book recounts Stalin's deportation of national
minorities to Kazakhstan, Siberia and the Soviet Far East during World War II and the
subsequent rehabilitation of many of them under Khrushchev. An account by a
dissident Soviet scholar, Aleksandr Moiseevich Nekrich, *The punished peoples: the
deportation and fate of Soviet minorities at the end of the Second World War*, translated
from the Russian by George Saunders (New York: Norton, 1978. 238p. maps) goes
over much of the same ground, but from a more emotionally involved standpoint.

307   **How Russia prepared. USSR beyond the Urals.**
Maurice Edelman.   Harmondsworth, England; New York: Penguin
Books, 1942. 127p. (Penguin Special, no. 110).
A veteran British socialist discusses how the USSR prepared for the struggle against
Hitler. Much of the book is concerned with a description of the industrial development
of western Siberia and the Soviet Far East.

308   **Dollars without the flag: the case of Sinclair and Sakhalin oil.**
Floyd J. Fithian.   *Pacific Historical Review*, vol. 39 (May 1970),
p. 205-22.
Charts the attempt by a small but aggressive US oil company to obtain and exploit a
monopoly over oil in northern Sakhalin in the early 1920s.

309   **The Soviet Ural–Kuznetsk combine.**
Franklyn D. Holzman.   *Quarterly Journal of Economics*, vol. 71, no. 3
(Aug. 1957), p. 368-405. maps.
A brief introduction to the pre-revolutionary history of industry in the region leads into
a survey of the 'most ambitious single project . . . ever attempted by the Soviets',
namely the linking of Urals iron ore to the Kuzbas coal deposits, 1400 miles away from
each other. Evaluation of the combine as an investment project leads to the conclusion
that it could be regarded as worthwhile only if it was necessary to develop industry in a
strategically invulnerable area. Many of the decisions about it had been irrational.
Other countries should not emulate this costly project. American contributions to this
project are the subject of *Project Kuzbas: American workers in Siberia, 1921-1926* by
J. P. Morray (New York: International Publishers, 1983. 204p.).

310   **The Irkutsk affair: Stalin, Siberian politics and the end of NEP.**
J. R. Hughes.   *Soviet Studies*, vol. 41, no. 2 (April 1989), p. 228-53.
Details of the socio-economic structure of Siberian society in the late 1920s, which was
overwhelmingly peasant, and of the changes in economic and administrative matters
brought about under the New Economic Policy (NEP) lead in to a discussion of Stalin's
impact during his visit in 1927-28. One thousand six hundred 'kulaks' [peasants] were
tried for allegedly hoarding grain. Subsequently the Irkutsk Communists, whom Stalin
regarded as dangerously degenerate and pro-peasant, revolted against this harsh
treatment. Nevertheless, elated by his success in procuring grain, Stalin used the

'Urals–Siberian method' to obtain agricultural produce elsewhere, and so precipitated the end of NEP.

311 **Communism in Yakutiya – the first decade (1918-1928).**
Edward Stuart Kirby. *Slavic Studies* (Sapporo), no. 25 (1980), p. 27-42.

Based on published Soviet sources and archive documents, this account traces the development of Soviet Yakutiya during the 1917-18 Revolution, War Communism and the New Economic Policy periods. The main stress is on economic conditions, including relations with Western firms operating in the region. It is worthwhile comparing this with 'Yakutiya and the future of the north' by Owen Lattimore, in his *Studies in frontier history: collected papers, 1928-1958* (London: Oxford University Press, 1962. p. 456-66).

312 **In search of Soviet gold.**
John D. Littlepage, Demaree Bess. New York: Harcourt, Brace, 1938; London: Harrap, 1939. 286p. Reprinted New York: Arno Press/New York Times, 1970.

Contains the rather critical reminiscences of an American with Alaskan experience who worked for the Soviet Gold Trust under Aleksandr Serebrovskii during the years of the first five-year plan and the beginnings of Stalinism (1927-37). 'Gold for the commissars: Charles Janin's Siberian ventures' by Donald Chaput (*Huntington Library Quarterly*, vol. 49 [1986], p. 385-400) is about Charles Henry Janin (1873-1938), an American specialist in gold-dredging and contributor of regular short articles about Siberian mining to the San Francisco journal *Mining and Scientific Press* (see item no. 710). From 1917 to 1929 he was employed as a consultant to the Soviet government and British mining interests in Siberia, before differences with the authorities led to his replacement by Littlepage. There are rare details about the mining industry in the 1920s in this article, based on Janin's papers in the Henry E. Huntington Library, San Mario, California.

313 **Russian engineer.**
John R. Westgarth. London: Denis Archer, 1934. 223p.

Sections of this memoir by a British consulting engineer working for the Soviet government from 1929 to 1931 refer to the problems of industrialization in the Kuznetsk region.

# Ethnography

## General

**314 Islamic peoples of the Soviet Union, with an appendix on the non-Muslim Turkic peoples of the Soviet Union.**
Shirin Akiner. London: Kegan Paul International, 1983. 462p. maps. bibliog.

Several sections of this reference work concern peoples in Siberia. Some, like the Tatars and Bukharans are Muslim; others including the Altaian, Yakut, Tuvinian, Khakass, Telengit, Teleut and Dolgan, appear in the appendix about non-Muslim peoples. See also *The non-Slavic peoples of the Soviet Union: a brief ethnographical survey*, translated from the Russian and edited by Konstantin Symmons-Symonolewicz (Meadville, Pennsylvania: Maplewood Press, 1972. 168p. bibliog.), which is derived from a Soviet text issued in 1968 and chapter 4 of which deals with Siberia, and *The peoples of the USSR: an ethnographic handbook* by Ronald Wixman (London: Macmillan, 1984. 246p. maps) which is arranged alphabetically like an extended glossary of ethnic names. The ethnonyms used in this present bibliography are derived largely from Wixman. Material about the current state of Soviet anthropology may be found in *Cahiers du monde russe et soviétique*, vol. 31, nos 2-3 (1990) all of which is devoted to this subject.

**315 Some problems of rural youth in Yakutia.**
I. A. Argunov. *Soviet Sociology*, vol. 18, no. 1 (1979), p. 16-24.

Consists of a translation of the results of Soviet fieldwork among young Even, Evenk and Yakut people, carried out between 1973 and 1976. Problems of acculturation, poor education, urban migration and an inability to engage in traditional occupations are noted. See also the earlier but still valuable 'Current ethnic processes taking place in northern Yakutiya' by Ilya Samoilovich Gurev (*Arctic Anthropology*, vol. 1, no. 2 [1963], p. 86-92). A similar study relating to the Khanty-Mansi and Yamalo-nenets national regions in western Siberia from 1970 to 1973 revealed problems caused by urban migration and oil field development. See 'On certain features of the social structure of the indigenous rural population of western Siberia' by V. G. Babakov (*Soviet Sociology*, vol. 17, no. 3 [winter 1978-79], p. 3-11).

316 **Soviet policy towards Siberian native peoples: integration, assimilation or russification?**
Dennis Bartels, Alice Bartels. *Culture* (Quebec), vol. 6, no. 2 (1986), p. 15-31. map. bibliog.

Western analysts investigate the depth of assimilation experienced by native people in Siberia through the results of questionnaires given to 58 academics, professionals, students and their families. Traditional ways were retained for many areas of life even today. Covering a far longer period is 'Russia's small peoples: the policies and attitudes towards the native northerners, seventeenth century to 1938' by Yuri Slezkine (PhD thesis, University of Texas, Austin, 1989 [available from University Microfilms, Ann Arbor, Michigan, order no. NHF89-20842]). News about problems facing Soviet minorities has begun reaching the Copenhagen-based International Work Group for Indigenous Affairs (IGWIA). See 'The big problems of small ethnic groups' by A. Pika and B. Prokhorov (*IWGIA Newsletter*, no. 57 [May 1989], p. 123-36). Increasing desperation and the onset of *glasnost* has led to the establishment of an Association of the Small Peoples of the North of the Soviet Union to champion their cause (see *Indigenous peoples of the Soviet north* (Copenhagen: IWGIA, 1990. [IGWIA Document, no. 67]).

317 **Paleoasiatic tribes of south Siberia.**
Waldemar Bogoras-Tan. In: *International Congress of Americanists, 22nd session: Atti*, vol. 1. Rome, 1928, p. 249-72. maps.

The author, whose name is quoted in the preferred form instead of the more correct Vladimir Germanovich Bogoraz, presents an analysis of the small groups regarded as being descendants of some of the earliest inhabitants of Siberia.

318 **Basic problems in social management of the development of the peoples of the north, in connection with the construction of the Baikal–Amur railroad.**
Vladimir Ivanovich Boiko. *Soviet Sociology*, vol. 19, no. 2 (1980), p. 3-26.

A Soviet sociologist presents a synopsis of his research into the ways in which the construction of the Baikal–Amur main railway in eastern Siberia is likely to impinge on the lives of the indigenous Evenk and Even peoples.

319 **Direction and motivations of potential migration of the peoples of the lower Amur.**
Vladimir Ivanovich Boiko. *Soviet Sociology*, vol. 9, no. 4 (spring 1971), p. 567-78.

A contemporary sociological investigation of the reasons why the Russian settlers and the Nanai (Gold) and Ulchi peoples should want to migrate. The main reasons are dissatisfaction with jobs and cultural facilities where they live. There is a tendency to congregate in larger communities. See also 'Changes in the social makeup of the minor peoples of the Far East' by Chuner Mikhailovich Taksami (*Soviet Sociology*, vol. 14, no. 3 [winter 1975-76], p. 26-43), translated from an article in *Sovetskaya etnografiya*

(Soviet Ethnography), no. 2 (1970), which includes changes in lifestyle, clothing, language use and social class.

320 **The native population of the Soviet north: language, education and employment.**
Arkadii Cherkasov. *Musk-Ox*, no. 30 (1982), p. 65-72. map.
Summarizes the pre-Gorbachev situation among the 'small peoples' of the Soviet north. A similar article originally published in *Sovetskaya etnografiya*, no. 4 (1978), containing data obtained by the University of Omsk West Siberian Historical and Ethnographic Expedition of 1975-77, is 'Contemporary ethnic processes in the southern and central zones of western Siberia' by N. A. Tomilov (*Soviet Sociology*, vol. 18, no. 2 [fall 1979], p. 58-82). The expedition discovered that cultural integration was under way in the Altai and other regions.

321 **Aboriginal Siberia: a study in social anthropology.**
Marie Antoinette Czaplicka. Oxford: Clarendon Press, 1914. 374p. maps. Reprinted Oxford: Clarendon Press, 1969. bibliog.
These are the more professional conclusions reached by the Oxford anthropologist who visited Siberia just before the outbreak of World War I and left a travelogue of her trip *My Siberian year* (q.v.). Fieldwork enabled her to shed light on many aspects of the lifestyle, religion and social organization of tribes inhabiting western and central Siberia. References to peoples of the Far East owe a good deal to work by Russian anthropologists. The terminology used is now dated, since the Soviet scientific community adopted different names for many groups. Details about the expedition and artefacts brought back may be found in 'The Siberian expedition' by Henry Usher Hall (*University of Pennsylvania Museum Journal*, vol. 17 [1916], p. 27-45).

322 **Tracing shamans in Siberia: the story of an ethnographical expedition.**
Vilmos Diószegi, translated from the Hungarian by Anita Rajkay Babó. Oosterhut, Netherlands: Anthropological Publications, 1960; New York: Humanities Press, 1968. 327p.
This is a readable account of a 9,000-km journey undertaken in 1957-58 by a Hungarian scholar to find out from Siberian evidence what the pre-Christian religion of his own people might have been like. He visited the Karagas (Tofalar), Soyot, Buryat Mongols and the Beltir (Abakan Tatars).

323 **Among the Samoyed in Siberia.**
Kai Donner, translated by Rinehart Kyler. New Haven, Connecticut: Human Relations Area Files Press, 1954. 176p. (Behavior Science Translations).
A Finnish linguist, the author made two trips to investigate the lives of indigenous peoples in northwestern Siberia just before World War I. References are made to the Selkup, Nenets and Ket.

324 **Educating the small peoples of the Soviet north: the limits of culture change.**
Ethel Dunn. *Arctic Anthropology*, vol. 5, no. 1 (1968), p. 1-31.
Demonstrates the successes and the failures of Soviet educational and propaganda policies among the minority peoples of Siberia. There is an important sequel: 'Education and the native intelligentsia in the Soviet north: further thoughts on the limits of culture change' (*Arctic Anthropology*, vol. 6, no. 2 [1970], p. 112-22. bibliog.) which charts educational advance, but is realistic about the limits to which change imposed from outside can go.

325 **Transformation of the economy and culture in the Soviet north.**
Stephen P. Dunn, Ethel Dunn. *Arctic Anthropology*, vol. 1, no. 2 (1963), p. 1-28. bibliog.
Since it approves the creation of an 'international soviet culture' which would result in the assimilation of minority peoples, this pioneer study of economic and culture change among the Siberian peoples may seem rather outdatedly pro-communist. Nevertheless it poses important questions and contains some useful analysis.

326 **Contributions to the anthropology of the Soviet Union.**
Compiled by Henry Field. *Smithsonian Miscellaneous Collections*, vol. 110, no. 13 (1948), p. 1-244.
This collection of materials is devoted to the physical anthropology of the indigenous peoples of Siberia, including the paleoasiatics, the Khakass, the Altai Kazakhs, the Kalmyk, the Ulchi, the Yakut and the Orochi. See also 'Anthropometry of the Siberian peoples' by Valerii P. Alekseev, in *The first Americans: origins, affinities, adaptations*, edited by William Laughlin and Albert B. Harper (New York: Gustav Fisher, 1979, p. 57-90).

327 **Crossroads of continents: cultures of Siberia and Alaska.**
William W. Fitzhugh, Aron Crowell. Washington, DC; London: Smithsonian Institution, 1988. 360p. maps. bibliog.
The result of a joint US–Soviet collaboration, this absolutely splendidly produced large-format book with many colour illustrations covers the prehistory, history, physical and social anthropology and languages of all the minor peoples inhabiting eastern Siberia, the Soviet Far East and Alaska. Information about the different aspects of life of each people is scattered throughout the text, so it is singularly unfortunate that there is no subject index. Details are included of the various scientific investigations carried out in the region, the Jesup North Pacific Expedition of 1897-1903 being perhaps the most important for our purposes. A large proportion of the illustrations are derived from the exhibits shown at a joint exhibition mounted by the Smithsonian Institution and Leningrad Museum.

328 **Russia, a compleat historical account of all the nations which compose that empire.**
Johann Gottlieb Georgi, translated by William Tooke. London: Printed for J. Nichols, 1780-83. 4 vols.

Johann Georgi (1738-1802) was one of the key German investigators of Siberia in the late eighteenth century. His account is painstaking and detailed and includes much information which would otherwise have perished.

329 **The Samoyed peoples and languages.**
Péter Hajdú, translated by Marianne Esztergar, Attila P. Csanyi. Bloomington, Indiana: Indiana University Press; The Hague: Mouton, 1963. 114p. bibliog. (Indiana University Publications: Ural and Altaic Series, no. 14).

An all-round investigation of the Samoyed (Samodiiskie) peoples inhabiting northern Siberia, this updated translation of a Hungarian book published in 1949 is an essential basis for understanding the distribution, culture and language of the people in question.

330 **Peoples of asiatic Russia.**
Waldemar Jochelson. New York: American Museum of Natural History, 1928. Reprinted New York; London: Johnson Reprint, 1970. 277p.

Though rather early this work includes a great deal of solid information on the Buryat, Chukchi, Koryak, Itelmen, Yukagir, Nivkh, Eskimo, Ket and Ainu.

331 **Peoples of the Soviet Far East.**
Walter Kolarz. London: George Philip; New York: Praeger, 1954. 193p.

This is a continuation of the author's *Russia and her colonies* (London: George Philip, 1952. 334p.) which should be consulted for general remarks about Soviet nationality policies. It concentrates on the Soviet drive towards the Far East, discusses the 'mystique' of colonization, and proceeds to survey Soviet policies towards the Koreans, Chinese and Japanese. There is a section on the aboriginal population including the Nanai, Udegei, Nivkh, Itelmen, Ainu, Even, Koryak, Chukchi, Yakut, Buryat Mongols, Tuvinian, Shor, Altaian and Khakass. The tone is markedly anti-Soviet, but for the era the range of sources used is impressive.

332 **The revolution in the north: Soviet ethnography and nationality policy.**
Kerstin Eidlitz Kuoijok. Uppsala, Sweden: 1985. 185p. (Acta universitatis Upsalensis. Studia multiethnica Upsalensia, no. 1).

Discusses the fate of the peoples of the Soviet north and east under the Bolsheviks. The view which emerges is markedly pro-Soviet. Also sympathetic towards the Soviet régime, but this time from a virulently anti-American viewpoint, is *Soviet but not Russian: the 'other' peoples of the Soviet Union* by William M. Mandel (Edmonton, Canada: Alberta University Press; Palo Alto, California: Ramparts Press, 1985) whose author was in the USSR as a student in the 1930s. Chapter seven deals with Siberia.

Evidence that all is not as well as these authors think is being made public during the era of *glasnost*.

333 **The native races of the Russian Empire.**
Robert Gordon Latham. London: Hippolyte Baillière, 1854. 340p. map. (The Ethnographical Library Conducted by Edwin Norris, Esq., vol. 2).
Though it uses old ethnonyms, this work is included because it demonstrates the state of ethnographical knowledge in the West in the mid-nineteenth century before investigations such as those of Czaplicka (q.v.) and the Jesup North Pacific Expedition. Chapter eight is on the Khanty and Mansi, chapter nine on Samoyed and Yukagir, chapter thirteen on the Altaian and Yakut, chapter nineteen on the Mongols, Evenk, Ainu, Koryak and Itelmen.

334 **The decorative art of the Amur tribes.**
Berthold Laufer. New York: AMS Press, 1975. 86p.
This is a reprint of material contained in part of the publications of the American Jesup North Pacific Expedition, issued in 1902 (for details of the Jesup Expedition see item no. 327). Well illustrated in colour, this pamphlet demonstrates the high level of art, under evident Chinese influence, attained by the indigenous peoples living along the Amur river.

335 **The peoples of Siberia.**
Edited by Maksim Grigorevich Levin, Leonid Pavlovich Potapov, English translation edited by Steven Dunn. Chicago, Illinois; London: University of Chicago Press, 1964. 948p. maps.
A translation of *Narody Sibiri* (Moscow: Izdatelstvo Akademii nauk SSSR, 1956) this illustrated work is fundamental for English-speaking students of Siberia's minority peoples. There is a great deal of information about the physical and social anthropology of each group, together with studies of their interrelationships and the effects of Russian and Soviet power on them. It is marred by outdated ideological concepts permeating the value judgements as a brief glance at recent Soviet statements would make evident. See for instance 'SOS for native peoples of the Soviet north' by Kathleen Mihalisko (*Radio Liberty Report on the USSR*, vol. 1, no. 5 [1989], p. 3-6).

336 **Collected works of Bronisław Piłsudski in five volumes.**
Bronisław Piłsudski, editors Toru Asai (et al.), supervising editor Alfred F. Majewicz. Berlin; Amsterdam: Mouton de Gruyter, 1988- .
An International Committee for the Restoration and Assessment of the Work of Bronisław Piłsudski consisting of Japanese and Polish scholars has undertaken this ambitious attempt to reissue all the anthropologist's works published between 1898 and 1936. They relate to the indigenous peoples of Sakhalin and the lower Amur region, particularly the Ainu, Nivkh, Oroch and Orok. Items originally published in Polish, Russian or Japanese will be translated into English; works originally published in English, German or French will remain in those languages. Volumes 3-5 will include previously unpublished materials. Preliminary work, edited by Alfred F. Majewicz and others, has already been published in various volumes of the Working Papers of the

Institute of Linguistics of Adam Mickiewicz University, Poznań, Poland, from 1984 onwards. (Please contact Dr Majewicz for further details.)

337 **Customary law of the nomadic tribes of Siberia.**
Valentin Aleksandrovich Ryazanovsky. Tientsin: [n.p.], 1938. 151p. Reprinted Bloomington, Indiana: Indiana University Press; The Hague: Mouton, 1965. (Indiana University Publications. Uralic and Altaic Series, no. 48).

Though in some ways dated, this survey of legal practices among the Turkic, Mongol and Tungus peoples in Siberia is unique in its area of investigation. It is an important aid to an understanding of the social functioning of the peoples in question, and raises many issues relating to cultural influences in the steppe zone. For more information about the author's work see 'The scientific works of Professor V. A. Riasanovsky in the sphere of the laws of the oriental peoples' by B. Rumyantsev (*Chinese Social and Political Science Review*, vol. 22, no. 1 [1938], p. 72-91) which includes references to the Yakut, Mongols, Kalmyk, Altai, Kazakh, Khanti and Mansi.

338 **People of the long spring.**
Yurii Rytkheu, photographs by Dean Conger. *National Geographic*, vol. 163, no. 2 (Feb. 1983), p. 206-23.

This is an unusual combination: a Chukchi author provides the text and an American cameraman the photographs. The article portrays the life of Siberian minorities such as the Nentsy and Yukagir in the early 1980s.

339 **Social and cultural dynamics of the peoples of the Soviet north.**
S. S. Savoskul, translated by Terence Armstrong, notes compiled by Caroline Humphrey. *Polar Record*, vol. 19, no. 119 (May 1978), p. 129-52. bibliog.

A Soviet anthropologist provides information about social and cultural change among the Itelmen, Ket, Eskimo, Evenk, Nanai, Khanty, Koryak, Yukagir, Nenets, Even, Dolgan, Selkup, Orok and Chukchi during the 1960s and 1970s.

340 **The natives of the lower reaches of the Amur river as represented in Chinese records.**
Wada Sei. *Memoirs of the Research Department of the Tokyo Bunko*, no. 10 (1938), p. 41-102.

Presents English versions of rare Chinese historical materials relating to aboriginal peoples such as the Nivkh who inhabit the lower Amur region.

341 **Population dynamics in northeastern Siberia, 1650/1700-1970.**
Demitri Boris Shimkin, Edith M. Shimkin. *Musk-Ox*, no. 16 (1975), p. 7-23. maps. bibliog.

Although this study has been acclaimed in other bibliographies, and it is true that it is based on significant research and includes useful maps and tables, insufficient attention has been given to pre-revolutionary studies of population decline among the aboriginal peoples of Siberia. More work needs to be done on this thorny topic.

342 **Social organization of the northern Tungus, with introductory chapters
concerning the geographical distribution and history of these groups.**
Sergei Mikhailovich Shirokogorov. Shanghai: Commercial Press,
1929. 427p. maps. bibliog. Reprinted Oosterhut: Anthropological
Publications, 1966.
This is a very wide-ranging study of the northern Tungus peoples including the Nanai,
based on fieldwork carried out in Transbaikalia in 1912-13, and in Mongolia and
Manchuria from 1915 to 1917. It includes the history, migrations, clan and social
organization, customs and laws of the groups in question.

343 **The psychomental complex of the Tungus.**
Sergei Mikhailovich Shirokogorov. London: Kegan Paul, Trench,
Trubner; Peking: Catholic University Press, 1935. 464p.
This other study by the Russian anthropologist is derived from the fieldwork
mentioned in item no. 342 above. It has been described as a 'monumental work on
Tungus shamanism' and a 'classic of thorough field investigation matched to creative
theoretical ideas'.

344 **The Soviet nationalities collection at Columbia University.**
Susan Cook Summer. *Slavic Review*, vol. 46, no. 2 (summer 1987),
p. 292-3.
This brief item is included because it informs the public of an important library
collection relating to all aspects of life of the Soviet minorities. Housed in the Lehman
Library of the School of International and Public Affairs of Columbia University, the
library includes 15,000 volumes in 47 languages and is growing at a rate of 500 items a
year. There are books in Yakut, Even and Evenk.

345 **The peoples of the Soviet north and their road to socialism.**
Vasilii Nikolaevich Uvachan, translated from the Russian by Sergei
Shcherbovich. Moscow: Progress Publishers, 1975. 227p.
A well-produced glorification of Soviet policies towards the indigenous minorities of
Siberia, this work includes some valuable factual information. It is an update of
*Peoples of the Soviet north* (Moscow: Foreign Languages Publishing House, 1960.
124p.). A similar work, but more limited in range, is 'Legislative, economic and
cultural policies of the USSR to encourage the development of the Chukchi and
Eskimo' by Innokentii Stepanovich Vdovin, translated by William Barr (*Musk-Ox*, no.
13 [1973], p. 41-8. map. bibliog.) which extols Soviet policies towards the Chukchi and
Eskimo from the Bolshevik Revolution until the late 1960s.

346 **The Siberian native peoples after the February Revolution.**
Elena Varneck. *American Slavic Review*, vol. 2 (1943), p. 70-88.
Despite its age this article is almost alone in providing a general introduction to the
policies of the Russian Provisional Governments of 1917 towards the minority peoples
of Siberia.

# Individual peoples

## Ainu

347 **The Saghalien trade: a contribution to Ainu studies.**
John Armstrong Harrison. *Southwestern Journal of Anthropology*,
vol. 10 (autumn 1954), p. 278-93.
Critical of Western literature on the Ainu, the author delves into 'fine' Japanese
sources to investigate the complex pattern of trade established between the Ainu, the
Japanese and peoples along the Amur littoral who were vassals of the Chinese. This
enables an assessment of the changes brought about in Ainu lifestyle from the
sixteenth century onwards which led to an eclipse of their society.

348 **Alone with the hairy Ainu, or 3,800 miles on a pack saddle in Yezo and a
cruise to the Kurile Islands.**
Arnold Henry Savage Landor. London: John Murray, 1893. 325p.
A well-seasoned traveller and editor of a series on world anthropology relates his
experiences of the Ainu in the late nineteenth century.

349 **The Ainu in the journal of E. E. Levenstern.**
T. K. Shafranovskaia, B. N. Komissarov. *Soviet Anthropology and
Archeology*, vol. 25, no. 4 (spring 1987), p. 53-64. bibliog.
This very individual journal was compiled by Levenstern during the visit of the sloop
*Hope* to Sakhalin in 1805. Facsimiles of eleven of his original drawings are included.

350 **The Ainu problem.**
Lev Yakovlevich Shternberg. *Anthropos*, vol. 24 (1929), p. 755-99.
A well-known Soviet investigator of the minority peoples of the Soviet Far East tries to
shed light on the origins of the Ainu by comparing them with other groups, including
the Nivkh.

351 **The Ainu of the northwest coast of southern Sakhalin.**
Emiko Ohnuki-Tierney. New York: Holt, Rinehart, 1974. 127p.
bibliog.
The published form of a University of Wisconsin PhD thesis, this book concerns itself
to a large extent with the world-view of the Ainu. The author has also published 'The
classification of the "habitual illnesses" of the Sakhalin Ainu' (*Arctic Anthropology*,
vol. 14, no. 2 [1977], p. 9-34 . bibliog.), which shows how data about apparently
insignificant illnesses can shed light on the cognitive structure of a people group. See
also his study of medical matters among the tribe: *Illness and healing among the
Sakhalin Ainu: a symbolic interpretation* (Cambridge: Cambridge University Press,
1981. 245p.) and a study of Ainu religion in 'The shamanism of the Ainu of the
northwest coast of southern Sakhalin' (*Ethnology*, vol. 12 [Jan. 1973], p. 15-30.
bibliog.).

352 **A visit to the Ainu of southern Sakhalin.**
N. Yakovlev. *Asiatic Review*, NS vol. 43 (July 1947), p. 276-9.
A Soviet ethnographer investigates the condition of the Sakhalin Ainu immediately after southern Sakhalin was ceded to the USSR after the Japanese defeat in 1945. A Western account of indirect interest, since it concerns the Ainu living in Hokkaido, is *Together with the Ainu, a vanishing people* by M. Inez Hilger, with the assistance of Chiye Sano and Midori Yamaha (Norman, Oklahoma: University of Oklahoma Press, 1971. 223p.).

# Buryat Mongols

353 **A journey in southern Siberia: the Mongols, their religion and myths.**
Jeremiah Curtin. Boston, Massachusetts: Little, Brown; London: Sampson, Low, Marston, 1909. 319p. map. Reprinted New York: Arno Press and New York Times, 1971.
A brief historical introduction leads in to an American anthropologist's account of the life, beliefs, folklore and horse sacrifices of the Buryat Mongols. Curtin worked for the Smithsonian Institution Bureau of Ethnology and was a fine linguist. He learned Buryat for the field trip which he undertook in 1900. Many photographs are included.

354 **Some contributions to the anthropology of the Buriats.**
George P. Kojeuroff. *Journal of the North China Branch of the Royal Asiatic Society*, vol. 58 (1927), p. 142-57. bibliog.
An overview of the history and present status of the Buryat Mongols leads the author, who has examined Buryat recruits for the Red Army, into a physical anthropological analysis. Tables and graphs are provided. There is also mention of the Russian *semeinye* [family] settlers who had migrated to Transbaikalia under the Tsars.

355 **Social organization of the Mongol-Turkic pastoral nomads.**
Lawrence Krader. Bloomington, Indiana: Indiana University Press; The Hague: Mouton, 1963. 412p. maps. (Indiana University Publications, Uralic and Altaic Series, no. 20).
Relevant sections of this thorough study of Mongol Turkic society include chapter 2 on the Buryats, chapter 3 on the Kazakhs and pages 272-86 on the Kazakhs of the Altai.

356 **Dawn in Siberia: the Mongols of Lake Baikal.**
G. D. R. Phillips. London: Frederick Muller, 1942. 196p.
The outcome of a visit to the Buryat Mongols in the mid-1930s, this book contains elements of history, particularly the Russian colonial penetration of the region, and information about the situation under Stalin. The author's socialist convictions pervade his account. For a more recent account by Caroline Humphrey (q.v.), see chapter eighteen of *The nationalities question in the Soviet Union*, edited by Graham Smith (London; New York: Longman, 1990).

# Chukchi

357  **The Chukchee.**
Waldemar Bogoras-Tan. *Memoirs of the American Museum of Natural History*, vol. 11, parts 1-3 (1904-9). (Publications of the Jesup North Pacific Expedition, vol. 7). Reprinted New York; London: Johnson Reprint, [*c.* 1970]. 733p. maps. bibliog.
Vladimir Germanovich Bogoraz (1865-1936) was a productive member of the Jesup North Pacific Expedition of 1897-1903. His rich study of the Chukchi is divided into three sections: material culture, religion and social organization. There are many illustrations in what amounts to a vast compendium of data about this people.

358  **Through the gold fields of Alaska to the Bering Straits.**
Harry De Windt.  New York: Harper Bros; London: Chatto & Windus, 1898. 312p. map.
Chapters nine to eleven of this work by De Windt (q.v.), a frequent traveller in and prolific writer on matters Siberian, provide an interesting impressionistic account of Chukchi life and customs. There is a glossary of vocabulary used by those Chukchi who lived at a village called Oumwaidjik.

359  **Cultural change among the Siberian Chukchi and Yakuts under the Soviet regime.**
Lydia Holubnychy.  *East Turkic Review*, no. 3 (1960), p. 82-101.
Though concentrating on the Chukchi and Yakut, this useful account of Soviet policies from 1917 to the late 1950s includes references to the numerical strength of all Siberian minorities. It also discusses education and publications in local languages of Siberia and the Soviet Far East. It is based on official Soviet sources. A brief but adequate survey is 'Three hundred years of Chukchi ethnic identity' by Dorothy Libby in *Man and cultures*, edited by Anthony F. Wallace (Philadelphia, Pennsylvania: University of Pennsylvania Press, 1960, p. 298-304. bibliog.).

360  **Ten months among the tents of the Tuski.**
William Hulme Heeper.  London: Murray, 1853. 417 p.
This detailed account of Chukchi life, beliefs and customs is especially valuable because it was published so early. Another pioneering account, by a man called 'the "dean" of Alaska natural history', is 'On the so-called Chukchi and Namollo people of eastern Siberia' by William Healy Dall (*American Naturalist*, vol. 15 [1881], p. 857-68). They may be helpfully contrasted with Bogoras's account (q.v.) to show increasing levels of russification in the later nineteenth century.

361 **Among the tundra people.**
Harald Ulrick Sverdrup, translated from the Norwegian by Molly
Sverdrup. La Jolla, California: Scripps Institution of Oceanography,
1978. 228p. maps. bibliog.
Though translated into English in 1939, this classic account of life among the reindeer
Chukchi by a member of Amundsen's expeditions just after World War I was
published in English only in the late 1970s. The author is said to have visited every
native settlement.

## Cossacks

362 **The Cossacks.**
Philip Longworth. London: Constable, 1969. Reprinted London:
Sphere Books, 1971. 408p. maps. bibliog.
There is no specialist work in English about the Cossacks in Siberia and the Far East.
There are short relevant sections in this general study of the Tsar's frontier troops. See
also *Tsar and Cossack, 1855-1914* by Robert H. McNeal (London: Macmillan, in
association with St. Antony's College, Oxford, 1987. 262p. maps. bibliog.) and *The
horsemen of the steppes: the story of the Cossacks* by Albert Seaton (London: Bodley
Head, 1985. 268p. maps. bibliog.) both of which have several sections devoted to the
Cossack regional forces in western Siberia, the Amur and the Far East.

## Eskimos

363 **The Eskimo of Siberia.**
Waldemar Bogoras-Tan. *Memoirs of the American Museum of
Natural History*, vol. 12 (1913), p. 417-56.
This broad-ranging (if brief) study of the small Siberian Eskimo group, forming part of
the publications of the Jesup North Pacific Expedition, continues the high standard s ℩
by Bogoraz in his work on the Chukchi (q.v.). See also his article 'Siberian cousins of
the Eskimo' (*Asia*, vol. 29, no. 1 [1929], p. 316-22. map).

364 **Air bridge to Alaska.**
Wilbur E. Garrett, photographs by Steve Rayner. *National
Geographic*, vol. 174, no. 4 (Oct. 1989), p. 504-9.
Rich in colour photographs, this is an account of the first trip made by Alaskan Yupik-
speaking Eskimos to their cousins in the USSR after the end of the Cold War. Hopes
are expressed that many more ties may be established.

365 **Early maritime trade with the Eskimo of Bering Strait and the
introduction of firearms.**
Dorothy Jean Ray. *Arctic Anthropology*, vol. 12, no. 1 (1975), p. 1-9.
Traces the process whereby trading with Western sailors led to the Eskimo in the
Bering Sea region to obtain the firearms which have subsequently had such a powerful
impact on their relationship with the natural environment.

# Even (Lamut)

366 **Perestroika reaches the reindeer herders of Siberia.**
Piers Vitebsky. *Geographical Magazine*, vol. 61, no. 6 (June 1989),
p. 22-5. bibliog.
Assistant Director for Research at the Scott Polar Research Institute in Cambridge,
the author reports on his recent visit to two state reindeer farms in the Yakut ASSR
in which the workers were Even. The details of herders' lives in this brief account
demonstrate that changes introduced by M. S. Gorbachev in Moscow are already
affecting very remote regions. Colour photographs are included. See also 'Centralized
decentralization: the ethnography of remote reindeer herders under perestroika'
(*Cahiers du monde russe et soviétique*, vol. 31, nos 2-3 [April-Sept. 1990], p. 345-56.
map).

# Evenk (Tungus)

367 **The origin of the Evenki shamanic instruments (stick, knout) of
Transbaikalia.**
Vilmos Diószegi. *Acta Ethnographica*, vol. 17 (1968), p. 265-311.
A Hungarian ethnographer investigating Siberian native religion attempts to trace the
origins of the ceremonial instruments used by the Evenk shamans of Transbaikalia.

368 **Indians in Siberia.**
J. Katser. *Arctic*, vol. 22, no. 1 (1969), p. 70-2.
A brief but compressed survey of the contemporary lives of the Evenk within the
Evenk National District in Krasnoyarsk Province of Siberia, this article has
information about their art and literature and depicts the central settlement of Tura.
Similar in intent is his 'Reindeer people of central Siberia' (*North*, vol. 16, no. 1
[1969], p. 31-4. map). *The vanishing Tungus* by Morton Friend (New York: Dial Press,
1973. 103p. map. bibliog.), though mainly intended for young people, is a serious
attempt to evoke the lifestyle of the Evenk in contemporary Siberia.

369 **On the ethnogenesis of the Tungus.**
Maksim Grigorevich Levin. *Arctic Anthropology*, vol. 1, no. 2 (1963),
p. 70-4. bibliog.
A famous Soviet ethnographer traces the process whereby the Evenk people came into
being.

# Gypsies

370 **The Siberian gypsies.**
V. J. Sanarov. *Journal of the Gypsy Lore Society*, 3rd series, vol. 49,
no. 3-4 (July-Oct. 1970), p. 126-37.
According to the 1959 census there were 11,600 gypsies in Siberia. The article traces
their migration there from Poland in the eighteenth century and presents details of
their trades, material culture, means of conveyance, food and dress. Romany words
are given for all the artefacts mentioned. Most gypsies now work as herdsmen in

collective farms. At the foot of the article it says 'to be continued', but the sequel seems never to have been published.

## Itelmen (Kamchadals)

371 **Kamchadal culture and its relationships in the old and new worlds.**
Chester Stevens Chard.   Madison, Wisconsin: University of Wisconsin
Press, 1961. 54p. (Society for American Archeology, Archives of
Archeology, no. 15).
Distilled from a University of California PhD dissertation of 1953 this booklet
compares the culture of the Itelmen of Kamchatka with other aboriginal cultures in
Siberia and Alaska. See also 'The Kamchadal: a synthetic sketch' (*Papers of the
Kroeber Anthropological Society*, no. 8-9 [1953], p. 20-44) which covers Itelmem
culture, lifestyle and religion.

## Jews

372 **The Birobidzhan affair: a Yiddish writer in Siberia.**
Israel Emiot [Israel Yanovsky-Goldwasser], translated from the
Yiddish by Max Rosenfeld, introduced by Michael Stanislawski.
Philadelphia, Pennsylvania: Jewish Publication Society of America,
1981. 205p.
A Jew who fled to the USSR in 1939 to escape the Nazis, the author went, in 1944, to
help the Birobidzhan project as a correspondent for the Jewish Soviet Antifascist
Committee. He was imprisoned in 1948. The work is in the main a poignant prison
memoir.

373 **The Jews of the Soviet Union: the history of a national minority.**
Benjamin Pinkus.   Cambridge: Cambridge University Press, 1988.
397p. bibliog.
This general history of the Soviet Jews has many references to Jews in Siberia, and
especially in Birobidzhan. English versions of relevant documents are included in a
companion volume *The Soviet government and the Jews, 1948-1967: a documented
study* (Cambridge: Cambridge University Press in association with the Hebrew
University of Jerusalem Institute of Contemporary Jewry and the Israel Academy of
Sciences and Humanities, 1984. 612p. bibliog.). See the indexes to both volumes.

374 **The Jews in the Soviet Union since 1917: paradox of survival.**
Nora Levin.   New York; London: New York University Press, 1988.
2 vols.
This study is particularly helpful about the early years of Birobidzhan, for which
chapters thirteen and twenty-two are relevant. A summary of developments in later
years is provided in 'Birobidzhan after forty years' by Lukasz Hirszowicz (*Soviet Jewish
Affairs*, no. 2 [1974], p. 38-47).

375 **The Jews in the Soviet Union.**
Solomon M. Schwarz.   Syracuse, New York: Syracuse University
Press, 1951. 380p.

Nora Levin (q.v.) writes that the chapter on Birobidzhan in this work is 'one of the best summaries in English'. See also his 'Birobidzhan: an experiment in Jewish colonization' in *Russian Jewry, 1917-1967*, edited by Gregory Aronson (et al.) (New York: Thomas Yoseloff, 1969, p. 337-59). The subject is also treated in 'The Birobidzhan project, 1927-1959' in *The Jews in the Soviet Union since 1917*, edited by Lionel Kochan (Oxford: Oxford University Press for the Institute of Jewish Affairs, 1970, p. 62-75. bibliog.).

# Ket

376 **Ethnological notes about the Yenisey-Ostjak (in the Turukhansk region).**
Kai Donner.   *Mémoires de la Société Finno-Ougrienne*, vol. 66 (1933),
p. 5-104.

Fieldwork studies in a remote region of northwest Siberia enabled this Finnish linguist and anthropologist to provide a detailed and thorough account of life among the Ket before the Stalin era.

377 **The Ket: a contribution to the ethnography of a central Siberian tribe.**
Priscilla Thornbury Lee.   PhD thesis, Stanford University, Stanford,
California, 1966. (Available from University Microfilms, Ann Arbor,
Michigan, order no. 67-17,455).

Based on published sources in Russian and English this rather short dissertation examines the Ket way of life and social organization, concluding with an investigation of acculturation under the Soviet régime. Appendices cover Ket kinship terminology, beliefs and legends and Soviet policies for the non-capitalist development of the 'small peoples of the north'.

378 **A sketch of the Ket, or Yenisei 'Ostyak'.**
Demitrii Boris Shimkin.   *Ethnos*, vol. 4, nos 3-4 (1939), p. 147-76.
map.

Provides a brief but accurate survey of the language, history, physical anthropology, religious beliefs and customs of the Ket.

# Khanty (Ostyak)

379 **Ethnicity without power: the Siberian Khanty in Soviet society.**
Marjorie Mandelstam Balzer.   *Slavic Review*, vol. 42, no. 4 (winter
1983), p. 633-48.

The author, an American social anthropologist, took part in an ethnographic expedition from Leningrad University to the northern Ob region in 1976. There she interviewed Khanty and Russians. Analysis of the fieldwork data revealed that the Khanty had undergone a 'selective adaptation [to Soviet conditions] without complete cultural disintegration'. Their culture was surviving, if in an attenuated form. For an account by a Khanty author of problems brought to his people by industrialization, see

**Ethnography.** Individual peoples

'Not by oil alone' by Yeremei Aipin (*IGWIA Newsletter*, no. 57 [May 1989], page 137 to the end).

380 **Rituals of gender identity: markers of Siberian Khanty ethnicity, status and belief.**
Marjorie Mandelstam Balzer. *American Anthropologist*, vol. 83, no. 4 (1981), p. 850-67.
Basing her analysis on data collected in 1976 (see item no. 379 above) the author focuses on traditional Khanty rites of passage.

## Koreans

381 **Koreans in the Soviet Union.**
Edited by Dae-Sook Suh. Honolulu, Hawaii: SUPAR and the Center for Korean Studies, University of Hawaii at Manoa, 1988.
This selection of studies on the Koreans in the USSR includes a paper by Teruyuki Hara 'The Korean movement in the Russian Maritime Province, 1905-22' and 'Koreans in the Soviet Far East, 1917-37' by Haruki Wada. See also 'The Korean minority in the Soviet Union' by John J. Stephan (*Mizan*, vol. 13, no. 3 [1971], p. 141-3) and 'Aspects of the linguistic assimilation of Soviet Koreans' by Seung-Chul Hur (*Journal of Slavic Studies* [S. Korea], vol. 3 [1989], p. 123-39).

## Koryak (Nymlyan)

382 **The Koriak.**
Waldemar Jochelson. *Memoirs of the American Museum of Natural History*, vol. 10, nos 1-2 (1908), p. 1-842. (Publications of the Jesup North Pacific Expedition, vol. 6).
The first section of this extremely detailed survey of the Koryak relates to religion and myths. The texts of over 100 of them are given in English translation, as are the texts of nine Itelmen myths. The second section covers material culture and social organization, with a summary of the effects of Russo-Koryak contacts.

383 **Koryak religion and society: an anthropological analysis.**
Paul J. Magnarella. *Arctic Anthropology*, vol. 9, no. 2 (1972), p. 24-31.
The author attempts to show that the structure of Koryak religion is a symbolical equivalent of the structure of Koryak society.

# Nanai (Gold)

384 **The occupational structure of the Nanai rural population.**
Vladimir Ivanovich Boiko. *Soviet Sociology*, vol. 12, no. 2 (fall 1973),
p. 69-83.

A translation of an article which appeared in *Izvestiya Sibirskogo otdeleniya Akademii nauk SSSR, seriya obshchestvennykh nauk* (News of the Siberian Section of the USSR Academy of Sciences, Social Science Series), no. 11 (1972), this article consists of the results of a sociological survey of the Nanai population of three collective farms. Of these, 13.4 per cent were urbanized; occupational differentiation was developing with education, yet 79 per cent of those gainfully employed were in manual pursuits.

385 **The Gold tribe, "fishskin Tatars" of the lower Sungari.**
Owen Lattimore. In: *Studies in frontier history: collected papers, 1928-58.* London: Oxford University Press, 1962, p. 339-402.

Reprinted from the *Memoirs of the American Anthropological Association* (1933), this paper presents a detailed survey of the numbers, history, ethnic affinity, physical characteristics, material culture, social organization, religion and language of the Nanai living on the Sungari river. There are also details of their relationships with the Chinese.

# Nenets (Yurak Samoyed)

386 **Winter trek.**
Yurii Simchenko, translated from the Russian by Vladimir Krivoshchekov. Moscow: Progress Publishers, 1990. 171p. map.

A Soviet ethnographer visits the Nenets living on the Gyda Peninsula to the northeast of the Taz Gulf on the lower reaches of the Ob river. The book is written in a popular narrative form, but is full of information about the lives and beliefs of Nenets reindeer herders, huntsmen and school teachers. The texts of several legends are included, as are many small line-drawings of artefacts, each with a brief explanation of their use. There is some speculation about the origin of the Samoyed peoples (Nenets, Enets and Nganasan). Concern about the impact of industrialization on this people is expressed in 'How to save the Yamal' by B. Prokhorov (*IGWIA Newsletter*, no. 58 [Aug. 1989], page 113 to the end).

# Nganasan (Tavgi Samoyed)

387 **The Nganasan: wild reindeer hunters of the Taimyr peninsula.**
Chester Stevens Chard. *Arctic Anthropology*, vol. 1, no. 2 (1963),
p. 105-21. map. bibliog.

A prolific American writer on Siberian ethnic minorities provides one of very few Western studies of a little-known indigenous people inhabiting north central Siberia.

388 **The Nganasan: material culture of the Tavgi Samoyeds.**
Andrei Aleksandrovich Popov, translated by E. K. Ristenen.
Bloomington, Indiana: Indiana University Press, 1966. 168p. (Indiana
University Publications, Uralic and Altaic Series, vol. 56).

This is a translation of the first part of a study of the Nganasan by the foremost Soviet
expert on this small people group, Andrei Aleksandrovich Popov (1902-60). The first
volume was published in 1948 by the USSR Academy of Sciences. It covers all aspects
of Nganasan material culture with the necessary obeisance to Stalinist formularies. The
second volume, covering Nganasan social structure and beliefs, was published only in
1984 and has not been translated into English. This is partly remedied by his 'The
"kuoika", guardian spirits of family and clan among the Nganasan', translated by L. L.
Sample (*Arctic Anthropology*, vol. 1, no. 2 [1963], p. 122-30), which is from a German
version published in Hungary.

# Nivkh (Gilyak)

389 **The Nivkh (Gilyak) of Sakhalin and the Lower Amur.**
Lydia Black. *Arctic Anthropology*, vol. 10, no. 1 (1973), p. 1-110.
map. bibliog.

This is a very detailed and wide-ranging study of many aspects of Nivkh life, drawing
upon Western and Soviet sources. The contemporary concern with ecology is also
included. In another article, 'The relative status of wife givers and wife takers in
Gilyak society' (*American Anthropology*, vol. 74 [Oct. 1972], p. 1244-8. bibliog.), she
investigates an aspect of marriage rites among the Nivkh.

# Orok

390 **The Oroks, past and present.**
Alfred Majewicz. *Sibirica*, no. 3 (1987), p. 41-3.

Originating in a paper given at the Second International Siberian Studies Conference
in London in 1986, this brief study of the Orok of Sakhalin is indicative only of its
author's expertise in the area.

# Poles

391 **Poles in Siberia in the eighteenth century.**
Richard Danik. *Irish Slavonic Studies*, no. 7 (1986), p. 27-40.

This is virtually the only study in English devoted to the Poles in Siberia, many of
whom made their way there under duress, but many of whom also contributed greatly
to the scientific and political development of Siberia. Fuller accounts may be found in
*Les polonais en Sibérie* by Bronisaw Pisudski (Le Puy, France, 1918) and
*Dzieje Polaków na Syberji [History of the Poles in Siberia]* by Michał Janik
(Kraków: Krakowska Spólka Wydawnicza, 1928. 472p.).

# West Siberian Tatars

392 **Essays on Tatar history.**
Boris Ischboldin.   New Delhi: New Book Society of India, 1963.
[n.p.].
Chapter eight on the Tatar kingdom of West Siberia deals with the history of this
people group, and in particular surveys their relationship with the Russians from 1580
onwards.

393 **Contemporary ethnic processes among Tatars in the cities of western
Siberia.**
N. A. Tomilov.   *Soviet Sociology*, vol. 13, no. 3 (winter 1974-75),
p. 17-38.
A well-known Soviet researcher into the history of the West Siberian Tatars pays
attention to the changes in their lifestyle going on during the 1970s.

# Tuvinan

394 **Nomads of southern Siberia: the pastoral economies of Tuva.**
Sevyan Izrailevich Vainshtein, edited and with an introduction by
Caroline Humphrey, translated by Michael Colenso.   Cambridge:
Cambridge University Press, 1980. 289p. maps. bibliog.
Translated from a Soviet work issued by the Academy of Sciences in 1972, this book
presents a detailed analysis of the pastoral economy of the native inhabitants of the
Tuva Republic. There are also some references to the Altaian.

# Yakut

395 **The Yakut.**
Waldemar Jochelson.   *Anthropological Papers of the American
Museum of Natural History*, vol. 33, part 2 (1933), p. 37-225. maps.
Another very thorough study resulting in part from the Jesup North Pacific Expedition,
this work covers the origins, habitat, physical anthropology, language, calendar,
religion, family structure, material culture and art of the Yakut together with an
account of their contacts with the Russian conquerors. A more recent account by Piers
Vitebsky may be found in chapter nineteen of *The nationalities question in the Soviet
Union*, edited by Graham Smith (London; New York: Longman, 1990).

# Yukagir (Odul)

396 **The Yukaghir and the yukaghirized Tungus.**
Waldemar Jochelson.   *Memoirs of the American Museum of Natural
History*, vol. 12 (1910-26), p. 1-469. (Publications of the Jesup North
Pacific Expedition, vol. 9).
Jochelson has again managed to provide a comprehensive study of virtually all aspects
of this aboriginal people. A vocabulary of Yukagir words is included.

397 **The tundra Yukaghirs at the turn of the century.**
Erukhim Abramovich Kreinovich, translated by Marguerita Rittman.
*Arctic Anthropology*, vol. 16, no. 1 (1979), p. 178-216. map. bibliog.

Translated from the Soviet journal *Strany i narody vostoka* (Countries and peoples of the East), no. 13 (1972), this article is very useful in broadening the amount of material available on the Yukagir in English. The turn of the nineteenth and twentieth centuries was a crucial period in the development of indigenous peoples in Siberia; some experts even believed that they would die out from neglect and bad treatment by local officials and merchants.

# Languages

## General

398 **The languages of the Soviet Union.**
Bernard Comrie. London: Cambridge University Press, 1981. 317p.
bibliog.
A fairly large proportion of this work is devoted to languages spoken in Siberia.
Comrie distinguishes three major groups which will be the basis for the subdivisions in
this present bibliography. The **Altaic** is divided into three groups *Turkic* (Yakut,
Dolgan, Altaian or Oirot, Tuvan, Tofalar or Karagas, Chulym Tatar, Khakas and
Shor), the *Mongolian* (Buryat) and the *Tungusic* (Evenk including Orochon, Even,
Negidal, Nanai, Ulcha, Orok or Ulta, Udege and Oroch). The **Uralic** includes *northern
Samoyedic* (Nenets, Enets and Nganasan), *southern Samoyedic* (Selkup, Kamas),
*Finno-Ugric* (the two Ob-Ugric languages Khanty and Mansi). The **Paleosiberian**
consists of a mixture of isolated language groups not related to the others (the
Chukotko-Kamchatkan group, Yupik Eskimo, Yukagir, Ket, Nivkh and Ainu).

399 **The contemporary linguistic situation in the non-Russian regions of
Siberia and its investigation.**
A. I. Fëdorov, translated by Arlo Schuttz. *Soviet Anthropology and
Archeology*, vol. 22, no. 1 (summer 1983), p. 39-50.
After extensive fieldwork with questionnaires a Soviet social anthropologist detects two
types of bilingualism among the minorities. One is the native language with a form of
Russian full of native words, the other is the native language plus literary Russian. The
latter is desirable, so whilst the children should be taught in their own language at
school, they should also be taught good standard Russian.

400 **The social functions of the languages of the peoples of the north and Far East of the USSR.**
Ilya Samoilovich Gurvich, Chuner Mikhailovich Taksami. *Soviet Anthropology and Archeology*, vol. 25, no. 3 (winter 1986-87), p. 35-52. bibliog.
Surveying the development of Soviet policy towards minority languages the authors raise the question of which dialect should be regarded as the standard one. They then note that native languages are used for traditional economic roles and family life, whilst Russian is used in contact with outsiders. Details are given of education in minority languages.

401 **National languages in the USSR: problems and solutions.**
Magomet Ismailovich Isaev, translated from the Russian by Paul Medov. Moscow: Progress Publishers, 1977. 430p. map. bibliog.
After describing the classification of the languages of the USSR, the author explains the evolution of Soviet language policy up to the mid-Brezhnev period. The Soviet people are a new historical community developing an 'interlanguage' and will not have the troubles experienced in the bourgeois world. Foreign opponents of Soviet policy are attacked. 'Native speech' by Anatolii Omelchuk (*Soviet Literature*, no. 10 [1988], p. 132-6). summarizes the history of devising alphabets for the minority Siberian languages and describes the level of teaching and publishing in them. The article is written from a pro-*glasnost* viewpoint.

402 **Multilingualism in the Soviet Union: aspects of language policy and its implementation.**
E. Glyn Lewis. The Hague; Paris: Mouton, 1972. 332p. map. bibliog. (Contributions to the Sociology of Linguistics, no. 3).
Probably one of the Western books which M. Isaev (q.v.) was attacking, this study analyses all aspects of Soviet language 'planning' after presenting a survey of the languages.

403 **Languages of the USSR.**
William Kleesman Matthews. Cambridge: Cambridge University Press, 1951. 178p. maps.
Still basically sound, this book covers much of the same ground as Comrie's (q.v.).

404 **An appraisal of the importance of the national languages among the north Siberian peoples.**
Poul Thoe Nielsen. *Folk*, vol. 14-15 (1972-73), p. 205-53. bibliog.
A succint and informative survey of the smaller peoples and the extent to which their languages are encouraged and spoken. Details of publishing are also provided.

405  **A guide to the world's languages. Vol. 1: Classification.**
Merritt Ruhlen.   London: Edward Arnold, 1987. 433p.
Briefly details each of the language groups included in the Comrie entry (q.v.),
together with information on how the languages came to be grouped as they are. Each
section has a map and bibliography for further reading. See also *The Cambridge
encyclopaedia of language* by David Crystal (Cambridge: Cambridge University Press,
1987) and the informative entries for each of the groups in the *Encyclopaedia
Britannica*.

# Altaic languages

406  **Buriat reader.**
James E. Bosson, supervised and edited by Nicholas Poppe.
Bloomington, Indiana: Indiana University Press, 1962. 259p. (Indiana
University Publications, Uralic and Altaic Series, no. 8).
Contains texts in the Turkic Buryat language which can be used in conjunction with
Nicholas Poppe's Buryat grammar (q.v.).

407  **Yakut manual.**
John R. Krueger.   Bloomington, Indiana: Indiana University Press,
1962. 389p. (Indiana University Publications, Uralic and Altaic Series,
no. 21).
This work begins with an area handbook about Yakutiya, its people and history, then
presents a grammar, graded reader and glossary for this variant of the Turkic language
group.

408  **Material on the Orochee language. the Gold (Nanai) language and the
Olchi (Nani) language.**
Ivan Alexis Lopatin.   Freiburg, Germany: Posieux, 1957. 109p. (There
is a microform edition in the series Micro Bibliotheca Anthropos,
vol. 26).
Provides introductory materials on three of the Tungusic languages of the Amur
region.

409  **The Turkic languages and peoples: an introduction to Turkic studies.**
Karl H. Menges.   Wiesbaden, Germany: Otto Harrassowitz, 1968.
248p. (Ural-Altaische Bibliothek, no. 15).
Brief historical introductions to the various peoples who speak Turkic languages leads
into a summary of their languages. Of interest are: Khakass, Buryat, Yakut and
Altaian.

410 **Materials for the study of the Orok (Uilta) language and folklore.**
Bronisław Piłsudski, transcribed and edited by Alfred F. Majewicz,
Elżbieta Majewicz. Poznań: Wydawnictwo Naukowe Uniwersytetu,
1985, 1987. (Adam Mickiewicz University Institute of Linguistics,
Working Papers, nos 16-17).
Preprints for the intended Collected Works of Piłsudski (q.v.), these volumes contain
phonetic and grammatical notes made by the great linguist, Orok texts and an
Orok–Polish dictionary. There are English translations throughout.

411 **Materials for the study of the Olcha (Ulča/Mangun/Năní) language and
folklore.**
Bronisław Piłsudski, transcribed from the manuscripts by Elżbieta
Majewicz under the supervision of and edited by Alfred F. Majewicz.
Sapporo, Japan: ICRAP; Poznań: Wydawnictwo Naukowe
Uniwersytetu, 1984-85. [unpaginated]. (Adam Mickiewicz University
Institute of Linguistics, Working Papers, [25]).
Continues the preprint presentation of materials on the language and folklore of the
aboriginal peoples of Sakhalin and the lower Amur region (see item no. 410 above).
An attempted reconstruction of the Olchan glossary appeared in *Lingua Posnansiensis*,
vol. 27 (1984), p. 71-96.

412 **Introduction to Altaic linguistics.**
Karl Poppe. Wiesbaden, Germany: Otto Harrassowitz, 1965. 212p.
(Ural-Altaische Bibliothek, no. 14).
A very detailed work, this book describes the history of the investigation of these
languages, including much information on the Turkic, Mongol and Tungusic groups.

413 **Buriat grammar.**
Nicholas N. Poppe. Bloomington, Indiana: Indiana University Press,
1961, 136p. (Indiana University Publications, Uralic and Altaic Series,
no. 2).
Provides a basic introduction to the grammar of the Buryat language, and is to be used
in conjunction with Bosson's texts (q.v.).

414 **Some features of the morphology of the Oirot, Gorno-Altai, language.**
Cyril Gordon Simpson. London: Central Asian Research Centre,
1955. 68p.
Short and specialized as it is, this is the only work I can find in English on the Altaian
language as spoken in the Mountain Altai region of southwest Siberia.

415 **Proceedings of the fifth meeting of the Permanent International Altaistic Conference.**
Edited by Denis Sinor. Bloomington, Indiana: Indiana University Press, 1962. [n.p.] (Indiana University Publications, Uralic and Altaic Series, no. 23). Reprinted New York: Greenwood Press, 1981.
This is the first of many *Proceedings of the Permanent International Altaistic Conference* which appeared in book form. They often include information about the languages and customs of the Altaic-speaking peoples.

# Uralic languages

416 **Survey of the Uralic languages.**
Compiled by Björn Collinder. Stockholm: Almqvist & Wiksell, 1957. 536p. 2nd ed., 1969.
Contains sections on Mansi (p. 319-44), Khanty (p. 345-63), Nenets (p. 421-54) and Selkup (p. 455-87). Each section briefly describes the main characteristics of the language in question.

417 **The Uralic languages: description, history and foreign influences.**
Edited by Denis Sinor. Leiden, The Netherlands; New York: E. J. Brill, 1988. 841p. (Handbuch der Orientalistik, Achte Abteilung. Handbook of Uralic Studies, vol. 1).
Several sections, notably pages 3-41 and 219-63 (Nenets, Nganasan), and pages 147-96 and 395-412 (Khanty and Mansi), contain descriptions of the present status and historical evolution of the languages of these Siberian peoples.

# Paleosiberian languages

418 **Chukchee.**
Waldemar Bogoras-Tan. In: *Handbook of American Indian Languages*, part 2. *Bulletin of the Bureau of American Ethnology*, no. 40 (1922), p. 631-903.
Includes comprehensive grammars of three different languages used by the Chukchee.

419 **Koryak texts.**
Waldemar Bogoras-Tan. *Publications of the American Ethnological Society*, vol. 5 (1917), p. 1-153.
Provides a wide variety of data on the various dialects of Koryak. Twenty-five folk tales and some songs are included in translation. There are also vocabularies from and into Koryak.

420 **A grammatical sketch of Siberian Yupik Eskimo.**
Steven A. Jacobson. Fairbanks, Alaska: [n.p.], 1977. [n.p.].
I have been unable to obtain this study, which is mentioned in Comrie (q.v.). Steven Jacobson has recently published a Yupik Eskimo dictionary (Fairbanks, Alaska: Native Language Center, University of Alaska, 1984).

421 **The Paleosiberian languages.**
Roman Jakobson. *American Anthropologist*, vol. 44, no. 4 (Oct.-Dec. 1942), p. 602-20.
Demonstrates the relationships between the various Paleosiberian languages, whose links seem to be more in their distinctness from other groups than in any internal homogeneity. Provides some linguistic and grammatical detail.

422 **Essay on the grammar of the Yukaghir language.**
Waldemar Jochelson. *American Anthropologist*, vol. 7, no. 2 (April-June 1905). p. 369-424.
Printed as a supplement to the *American Anthropologist*, this work is another product of the Jesup expedition to the North Pacific. There is a linguistic map showing the distribution of two dialects of the language in the past and when the author was there.

423 **Brief remarks on the structure of the Nymlyan (Koryak) language and its dialects.**
G. M. Korsakov, S. N. Stebnitskii, English translation by J. R. Krueger. Alexandria, Va: [n.p.], 1952. 88p.
I have not seen this. It is mentioned (as item 3: 259) in Jakobson's bibliography (q.v.).

424 **Ainu prayer texts.**
Bronisław Piłsudski, facsimile of the manuscript edited by Alfred Majewicz. Sapporo, Japan: ICRAP; Poznań: Wydawnictwo Naukowe Uniwersytetu, 1984-85. 4 vols. (Adam Mickiewicz University Institute of Linguistics, Working Papers, nos 10-13).
Contains the full text of the notes made by Piłsudski on Ainu prayers.

425 **Materials for the study of the Ainu language and folklore.**
Bronisław Piłsudski, under the supervision of J. Rozwadowski.
Cracow: Imperial Academy of Sciences (Spasowicz Fund), 1912.
242p. bibliog.

A major work by a Polish linguist and anthropologist (q.v.), it includes Ainu texts and English translations with a grammatical introduction and notes. The work has recently been added to by *An Ainu–English index dictionary to B. Piłsudski's "Materials for the Study of the Ainu Language and Folklore"* of 1912, compiled by Elżbieta Majewicz (Poznań: Wydawnictwo Naukowe Universytetu, 1986. 780p.).

426 **Dictionary of western Kamchadal.**
Dean Stoddard Worth. *California University Publications in Linguistics*, vol. 59 (1969), p. 1-320.

An exhaustive work, this book includes a brief introduction to the language of the Itelmen, aboriginal inhabitants of Kamchatka, followed by a Kamchadal–English dictionary and a brief English–Kamchadal root list.

427 **Kamchadal texts collected by W. Jochelson.**
Edited by Dean Stoddard Worth. The Hague: Mouton, 1961. 284p. (Janua Linguarum, Series Maior, no. 2).

Provides a brief introduction to the language of the Itelmen in relation to other Paleosiberian languages, then presents the texts of forty-one documents in Kamchadal and English.

428 **Kamchadal and asiatic Eskimo manuscript collection.**
Avram Yarmolinsky. *Bulletin of the New York Public Library* (Nov. 1947), p. 659-69.

This is an illustrated account of Jochelson's collection of texts from the northeast Asian mainland. See item no. 427 above.

# Folklore and Oral Literature

### 429   A Siberian narrator.
Mark K. Azadovskii. In: *The study of Russian folklore*, edited and translated by Felix J. Oinas, Stephen Soudakoff. The Hague; Paris: Mouton, 1975, p. 79-89. (Slavistic Printings and Reprintings, Textbook Series, 4; Indiana University Folklore Institute, Monograph Series, vol. 25).

This is an abridged translation from a book by a noted Soviet folklorist and bibliographer, Mark Azadovskii (1888-1954). The excerpt concerns a Russian peasant woman storyteller from the Lena river region, Natalya O. Vinokurova. It mainly depicts her method of telling stories, but also includes short excerpts from some of the stories. The brief editorial introduction has information about Siberian tellers in general.

### 430   Chukchee tales.
Waldemar Bogoras-Tan. *Journal of American Folklore*, vol. 41, no. 161 (1928), p. 297-452.

Consists of English translations of some of the tales collected by Bogoras during his Jesup ramblings among the Chukchi.

### 431   The folklore of northeastern Asia, as compared with that of northwest America.
Waldemar Bogoras-Tan. *American Anthropologist*, NS vol. 4 (1902), p. 577-683.

As the title suggests this article compares the folklore traditions of the indigenous peoples on both sides of the Bering Strait.

432  **Tales of the Yukaghir, Lamut and russianized natives of eastern Siberia.**
Waldemar Bogoras-Tan.  *Anthropological Papers of the American Museum of Natural History*, vol. 20, part 1 (1918), p. 1-148.
This is another publication of material collected by the intrepid anthropologist, and this time the tales are from the Yukagir, Even and assimilated natives of the northeast region of Siberia.

433  **Siberian and other folk tales: primitive literature of the empire of the Tsars.**
Collected and translated, with an introduction and notes, by Charles Fillingham Coxwell.  London: C. W. Daniel, 1925. 1056p. map. bibliog.
An introduction comparing the folklore of the various peoples of the USSR leads in to an extensive publication of translations of tales from many areas. From the Paleoasiatic peoples there are eleven Chukchi tales, five Yukagir stories and a short note on Koryak mythology. The Mongol-Turkic peoples are represented by five Tungus (Even), eleven Buryat, eight Yakut and six Altaian tales. Four Khanty tales from the Finno-Ugrians conclude the list of relevant items. However, many of the sixty-eight Russian stories and fairy tales will have been told around winter stoves by the peasant emigrants to Siberia. Each section is followed by brief notes putting the stories in context.

434  **Popular beliefs and folklore tradition in Siberia.**
Edited by Vilmos Diószegi.  Bloomington, Indiana: Indiana University Press; The Hague: Mouton, 1968. 498p. (Indiana University Publications, Uralic and Altaic Series, no. 57).
This illustrated but highly academic work contains data about the folk tales and beliefs of the Khanty, Mansi, Enets, Nganasan, Ket, Altaian, Shor, Tuvinian, Evenk, Nanai, Nivkh and Siberian Eskimos. There are elements of ethnography, folklore, linguistics, history, archaeology and religious studies in this broad work which contains over thirty articles.

435  **Ainu folklore: traditions and culture of the vanishing aborigines of Japan.**
Carl Etter.  Chicago, Illinois: Wilcox & Follett, 1949. 234p.
Contains a great deal of information about the folklore and culture of the Ainu of Japan and Sakhalin Island.

436  **Gold Khan.**
Translated by Norman Cohn.  London: Secker & Warburg, 1946. 180p.
This is a very rare English version of Turkic heroic oral folk poetry from Siberia. The six poems were collected from people living near the Abakan River in the Minusinsk area of southwest Siberia, the Koybal, Kachin and Sagai branches of the people known by the collective ethnonym Khakass. The book's title is derived from that of the first poem, which is about the legendary Altyn, or golden, khan [ruler].

### 437 Finno-Ugric, Siberian

Uno Holmberg. In: *The mythology of all races*, edited by John Arnott MacCulloch, vol. 4. London: Harrap; Boston: Archeological Institute of America, Marshall Jones, 1927. 587p. map. bibliog.

Author of numerous works in Finnish and German about the beliefs of the minority peoples of Siberia, Uno Nils Oskar Harva (formerly Holmberg, 1882-1949) provides here a detailed overview of the myths of all the Finno-Ugric peoples and Siberian minorities, including the Chukchi, Koryak and Itelmen.

### 438 Folktales of the Amur: stories from the Russian Far East.

Dmitrii Nagishkin, translated from the Russian by Emily Lehrman. New York: Harry N. Abrams; Leningrad: Aurora Art Publications, 1980. 224p.

This colour illustrated publication contains thirty-one tales from the Amur region of the Soviet Far East.

### 439 Ainu folklore.

Bronisław Piłsudski. *Journal of American Folklore*, vol. 25, no. 95 (1912), p. 72-86.

Provides an overview of traditional Ainu folklore based on materials collected by the great Polish anthropologist and linguist.

### 440 The Gilyaks and their songs.

Bronisław Piłsudski. *Folklore. Transactions of the Folk-Lore Society* (London), vol. 24, no. 4 (1913), p. 477-90.

Contains a series of translations of Nivkh songs collected by Piłsudski during his anthropological investigations along the Amur river. A much more recent addition to our knowledge of the Nivkh poetic experience is 'Ten Nivkh (Gilyak) erotic poems' by Robert Austerlitz (*Acta ethnographica Academicae scientarum Hungaricae*, vol. 33 [1984-85], p. 33-44).

### 441 South Siberian oral literature: Turkic texts.

Friedrich Wilhelm Radloff. Bloomington, Indiana: Indiana University Press, 1967. 2 vols. (Indiana University Publications, Uralic and Altaic Series, no. 79, i-ii).

Though the text of these oral literary pieces from Turkic peoples including the Altaian and Shor is in Turkic with German parallel texts, Denis Sinor's introduction about the famous linguist and traveller Radloff (1837-1918; the Russian version of whose name was Vasilii Vasilevich Radlov) is in English.

### 442 N. K. Rerikh and the legend of Belovod'e (the White Waters).

S. S. Savoskul. *Soviet Anthropology and Archeology*, vol. 22, no. 4 (spring 1984), p. 3-29. bibliog.

From *Sovetskaya etnografiya* (Soviet Ethnography), no. 6 (1983), this article explains how in the mid-1920s when Nicholas Roerich travelled in the Altai mountains (see his *Altai–Himalaya: a travel diary*. New York: Stokes, 1929; London: Jarrolds, [c. 1930]) a legend was still current among Russian peasants in the Bukhtarma district that beyond the hills somewhere there was a magical 'Land of White Water' where freedom could be found. Roerich related this to his own mystical quest. Savoskul had visited the region and had talked with old-timers about Roerich and the legend, also visiting the Roerich museum at Verkhnyi Uimon.

### 443 The oral epic of Siberia and Central Asia.

G. M. H. Shoolbraid. Bloomington, Indiana: Indiana University Press, 1975. 176p. bibliog. (Indiana University Publications, Uralic and Altaic Series, no. 111).

A thorough treatise on the oral epic of the nomadic peoples of the south Siberian region, this work includes a detailed bibliography for further investigation.

### 444 The horse in Evenki folklore.

G. M. Vasilevich. *Central Asiatic Journal*, vol. 10, nos 3-4 (Dec. 1965), p. 320-32.

A paper read at the seventh meeting of the Permanent International Altaistic Conference, this item provides rare insight into Evenk folklore.

# Religion

## General

**445 Encyclopaedia of religion and ethics.**
Edited by James Hastings. Edinburgh: T. & T. Clark; New York:
C. Scribner's Sons, 1908-26. 13 vols.

There is a special section on the religions of Siberia in this multi-volume reference work (vol. 11, p. 488-96), but careful study of the index will make it clear that scattered references often using dated ethnonyms (including Ainu, Buryat Mongols, Chukchi, Eskimo, Gilyak, Kamchadal [i.e. Itelmen], Koryak, Ostyak [i.e. Khanty], Samoyed [i.e. Nenets or Nganasan] , Tungus [usually Evenk] and Yukaghir) occur in many places. The articles, written by Russian and Western experts of the period such as Marie-Antoinette Czaplicka and Dmitrii Aleksandrovich Klements (1848-1914), retain their interest despite the complications of nomenclature.

**446 Aspects of religion in the Soviet Union, 1917-1967.**
Edited by Richard H. Marshall, Jr. Chicago, Illinois; London:
Chicago University Press, 1971. 489p.

As well as covering general Soviet legislation and practice towards religion, this volume includes a section on the religions of the Siberian peoples (pages 421-31) which concentrates on shamanism and Buddhism.

**447 The modern encyclopaedia of religions in Russia and the Soviet Union.**
Edited by Paul D. Steeves. Gulf Breeze, Florida: Academic
International Press, 1989- . [? vols.]

Intended to provide a broad survey of religious beliefs within the Russian Empire and the USSR in many volumes, this work will include articles on Siberia, such as one written by the author of this present bibliography, entitled *Burkhanism*, which discusses a religio-nationalist movement developed by the Altaian in 1904.

# Buddhism

448 **Buddhism in the Soviet Union: annihilation or survival?**
Hans Bräker, translated from the German by G. M. Ablitt. *Religion in Communist Lands*, vol. 11, no. 1 (1983), p. 36-48.
Buddhism in the USSR is concentrated mainly in the Buryat Autonomous Soviet Republic and areas immediately around it. This rare, illustrated Western investigation demonstrates that even before the era of *glasnost* traces of Buddhist practice were evident.

449 **The Buddhists in the USSR.**
Nicholas N. Poppe. In: *Religion in the USSR*, edited by B. Ivanov.
Munich, Germany: Institute for the Study of the USSR, 1960.
p. 168-79.
Deals with an earlier phase in Soviet Buddhist history than that covered in item no. 448 above. See also his 'The destruction of Buddhism in the USSR' (*Bulletin of the Institute for the Study of the USSR*, vol. 7 [1956], p. 14-20).

# Christianity

450 **Revolution and emigration: the Russian files of the British and Foreign Bible Society, 1917-1970.**
Stephen K. Batalden. In: *The study of Russian history from British archival sources*, compiled by Janet M. Hartley. London; New York: Mansell, 1986, p. 147-72.
Provides details about the files of Russian material built up by the British and Foreign Bible Society. Some of the data refer to Siberia, where the Bible Society had branches before the Revolution. See, for instance, the *111th Report of the British and Foreign Bible Society* (London, 1915), pages 103-20 of which contain a very useful report on colportage, sales in book shops, and donations by interested persons within Siberia.

451 **Shamans, lamas and evangelicals: the English missionaries in Siberia.**
Charles R. Bawden. London: Routledge & Kegan Paul, 1985. 382p. bibliog.
The culmination of years of research work, this book examines the attempts by evangelical Christians such as Stallybrass (q.v.) from the London Missionary Society to convert the Buryat Mongols from 1817 to 1840, and the later efforts under Gilmour (q.v.). Related material had appeared elsewhere, for instance see 'English mission schools among the Buryats' (*Zentralasiatische Studien*, no. 16 [1982], p. 211-50).

452 **The foreign missions of the Russian Orthodox Church.**
Serge Bolshakoff. London: Society for the Propagation of Christian
Knowledge; New York: Macmillan, 1943. 120p. bibliog.
This general study of Russian Orthodox missionary activities contains sections on the
various missions operating in Siberia and the Far East, including pages 57-61 on the
Altai Mission, the most successful of them all.

453 **With God in Russia. My 23 years as a priest in Soviet prison and labour
camps in Siberia.**
Walter J. Ciszek, with Daniel Flaherty. London: Peter Davis; New
York: America Press, 1964. 302p. map. Reprinted Garden City, New
York: Image/Doubleday, 1966. 357p.
An American-born Catholic priest, Father Ciszek sought admission to the USSR
incognito in 1939 with a group of Polish refugees from Nazism. He was hoping to
evangelize and to serve Poles in his priestly capacity, but was discovered by the NKVD
[People's Commissariat for Internal Affairs] and imprisoned as a Vatican spy. The
book relates his experiences. Allowed to leave the far north in 1958 he was harrassed
by local officials in Krasnoyarsk when he tried to work in a parish there, and was sent
to Abakan, centre of the Khakass Autonomous Region before his eventual release in
1963.

454 **Colonialism and Siberian development: the Orthodox mission to the
Altay, 1830-1917.**
David Norman Collins. In: *The development of Siberia: people and
resources* (q.v.), p. 50-71. bibliog.
Analyses the aims, methods and results of the Russian Orthodox Mission to the
Altaian people from its inception under Archimandrite Makarii (Glukharev) in 1830 to
the Revolution of 1917.

455 **The role of the Orthodox missionary in the Altai: Archimandrite
Makary and V. I. Verbitsky.**
David Norman Collins. In: *Church, nation and state in Russia and
Ukraine*, edited by Geoffrey Hosking. London: Macmillan, 1990,
p. 96-107. bibliog.
Through a biographical study of two long-serving missionaries, Archimandrite Makarii
(Glukharev, 1792-1847) and Father Vasilii Ivanovich Verbitskii (1827/8-90), the article
investigates the roles of the black and white clergy (that is monastic and married
clergy) in the Russian Orthodox Mission to the Altaian.

456 **A song in Siberia.**
Anita Deyneka, Peter Deyneka. Elgin, Illinois: David C. Cook, 1977;
London: Collins, 1978. 230p. map.
Catalogues the harrassment of an unregistered Baptist church community in Barnaul in
the Altai region from the 1960s to the mid-1970s. Though written in a popular form,
the work contains the texts of numerous appeals and letters addressed to the Soviet
authorities and world leaders. References to similar events in Kulunda, western

Siberia, may be found in *Faith on trial in Russia* by Michael Bourdeaux (London: Hodder & Stoughton, 1971, p. 86-99).

457 **Russian missions: an historical sketch.**
Georges Vasilevich Florovsky. *The Christian East*, no. 1 (1933), p. 30-41. Reprinted in *Aspects of church history*, vol. 4 of his *Collected Works*. Belmont, Massachusetts: Nordland [Notable and Academic Books], 1975, p. 139-55.

This general survey of Russian Orthodox missionary activity by a famous Russian émigré theologian and ecclesiastical historian contains a useful section on missions to Siberia and the Far East.

458 **St. Innocent: apostle to America.**
Paul D. Garrett. Crestwood, New York: St. Vladimir's Seminary Press, 1979. 345p. bibliog.

This biography of Ivan Popov (1797-1878), a sacristan's son from eastern Siberia who under the monastic name Innokentii rose to be the first Orthodox bishop of Alaska and later Metropolitan of Moscow, contains a good deal of material relating to Siberia. This includes information on parish life in Irkutsk diocese during his youth, and a lengthy section about his work in the Amur, Kamchatka and Okhotsk regions in the 1850s and 1860s. Another English work on Innokentii is *Innocent of Moscow, the apostle of Kamchatka and Alaska* by Charles Reuben Hale, privately printed in 1877.

459 **Among the Mongols.**
James Gilmour. London: Religious Tract Society, 1883. 382p. map. Reprinted New York: Praeger, 1970.

The Reverend James Gilmour (1843-91), a Scot, went to China as a missionary in 1870 to revive work among the Mongols. Earlier British missionaries had worked in Buryatiya from 1817, but their activities had been ended by the Russians for political reasons in 1841. He traced the remnants of the old mission and attempted to convert Buryats, though most of his work was outside Russia. For the earlier mission, see *Memoir of Mrs. Stallybrass, wife of the Rev. Edward Stallybrass, missionary to Siberia* by E. Stallybrass (London, 1836); *First-fruits of a mission to Siberia by the Revs. Messers. Yuille, Stallybrass, and Swan, agents of the London Missionary Society* by J. C. Brown (Cape Town, 1847); *Reminiscences of the mission in Siberia* by Mrs Swan [anon.] (Edinburgh, [n.d.]); and Bawden (item no. 451 above).

460 **Ruling Siberia. The Imperial power, the Orthodox Church and the native people.**
Oleg Kobtzeff. *Sibirica* (Lancaster), no. 2 (1986), p. 6-15.

All too brief, this article about the relationship between the Tsarist government and the Russian Orthodox Church in their treatment of Siberia's minorities is a pioneer attempt to cover important ground. It was also published in *St. Vladimir's Theological Quarterly*, vol. 30, no. 2 (1986), p. 269-80.

461 **The life and labors of schema monk Zosima, by his disciple.**
Anonymous. Etna, California: Nikodemos Orthodox Publication
Society, 1979. [n.p.].
Contains a hagiography of Zosima (Zakarii Vasilevich Verkhovskii) and another
monk, Basilisk, who pursued a contemplative lifestyle in Siberia in the late eighteenth
century. See also *The northern thebaid: monastic saints of the Russian north*,
introduced by I. M. Kontzevitch (Platina, California: St. Herman of Alaska
Brotherhood, 1975).

462 **On sledge and horseback to outcast Siberian lepers.**
Kate Marsden. London: Record Press, 1892. 243p. Reprinted with an
introduction by Eric Newby. London: Century Hutchinson, 1986.
This autobiographical work traces the experiences of a member of the British Royal
Nursing Association who went to Siberia in 1891 to treat lepers, hoping to find a herb
with therapeutic properties and to establish a model leper colony. The work is in some
respects a travelogue, and in others an account of her investigations in Yakutsk and
Vilyuisk. Numerous illustrations and documentary texts, including her official reports
are included. Her *My mission to Siberia: a vindication* (London: E. Stanford, 1921.
54p.) was written to end the persecution which she claimed had doggeed her since the
Siberian trip.

463 **The Siberian seven.**
John Pollock. London: Hodder & Stoughton, 1979. 252p.
This account by a well-known writer on Christian themes presents the harrowing
details of persecution of Siberian Pentecostals, the Vashchenko and Chmykhalov
families, from 1962 until 1978 when they sought refuge in the American embassy in
Moscow. An earlier book also by Pollock, *The Christians from Siberia* (London:
Hodder & Stoughton, 1964. 190p.), gave details of a first attempt to emigrate from the
USSR which led to their subsequent torments.

464 **A short account of the historical development and present position of
Russian Orthodox missions.**
Eugene Smirnoff. London: Rivingtons, 1903. 85p. Reprinted Willits,
California: Eastern Orthodox Books, [n.d.] and Welshpool, Wales:
Stylite Publishing, 1986.
A clergyman attached to the Imperial Russian Embassy in London, Smirnoff prepared
this study of missionary activity by the Church in Russia to inform Western Christians
about the situation. It is the first account in English to go into any detail about missions
in Siberia.

465 **Eastern Orthodox mission theology today.**
James J. Stamoolis. Maryknoll, New York: Orbis Books, 1986. 194p.
bibliog. (American Society of Missiology Series, no. 10).
In assessing the stance and methods to be adopted towards missionary work by the
Orthodox churches in the late twentieth century, the author draws on the experiences
of Russian missionaries, including those who were active in Siberia and the Russian
Far East before the 1917 Revolution (see chapters 4-5).

466 **Orthodox missions past and present.**
Nikita Struve. *St. Vladimir's Seminary Quarterly*, vol. 7, no. 1 (1963),
p. 31-42.
A brief overview of the experiences of Russian Orthodox missions in general, this
article contains a section on Siberia. See also Struve's more specific article 'Macaire
Gloukharev: a prophet of Orthodox mission' (*International Review of Mission*, vol. 54
[1965], p. 3-8, 14) which is devoted to the founder of the Altai mission.

467 **Czars, Soviets and Mennonites.**
John B. Toews. Newton, Kansas: Faith & Life Press, 1982. 221p.
This study of the Mennonites in Russia includes information on the Siberian groups.
See also *Siberian diary of Aron P. Toews*, edited by Lawrence Klippenstein (Winnipeg,
Canada: CMBC Publications, 1984. 177p.) and *The Mennonite Encyclopaedia*
(Hillsboro, Kansas: Mennonite Brethren, 1955, 1976. 4 vols).

468 **Three generations of suffering.**
Georgii Petrovich Vins, translated with an introduction by Jane
Ellis. London: Hodder & Stoughton, 1976. 222p.
This documentary biography of the Vins family by Georgii, one of the founders of the
Council of Evangelical Christian-Baptist Churches whose members refused to register
with the Soviet authorities and were thus subjected to intense persecution, contains
information about evangelical and evangelistic activity in Siberia and the Far East from
the 1920s to the 1970s.

469 **The Mongolian mission of the London Missionary Society.**
D. S. M. Williams. *Slavonic and East European Review*, vol. 56, no. 3
(July 1978), p. 329-45.
This article is based on a close study of the correspondence from the British
missionaries serving in Buryatiya in the early nineteenth century with the London
Missionary Society. The letters, which are quoted at some length, are preserved in the
Society's archives. Though published earlier than Bawden's work (q.v.) it is worth
inclusion here because of its extensive reliance on primary material.

470 **The Doukhobors.**
George Woodcock, Ivan Avakumović. London: Faber & Faber, 1968.
382p.
Though this study of the Doukhobors, a Christian pacifist sect, is mainly concerned
with their emigration to Canada in the late nineteenth century and their subsequent
treatment there, a considerable body of the text refers to their experiences of
persecution within the Russian Empire. Some of them were exiled to Siberia, and
small colonies totalling possibly 2,000 people in the early 1900s were established along
the Amur river. See the index for relevant references.

# Shamanism

471 **Shamanism among the Turkic peoples of Siberia.**
N. A. Alekseev. *Soviet Anthropology and Archeology*, vol. 28, no. 1 (summer 1989), p. 56-107. bibliog.
A translated excerpt from a book published by the Soviet Academy of Sciences in Novosibirsk in 1987, this article surveys the shamanist rites of the Yakut, Altaian, Kumandin, Khakass, Kachin, Sagai, Shor, Tofalar and Tuvinian. The author then analyses the significance of the shaman in the life of the peoples in question.

472 **The route to eternity: cultural persistence and change in Siberian Khanty burial ritual.**
Marjorie Mandelstam Balzer. *Arctic Anthropology*, vol. 17, no. 1 (1980), p. 77-89. map. bibliog.
Fieldwork among the Khanty of western Siberia demonstrates that a syncretistic form of burial rite has been developed with some Orthodox Christian and some pagan elements. The old values were still evident despite Soviet attempts to overcome any vestiges of religion. Balzer's subsequent researches have led to the publication of a book which appeared just as the present bibliography was going to press, namely *Shamanism: Soviet studies of traditional religion in Siberia and Central Asia* (Armonk, New York: M. E. Sharpe, 1990. 197p.).

473 **Chukchee mythology.**
Waldemar Bogoras-Tan. *Memoirs of the American Museum of Natural History*, vol. 12, part 1 (1910), p. 1-197. (Publications of the Jesup North Pacific Expedition, vol. 7, part 1).
Contains the texts of many Chukchee incantations, myths and songs in Chukchee and English translation, plus five tales by russianized Yukagir and Chuvantsy, relatives of the Yukagirs.

474 **The cult of the bear and Soviet ideology.**
Boris Chichlo. *Religion in Communist Lands*, vol. 13, no. 2 (1985), p. 166-81.
A Soviet ethnographer now resident in the West discusses the fate of the bear cult in Siberia under the Communists. Earlier studies which still retain scientific value are 'Bear worship among the Turkish tribes of Siberia' by N. P. Dyrenkova (*Proceedings of the 23rd International Conference of Americanists* [New York, 1930]); 'Bear ceremonialism in the northern hemisphere' by A. Irving Hallowell (*American Anthropologist*, vol. 28 [1926], p. 1-175); and the very rare *The bear worshippers of Yezo and the Island of Karafuto (Saghalien), or the adventures of the Jewett family and their friend Oto Nambo* by Edward Greey (Boston: Lee & Shephard; New York: C. T. Dillingham, 1884. 304p.).

475 **Shamanism in Siberia.**
Edited by Vilmos Diószegi, M. Hoppál, translated by S. Simon.
Budapest: Akadémiai Kiadó, 1978. 531p. (Bibliotheka Uralica, no. 1).
Consists of thirty articles by an international group of scholars about aspects of
shamanism among Siberian peoples including the Buryat Mongols, Nentsy, Ket,
Tuvans, Yakut, Nganasan, Selkup, Yukagir, Koryak, Chukchi, Enets, Nanai and
Dolgan. In 'Tuva shamanism' by Vilmos Diószegi (*Acta Ethnographica*, vol. 11 [1962],
p. 143-90) the Hungarian investigator of the religion of the Siberian peoples
concentrates on Tuvan shamanist practices.

476 **The shaman: patterns of Siberian and Ojibway healing.**
John A. Grim. Norman, Oklahoma: University of Oklahoma Press,
1983. 258p. bibliog. (Civilization of the American Indian Series,
no. 165).
This comparative study of Siberian and American indigenous religious beliefs
investigates the cosmological, sociological, anthropological and psychological aspects
of those beliefs. A comprehensive picture of the shaman's role emerges, but no sources
in Russian are used. See also 'Shamanism of the native tribes of Siberia' by Immanuel
Moses Casanowicz (*Annual Report of the Smithsonian Institution for 1924* [1925],
p. 415-34), a brief illustrated overview of shamanism in Siberia which was also
published as a separate pamphlet.

477 **The mythology of the Koriak.**
Waldemar Jochelson. *American Anthropologist*, NS vol. 6 (1904),
p. 413-25.
Consists of a brief specialized study of the religious mythology of the Koryak of
northeastern Siberia collected by the author during the Jesup expedition.

478 **The shamanistic tradition of the Buryats (Siberia).**
Lawrence Krader. *Anthropos*, vol. 70, nos 1-2 (1975), p. 105-44.
Building upon former work published as 'Buryat religion and society' (*Southwestern
Journal of Anthropology*, vol. 10 [1954], p. 322-51), Krader presents an account of
Buryat Mongol shamanist belief and practice.

479 **The cult of the dead among the natives of the Amur basin.**
Ivan Alexis Lopatin. The Hague: Mouton, 1960. 211p. map. (Central
Asiatic Studies, no. 6).
A noted student of the languages of the Amur tribes here provides a survey of their
religious beliefs.

480 **Studies in Siberian shamanism.**
Edited by Henry N. Michael. Toronto, Canada: University of
Toronto Press, published for the Arctic Institute of North America,
1963. 229p. (Anthropology of the North: Translations from Russian
Sources, no. 4).
These translations of five studies undertaken in the 1920s and 1930s by Soviet
investigators provide extensive details of religious beliefs among the Ob Ugrian, Evenk
and Enets peoples. Marxist–Leninist concepts intrude in places.

481 **Buryat shamanism: history, structure, and social functions.**
T. M. Mikhailov. *Soviet Anthropology and Archeology*, vol. 28, no. 2
(fall 1989), p. 9-19.
Briefly summarizes the results of extensive reasearch into Buryat animism. See also
'A description of Buriat shamanism' by Jorma Partanen (*Journal de la société finno-
ougrienne*, vol. 51 [1941-42]).

482 **Shamanism in Siberia and European Russia, being the second part of
Shamanstvo.**
Viktor Mikhailovich Mikhailovskii, translated by Oliver Wardrop.
*Journal of the Royal Anthropological Institute of Great Britain*, vol. 24,
no. 1 (Aug. 1894), p. 62-100; vol. 24, no. 2 (Nov. 1894), p. 126-58.
Despite its age this item is included because it is a translation from a pre-revolutionary
Russian source otherwise unavailable to Western readers. Subsequent publications
have not rendered the contents invalid.

483 **Ritual and folklore in Siberian shamanism: experiment in a comparison
of structures.**
E. S. Novik, *Soviet Anthropology and Archeology*, vol. 28, no. 2 (fall
1989), p. 20-100. bibliog.
Consists of a translation of part of a book published in 1984. It presents a generalized
study of the relationship between rituals and folklore among many minorities including
the Buryat Mongols, Even, Evenk, Oroch, Nivkh, Yakut, Ket, Dolgan, Nganasan,
Ainu and Nanai.

484 **General theory of shamanism among the Tungus.**
Sergei Mikhailovich Shirokogorov. *Journal of the North China Branch
of the Royal Asiatic Society*, vol. 54 (1923), p. 246-9.
An eminent ethnographer attempts to develop a coherent theory about the nature of
shamanism among the Tungus tribes, which include the Evenk.

485 **The rite technique of the Siberian shaman.**
Anna-Leena Siikala. *F. F. Communications* (Helsinki), vol. 93 (2),
no. 220 (1978), p. 1-385. bibliog.
Based on an academic dissertation for the University of Helsinki, this work provides a
thorough investigation into the methods employed by shamans in Siberia in pursuance
of their craft.

# Social Issues

486 **Selections from the journal** *Economics and Applied Sociology.*
Introduced by Gregory Andrusz. *Soviet Sociology*, vol. 25, no. 4
(spring 1987), p. 1-90.

Contains translations of important articles from the Siberian Branch of the Soviet
Academy of Science's journal *Izvestiia Sibirskogo otdeleniya Akademii nauk, seriya
ekonomiki i prikladnoi sotsiologii* (News of the Siberian Section of the Soviet Academy
of Sciences, Series on Economics and Applied Sociology). The articles, based on
fieldwork in Siberia, cover issues such as the standard of living in Siberia, rural family
dynamics, organizing settlement patterns for a territorial production complex, and the
use of incentives in the workplace. Frank discussion of contemporary problems leads to
sometimes imaginative proposals for overcoming them.

487 **Regional variation in the commune: the case of Siberia.**
John Channon. In: *Land commune and peasant community in Russia:
communal forms in Imperial and early Soviet society*, edited by Roger
Bartlett. London: Macmillan, in Association with the School of
Slavonic and East European Studies, University of London, 1990,
p. 66-85.

As evidence of the increasing maturity and sophistication of Western studies of Siberia
this article adds a great deal to the English-language historiography of peasant society
before the 1917 Revolution. It is noteworthy that the commune in Siberia varied in
different areas, and that it was not in decline by 1914.

488 **Slavery in Russia, 1450-1725.**
Richard Hellie. Chicago, Illinois; London: University of Chicago
Press, 1982. 776p. bibliog.

Slavery, which existed in Siberia among the indigenous peoples and was practised to
some extent among the Russian population in the seventeenth and eighteenth
centuries, has never been investigated at depth in the West. Some information about it
may be gained from scattered references in this general book.

489 **Traditional forms of investigation and trial among the Russian peasants
of western Siberia in the eighteenth and the first half of the nineteenth
centuries.**
Nina Adamovna Minenko. *Soviet Anthropology and Archeology*, vol.
21, no. 3 (winter 1982-83), p. 55-79.

A respected researcher into the lives of Russian peasants in pre-revolutionary western
Siberia here provides a rare glimpse into common law procedures conducted within the
village commune. The system was 'quite democratic at first'.

490 **The open-air museum in the village of Cherkekh.**
S. G. Safronov. *Soviet Anthropology and Archeology*, vol. 23, no. 1
(summer 1984), p. 66-76.

Translated from the journal *Sovetskaya etnografiya* (Soviet Ethnography), this
illustrated article describes the buildings and exhibits in a museum opened in Yakutiya
in late 1977. Partly inspired by the Yakut writer Suorum Omollon (pseud. D. K.
Svitsev), the sixteen-hectare museum site includes buildings which relate to the life of
Decembrist and other revolutionary exiles. It also contains material about everyday
life, including examples of traditional Yakut summer and winter dwellings.

491 **My childhood in Siberia.**
Tatiana Tchernavin. London: Oxford University Press, 1972. 112p.

Though intended for schoolchildren, this account of a young Russian girl's experiences
is unusual and rather interesting. She was born in 1887. Her father was appointed
professor of botany at Tomsk University. The book relates fascinating detail about pre-
revolutionary social life in provincial (but human) Tomsk, and records the near
drowning of her mother during a shipwreck on the Ob river.

# Exile and Imprisonment

## From the seventeenth century to 1916

492 **Rebel on the bridge. A life of the Decembrist Baron Andrey Rozen (1800-84).**
Glynn R. V. Barratt. London: Paul Elek, 1975. 310p. bibliog.

One of few full-length biographies in English about the Decembrists, who were exiled to Siberia after an abortive coup attempt in 1825, this work includes three chapters on the Siberian period of Baron Rozen's exile. He spent ten years there, from 1827 to 1837, mostly in Transbaikalia but also in Kurgan in the west. Many quotations from letters are included. An autobiographical account appeared too: *Russian conspirators in Siberia, a personal narrative by Baron R---, a Russian Dekabrist*, translated from the German by Evelyn St. John Mildmay (London: Smith, Elder, 1872. 272p.).

493 **Memoirs of a revolutionary.**
Eva Lvovna Broido, translated and edited by Vera Broido. London: Oxford University Press, 1967. 150p.

The author, a young Menshevik, was exiled to Siberia in 1899. There she married and had children, participated in a 1904 protest against the severity of conditions which ended in bloodshed, escaped, but was sent to Siberia again in 1915. Her account should be compared with her husband's: *My exile to Siberia and escape* by Mark Isaevich Broido (London: On behalf of the Society of Friends of Russian Freedom by T. Laurie, [c. 1905]. 40p.).

**Exile and Imprisonment.** From the seventeenth century to 1916

494  **Russian nihilism and exile life in Siberia. A graphic and chronological history of Russia's bloody nemesis, and a description of exile life in all its true but horrifying phases. . .**
James William Buel. Philadelphia, Pennsylvania: Historical Publishing Co., 1883. 574p. Also published in Philadelphia by West Philadelphia Publishing Co. in 1889. A later version entitled *A nemesis of misgovernment* was published in Philadelphia in 1900. 589p.

A journalist from Illinois reports at length about the horrors which he encountered on a journey to the Siberian exiles in 1882. See also the rather later account *Prisoners of Russia: a personal study of convict life in Sakhalin and Siberia* by Benjamin Douglas Howard (New York: D. Appleton & Co., 1902. 389p.).

495  **Bakunin's escape from Siberia.**
Edward Hallett Carr. *Slavonic and East European Review*, vol. 15 (Jan. 1937), p. 377-88.

Based on published sources in Russian this article is the result of a detailed investigation of events surrounding the anarchist Bakunin's escape from Siberian exile in 1861. While Muravëv-Amurskii, his second cousin, was ruling eastern Siberia, Bakunin was in a privileged position. Later he fled by sea. Carr tries to clear up some of the ambiguities surrounding Bakunin's actions. A more general survey of his period in exile is provided in chapter 18 of *Michael Bakunin*, also by Carr (London: Macmillan, 1937. 501p.).

496  **Sixteen years in Siberia. Some experiences of a Russian revolutionist.**
Lev Deich, translated by Helen Chisholm. London: Murray, 1903. 372p. Reprinted Westport, Connecticut: Hyperion Press, 1977.

Introduced by a helpful translator's preface this memoir of a Russian social democrat is slightly misnamed, since only pages 148 onwards deal with Siberia. The account of travel to and prison and exile life in Siberia in the 1880s and 1890s is colourful and broad ranging. Having helped to collect data for the 1897 census and archaeological information, Deich worked on the Trans-Siberian Railway at Stretensk for two years, then helped with a newspaper in Blagoveshchensk. The account of the infamous massacre of Chinese residents in 1900 is noteworthy.

497  **Prison life in Siberia.**
Fëdor Mikhailovich Dostoevsky, sole and authorised translation by H. Sutherland Edwards. London: Maxwell, [1888]. 368p.

This semi-fictionalized account of life in Tsarist prisons in Siberia was entitled *Notes from the house of the dead* in Russian. Purporting to be the posthumously published memoirs of a prisoner, it provides a vivid picture of convict life in the late nineteenth century. Later translations were *The house of the dead, or prison life in Siberia*, with an introduction by Julius Bramont (London: Dent, 1914) and *The house of the dead*, translated by Constance Garnett (London: Heinemann, 1948). Interesting letters written by Dostoevsky, describing life in prison, were published in *Selected letters of Fedor Dostoevsky*, edited by Joseph Frank and David Goldstein, Andrew R. MacAndrew translator (New Brunswick, New Jersey; London: Rutgers University Press, 1987, p. 55-65). For details of the exile, see *Dostoevsky: a biography* by Leonid Grossman, translated by Mary Mackler (London: Allen Lane, 1974, p. 169-85) *and Dostoevsky: the years of ordeal* by Joseph Frank (London: Robson Books, 1983, p. 69-86).

498 **Revelations of Siberia by a banished lady.**
Ewa Félinska, edited by Colonel Lach Szyrma.   London: Colburn & Co., 1852. 2 vols. 2nd ed., 1854.
Translated from a Polish edition published in Wilno in 1852, this book tells of the experiences of a Polish woman, Ewa Wendorff (1739-1859), in Siberia.

499 **The Decembrists in Siberian exile.**
Jeanne Meakin Haskett.   PhD thesis, Ohio University, 1962.
(Available from University Microfilms, Ann Arbor, Michigan, order no. 63-00054).
This research into the fate of the Decembrists in Siberia remains unpublished, apart from an article 'The Decembrist N. A. Bestuzhev in Siberian exile, 1826-55' (*Studies in Romanticism*, vol. 4, no. 4 [1965], p. 185-205). See also 'The Decembrists in Siberia' by K. E. Birkett (MLitt dissertation, University of Glasgow, 1988).

500 **Siberia and the exile system.**
George Kennan.   New York: Century; London: James R. Osgood, McIlvaine, 1891. 2 vols. Reprinted New York: Russell & Russell, 1970.
An abridged edition, with an introduction by George Frost Kennan was published in Chicago, Illinois: University of Chicago Press, 1958. 243p.
The archetypal study of Tsarist penal policies in Siberia, this work documented the arbitrariness and slovenly cruelty of the prison and exile systems. The journey was undertaken in 1885-86 in the company of George Frost, an American journalist. A fascinating study of George Kennan (1845-1924) and his attitude to Russia is 'George Kennan and Russia, 1865-1905' by Frederick Francis Travis (PhD thesis Emory University, Atlanta, Georgia, 1974 [available from University Microfilms, Ann Arbor, Michigan. Order no. 75-11140]).

501 **King stork and king log: at the dawn of a new reign. A study of modern Russia.**
Sergei Mikhailovich Kravchinskii-Stepnyak.   London: Chatto & Windus, 1905. 347p.
A Russian revolutionary populist concentrates on the seamier side of Russian life, namely administrative exile and imprisonment. Chapter thirteen discusses massacres in Yakutsk, and the Kara tragedy. The text includes quotations from official documents.

502 **The forgotten village: four years in Siberia.**
Theodore Kröger.   London: Hutchinson, 1936. 320p.
A German military doctor, the author was trapped in Russia by World War I, and spent four years interned in Siberia. The book includes insights into exile life deeper than those gained by mere observers.

503 **Lenin in Siberia: records, documents and recollection.**
Translated from the Russian by Raissa Bobrova. Moscow: Progress Publishers, 1983. 327p.
This illustrated compilation of materials relating to Lenin's exile in Siberia from 1897 to 1899 gives a very clear impression of an era when conditions were far more liberal than they were to become under Lenin's successors in the USSR.

504 **Women in exile: wives of the Decembrists.**
Anatole Gregory Mazour. Tallahassee, Florida: Diplomatic Press, 1975. 133p. map. bibliog.
This investigation of the fates of the wives who elected to follow their Decembrist husbands into exile provides fascinating insights into the mores of the period. The appendices include relevant documents from 1827 to 1850, and a biographical glossary. *The princess of Siberia: the story of Maria Volkonsky and the Decembrist exiles* by Christine Sutherland (London: Methuen; New York: Farrar, Straus, Giroux, 1984. 339p. maps. bibliog.) provides a more detailed study of one wife, who during her 26 years in Siberia participated in school teaching, theatricals and ethnographical investigation.

505 **My escape from Siberia.**
Rufin Piotrowski, translated by E. S. [*sic*] London: Routledge, Warne & Routledge, 1863. 386p.
Piotrowski (1806-72) was one of many Poles exiled to Siberia for anti-Russian activities. Tracing his escape from exile, this is an abridged translation of the Polish work published in Poznan in 1860. See also his *The story of a Siberian exile* (London: Longman, Green, Longman, Roberts & Green, 1863. 321p.).

506 **N. G. Chernyshevskii.**
Francis Ballard Randall. New York: Twaye Publishers, 1967. 178p.
Nikolai Gavrilovich Chernyshevskii (1828-89) was exiled to Siberia for the last fourteen years of his life. In chapter seven of this biography his time in Nerchinsk and then Vilyuisk is described. See also *Chernyshevskii: the man and the journalist* by William F. Woehrlin (Cambridge, Massachusetts: Harvard University Press, 1971, p. 321-6).

507 **The life of a Russian exile: the remarkable experience of a young girl, being an account of her peasant childhood, her girlhood in prison, her exile to Siberia, and escape from there.**
Mariya Suklova, translated by Gregory Yarros. New York: Century Co., 1914; London: Heinemann, 1915. 251p.
The subtitle adequately explains this work.

508 **Decembrists in exile.**
Joseph L. Sullivan. *Harvard Slavic Papers*, vol. 4 (1957), p. 93-106.
Though brief, this article presents an overview of the major figures associated with the Decembrist movement in their Siberian period.

509 **My flight from Siberia, 1907.**
Leon Trotsky, translated from the Russian by Malcolm Campbell.
Colombo, Sri Lanka: Young Socialist Publications, 1969. 56p. map.

Reprinted from a version published in Berlin in 1923, this pamphlet consists of a typically vivid account by Lev Davydovich Trotskii (1879-1940) of his dramatic winter-time escape from permanent exile in the northern Ob region in 1907. Trotsky's autobiography *My life: an attempt at an autobiography*, with an introduction by Joseph Hansen (New York: Pathfinder Press, 1970; Harmondsworth, England: Penguin Books, 1975) contains more sober yet still well-written accounts of his first exile to Siberia and successful escape (chapters 9-10) and the second episode which formed the subject of the the above pamphlet (chapter 15). Joseph Stalin (1879-1953), Trotsky's arch-rival for the Bolshevik leadership, was also exiled to Siberia more than once. An account of his experiences there may be found in chapters five and thirteen of a hostile American study, *The young Stalin: the early years of an elusive revolutionary* by Edward Ellis Smith (London: Cassell, 1968).

510 **Siberian exile in the eighteenth century.**
Alan Wood. *Siberica* (Portland, Oregon), vol. 1, no. 1 (summer 1990), p. 38-63. bibliog.

Part of a broader study of Siberia and the exile system, this article is a judicious summary of the existing state of knowledge about the extent of exile in the eighteenth century, based on Tsarist and Soviet publications. For an earlier period see *Avvakum's Siberian exile, 1653-64* (item no. 13, pages 11-34. bibliog.).

511 **Chernyshevskii, Siberian exile and oblastnichestvo.**
Alan Wood. In: *Russian thought and society, 1800-1917: essays in honour of Eugene Lampert*, edited by Roger Bartlett. Keele, England: University of Keele, 1984, p. 42-66.

The first half of this essay discusses the harmful effects on the exiled populist writer Nikolai Gavrilovich Chernyshevskii (1828-89) of abortive attempts to free him by sympathizers, and the failed insurrection by Poles near Lake Baikal in 1865. The second half introduces the regionalist movement whose proponents wished to set up an autonomous, or even independent, Siberia and presents a brief account of the 1865 independence scare.

512 **Crime and punishment in the house of the dead.**
Alan Wood. In: *Civil rights in Imperial Russia*, edited by Olga Crisp, Linda Edmondson. Oxford: Clarendon Press, 1989, p. 215-33.

A survey of the pre-revolutionary Russian exile and prison system, with special reference to Siberia, this essay develops themes outlined in items 510 and 511 above, and in the following: 'Siberian exile in Tsarist Russia' (*History Today*, vol. 30 [1980], p. 19-24); 'The use and abuse of administrative exile to Siberia' (*Irish Slavonic Studies*, no. 6 [1985], p. 65-81); 'Sex and violence in Siberia: aspects of the Tsarist exile system' in *Siberia: two historical perspectives*, by John Massy Stewart and Alan Wood (London: Great Britain–USSR Association and the School of Slavonic and East European Studies, 1984, p. 23-42); and 'Administrative exile and the criminals' commune in Siberia' in *Land commune and peasant community in Russia*, edited by Roger Bartlett (London: Macmillan in Association with the School of Slavonic and East European Studies, 1990. p. 395-414).

513 **The road to oblivion.**
   Vladimir Mikhailovich Zenzinov, with the collaboration of Isaac Don
   Levine. New York: McBride, 1931. 250p. maps. Also published
   London: Cape, 1932. 287p.

A leader of the Socialist Revolutionary Party, Zenzinov was exiled to the remote
northeast of Siberia in 1906. This memoir abounds with details of the lives of Russian
settlers, native people, geographical scenes and local delicacies. Zenzinov relates the
story of his escape via the Sea of Okhotsk and tells of his second period in Siberian
exile, this time in Russkoe uste, far up in the north of the Lena region, where he
remained from 1912 until 1917. An article entitled 'With an exile in arctic Siberia: the
narrative of a Russian who was compelled to turn polar explorer for two years'
(*National Geographic*, vol. 46 [Dec. 1924], p. 695-718. map) relates with some gusto
his travel among Yakut and Evenk, bird migrations, goose hunting and an attempted
escape during the second period.

# The post-1917 period

514 **Involuntary journey to Siberia.**
   Andrei Alekseevich Amalrik, translated from the Russian by Manya
   Harari, Max Hayward. London: Collins & Harvill Press, 1970. 282p.

Abridged from the Russian original, this is a memoir by a Soviet intellectual about his
experiences of exile in the late 1960s. Amalrik (1938-80) was sent to work on a
collective farm at Novokrivosheino near Tomsk. The account is rather matter-of-fact,
but includes details about Siberian peasant life which are rare for this period. His
revelations about food shortages and agricultural inefficiency are hardly unexpected,
but authentic enough. His *Notes of a Russian revolutionary*, translated by Guy Daniels,
with an introduction by Susan Jacoby (London: Weidenfeld & Nicolson, 1982. 343p.)
contains information about a second period in Siberia, this time spent in the far
northeast in Magadan in the mid-1970s.

515 **Shipwreck of a generation: the memoirs of Joseph Berger.**
   Joseph Berger. London: Harvill Press, 1971. 286p.

Joseph Berger (1904- ), a Jewish Communist, was imprisoned in Mariinsk in western
Siberia in 1935. Later he was employed in building the Tashtagol railway in Gornaya
Shoriya in the Sayan mountains, spent time at Dudinka in the far north, and in 1948
ended up at the Aleksandrovsk maximum security prison near Irkutsk. In 1951 he was
released from prison but had to stay in Siberia, living at Maklakovo near Eniseisk.
Rehabilitated in 1956 he emigrated to Poland and then Israel. The text concentrates on
the characteristrics of different types of prisoners whom he met, rather than on his
personal experiences. It is valuable as an epitome of prison life in Stalin's Siberia.

516 **The Russian enigma.**
Ante Ciliga, part one translated by Fernand G. Fernier and Anne Cliff,
part two translated by Margaret and Hugo Dewar. London: Ink
Links, 1979. 573p.

A Yugoslav born in 1898, Ciliga worked for Comintern, but was imprisoned for
Trotskyite activities in 1930. Subsequently he spent over two years in Siberian exile.
Part two of this publication contains his Siberian reminiscences. Details of life among
exiles and the problems of everyday life in Krasnoyarsk are followed by a fascinating
picaresque sequence about a winter journey via a machine-tractor station to Eniseisk,
his second place of exile. Released to Europe, he considered his years in the USSR the
richest of his life.

517 **Kolyma: the arctic death camps.**
Robert Conquest. London: Macmillan, 1978. 256p. maps. bibliog.

An exhaustive investigation of the infamous Kolyma camp system in the far northeast
by a tireless Western exposer of Soviet illegalities, this book also takes the opportunity
to slam the favourable reports on the region made by the Americans Henry A. Wallace
and Owen Lattimore in 1944 (q.v.). The Kolyma system contained at least 120 full-
scale camps with a capacity for roughly 400,000 prisoners, with a death toll so high that
some 3,000,000 may have perished there. More general accounts may be found in
*Forced labor in the Soviet Union* by David J. Dallin and Boris Ivanovich Nicolaievsky
(New York: Yale University Press, 1947; London: Hollis & Carter, 1948. 331p.
bibliog.) and *Forced labor in the Soviet Union* (Washington, DC: Department of State
Publications, 1952. 69p.). However. see also 'On assessing the size of forced
concentration camp labour in the Soviet Union, 1929-1956' by Stephen G. Wheatcroft
(*Soviet Studies*, vol. 22, no. 2 [April 1981], p. 265-95) as well as updates in the same
journal during 1989.

518 **A sparrow in the snow.**
Sylva Darel, translated from the Russian by Barbara Norman. New
York: Stein & Day, 1973; London: Souvenir Press, [1974]. 216p.

This book presents exile life in Siberia from a very unusual point of view. It consists of
a young girl's experiences as she grows up in Siberian exile during the last years of the
Stalin era.

519 **Into the whirlwind.**
Eugenia Ginzburg, translated by Paul Stevenson, Manya Harari.
London: Collins Harvill, 1967; Harmondsworth, England: Penguin
Books, 1968. 348p. There was also another edition translated by Paul
Stevenson and Max Hayward, New York: Harcourt, Brace & World,
1967. 418p. map. The second volume was published as *Within the
whirlwind*, translated by Ian Boland. London: Collins & Harvill Press,
1981. 423p. map.

Profound, poignant and sensitive, this memoir tells of one woman's experiences in
prison and exile from 1937 to 1955. Volume one becomes strictly relevant only at the
end when the prisoners are sent by sea to the Kolyma camps. Volume two tells of
subsequent experiences, including religious conversion, and eventual release.

520 **Years off my life.**
Aleksandr Vasilevich Gorbatov, translated from the Russian by
Gordon Clough, Anthony Cash.   London: Constable; New York,
W. W. Norton, 1964. 222p.
Consists of an abridged version of the excerpts from the author's memoirs about his
experiences of repression under Stalin which had appeared in the Soviet journal *Novyi
mir* (New World) in March–May 1964.

521 **Paying guest in Siberia.**
Maria Hadow.   London: Harvill Press, 1959; London; Glasgow:
Collins, Fontana Books, 1961. 189p.
This rather homely, unremarkable human document is the memoir of a Polish woman
deported with her mother to southern Siberia or northern Kazakhstan (the
geographical details are vague) in 1940. She relates her experiences trying to make
ends meet working in a collective farm, knitting garments for sale, and living to some
extent off parcels from home. A good deal of attention is paid to the horrors of insect
infestation. In 1942 she was deported to Iran.

522 **The endless steppe.**
Esther Hautzig.   New York: Thomas Y. Crowell, 1968; London:
Hamish Hamilton, 1969. 214p.
A girl from a religious Jewish family deported from Vilna finds herself in the middle of
the steppes at Rubtsovsk with her family. After working in the gypsum mines and
collective farms, the family are amnestied and take up free work in industry. They
make their own hut. Looming starvation, the pangs of teenage love, school conditions,
and the joy of return to Poland in 1946 are quite effectively depicted.

523 **Soviet Russia fights crime.**
Lenka von Koerber, translated from the German by Mary Fowler.
London: G. Routledge & Son, 1934; New York: Dutton, 1935. 240p.
This is a record of impressions gathered by a German prison official on a visit to the
USSR. She visited the jail in Tyumen, in western Siberia. Her impressions of the jail
may be compared with those of George Kennan (q.v.).

524 **Eleven years in Soviet prison camps.**
Elinor Lipper, translated from the German by Richard and Clara
Winston.   London: Hollis & Carter, 1951. 310p. map. Also London:
World Affairs Book Club, [1951].
An account by a Swiss-German Communist who was sent to the Kolyma camps in 1937
and remained in the Soviet Far East until 1948. Like Eugenia Ginzburg (q.v.) she
provides details of the rail and sea route via Irkutsk and Vladivostok to Magadan.

525 **Kolyma: gold and forced labor in the USSR.**
Silvester Mora. Washington, DC: Foundation for Foreign Affairs, 1949. 66p. (Foundation Pamphlet, no. 7).
The author's real name was Kasimierz Zamorski (1914- ). He provides a general analysis of the slave-labour system established in the Soviet Far East, based on the evidence of sixty-two released Polish prisoners.

526 **Hell in Siberia.**
Karl Nork, translated from the German by Eleanor Brockett.
London: R. Hale, 1957; London: John Spencer & Co, 1959. 222p. (World War II Series, no. 75).
The author was a German officer attached to an anti-Soviet Cossack division in World War II. He was sent to labour camps when he fell into Stalinist hands.

527 **Beria's gardens: ten years' captivity in Russia and Siberia.**
Unto Parvilahti, translated from the Finnish by Alan Blair. London: Hutchinson, 1959; New York: Dutton, 1960. 286p.
Another camps memoir, this account by a Finn (1907- ) concerns his experiences in Dudinka in the northern Enisei region from 1950 to 1954. His descriptions of the Enisei, particularly the break-up of ice as the thaw begins, are memorable. He also writes about a timber works in Igarka.

528 **It happens in Russia: seven years forced labour in the Siberian goldfields.**
Vladimir Petrov, translated from the Russian by Mirra Ginsburg.
London: Eyre & Spottiswood, 1951. 470p. map.
Parts two to four of Book 1 of this work present another bleakly authentic account of life in the Kolyma camps during the Stalin era. The trip through Siberia to Vladivostok, then by sea to the Dalstroi goldfields is described in some detail, but most of the section refers to life in the mines. Book 2, which deals with his escape, begins with the return journey to Siberia proper via Irkutsk and a Novosibirsk replete with Volga Germans exiled with the onset of World War II. Conquest's *Kolyma* (q.v.) relies heavily on this account as well as on Lipper (q.v.), Ginzburg (q.v.), Gorbatov and Solomon (q.v.). The American version of Petrov's work was entitled *Soviet gold: my life as a slave laborer in the Siberian mines* (New York: Farrar, Straus, 1949. 426p. map).

529 **Exiled to Siberia.**
Anita Preiss. Manitoba, Canada: Anita Press, 1972. 82p.
This privately published account of a Ukrainian's experiences as an exile until 1967 has the text in German at the rear of the same book, with a separate pagination.

530 **Sixteen years in Siberia: memoirs.**
Rachel Rachlin, Israel Rachlin, translated from the Danish and with a
foreword by Birgitte M. de Weille. Tuscaloosa, Alabama; London:
University of Alabama Press, 1988. 251p. maps.

Sent to Siberia from Lithuania in 1941 after the Soviet invasion, the Rachlins remained
there until 1957. This Jewish couple were sent to Biisk in the Altai in southwest Siberia
and then to northen Yakutiya. Fresh and intimate in style, their book is unique in that
the partners alternate, writing passages in turn about the same incidents.

531 **The first guidebook to prisons and concentration camps of the Soviet
Union.**
Abraham Shifrin. Uhlingen, Germany; Seewis, Switzerland:
Stephanus Edition, 1980. 378p. maps.

Commissioned by the Research Center for Prisons, Psychprisons and Forced Labor
Concentration Camps of the USSR, this thorough and detailed reference work
translated from Russian includes illustrations, maps and other information about all
the relevant institutions in the USSR in the late 1970s. Many entries refer to Siberia
and the Soviet Far East.

532 **The profits of slavery: Baltic forced laborers and deportees under Stalin
and Khrushchev.**
Adolfs Šilde, translated from the Latvian by Valdemars Kreicbergs,
edited by Herman Stein and Peter Williams. Stockholm: Latvian
National Foundation in Scandinavia, [1959]. 302p. map.

The title of this work is self-explanatory. There are references to Siberia and the Soviet
Far East scattered throughout, but especially in chapters 3 and 4.

533 **Magadan.**
Michael Solomon. New York: Auerbach Publishers; Montreal,
Canada: Chateau Books, 1971. 243p.

A Romanian Jewish journalist, Solomon was arrested in 1946 after returning from
service with the British. He spent seventeen years at hard labour, much of the time in
the far northeastern slave-camp complex.

534 **The Gulag Archipelago, 1918-1956: an experiment in literary analysis.**
Aleksandr Isaevich Solzhenitsyn, translated from the Russian by
Thomas P. Witney (volume three translated by H. T. Willetts).
London: Collins, Fontana, 1974-78. 3 vols.

This monumental *tour de force* about the whole grisly subject of Soviet terror, prisons,
slave-labour camps and exile has many details about the Siberian experience scattered
through it. A mere glance at the maps is enough to show how widespread the camps
were. Gruesome; to be read only by the stout of heart.

535 **7000 days in Siberia.**
Karlo Stajner.   New York: Farrar, Straus, Giroux, 1988; London:
Corgi Books, 1989. [n.p.].

Karlo Stajner (1902- ) provides yet another account of a lengthy enforced visit to Siberia. An Austrian Communist who took a Serbian name, he emigrated to the USSR in 1932 only to end up with two consecutive ten-year sentences to the Gulag. He was held in Dudinka and Norilsk, and in 1956 was amnestied and obliged to settle 'for life' in the Krasnoyarsk region. The depiction of the camps is stark and immediate. See also *Sonechka: a life in Siberia* by Sonia Terry and A. Frank (Kensington, Maryland: A. Frank, 1987).

536 **The silver madonna, or the odyssey of Eugenia Wasilewska.**
Eugenia Wasilewska.   London: Allen & Unwin, 1970; New York:
John Day, 1971. 216p. maps.

The odyssey of a Polish woman transported to Siberia, this work ends with an account of her escape after many wanderings.

537 **Ten years in Russia and Siberia.**
Johannes Henricus Wigmans, translated from the Dutch by Arnout de
Waal.   London: Darton, Longman & Todd, 1964. 234p. map.

Deserting to the Russians to escape from service in the *Wehrmacht* [German armed forces] did not help Wigmans. He was imprisoned, then spent five years in a Siberian prison camp before being released. The revulsion he felt towards the Soviet system did not prevent him seeing kindness in individual Russians.

# Population, Settlement and Urban Development

## From the seventeenth century to 1916

538 **Russian settlement in the north.**
Terence Armstrong.   Cambridge: Cambridge University Press, 1965.
223p. maps. bibliog.

Covering the pre- and post-revolutionary eras this is a most valuable all-round study of Russian settlement in northern Siberia. Unfortunately the author's intention to concentrate on the Arctic region meant that he had to exclude the whole of the thickly settled funnel-shaped zone along the Trans-Siberian Railway.

539 **The Trans-Siberian and urban change in Siberia in a space–time framework, 1885-1913.**
Elena A. Baranov.   PhD thesis, University of Kansas, 1987.
(Available from University Microfilms, Ann Arbor, Michigan, order no. NHF 88–13384).

This study, which I have not seen, appears to be an important contribution to Siberian settlement history, assessing the effects of railway construction on urban developments along the railway line.

540 **Subjugation and settlement in seventeenth and eighteenth century Siberia.**
David Norman Collins.   In: *The history of Siberia from Russian conquest to revolution* (q.v.), p. 37-56.

Investigates the nature and methods of Muscovite colonial policies in Siberia to the end of the eighteenth century, with special reference to Russo-Teleut relations. The picture which emerges is of a complex interaction between state and private initiative, Russians of various social strata and aboriginal inhabitants, rather than the crude stereotypes of brutal military subjugation or entirely peaceful peasant settlement current at various times.

541 **Peasant colonisation of Siberia: a study of the growth of Russian rural society in Siberia, with special emphasis on the years 1890 to 1918.**
Herbert J. Ellison. PhD thesis, London University, 1955.

Valuable in its gathering of information about peasant migration to Siberia, particularly in the era of the Trans-Siberian Railway, this study has now been rendered somewhat dated by the amount of Soviet research into the problem which burst upon the scene following Khrushchev's destalinization in the mid-1950s.

542 **Feeding the Russian fur trade: provisionment of the Okhotsk seaboard and the Kamchatka peninsula, 1639-1856.**
James R. Gibson. Madison, Wisconsin; Milwaukee, Wisconsin; London: University of Wisconsin Press, 1969. 337p. maps. bibliog.

Almost unique among Western studies of Siberia to date this work uses Soviet archive material extensively. Gibson's thorough analysis of transportation routes, agricultural problems and the difficulties of provisioning Russia's settlements in the Far East has no parallel anywhere.

543 **On the geography of pre-revolutionary colonization and migration processes in the southern part of the Soviet Far East.**
Vadim Vyacheslavovich Pokshishevskii. *Soviet Geography*, vol. 4, no. 4 (April 1963), p. 17-31. map. bibliog.

One of very few English-language accounts of the population of the Amur and Ussuri regions under the Tsars, this article contrasts Cossack overland settlement with the maritime transportation of peasants from European Russia. The locational pattern of cities, urban growth and the sequence of rural settlement are included.

544 **Ukrainian peasant colonization east of the Urals, 1896-1914.**
Ihor Stebelsky. *Soviet Geography*, vol. 25, no. 9 (Nov. 1984), p. 681-94. maps. bibliog.

A valuable contribution to the study of peasant colonization in Siberia and northern Kazakhstan before World war I, this article provides information about the destinations of Ukrainian emigrants (who formed 50 per cent of the total), the conditions encountered and evidence still remaining of the early Ukrainian settlements. There are several tables of figures.

545 **The great Siberian migration: government and peasant in resettlement from emancipation to the First World War.**
Donald Warren Treadgold. Princeton, New Jersey: Princeton University Press, 1957. 278p. maps. bibliog. Reprinted Westport, Connecticut: Greenwood Press, 1976.

An important pioneering study of the reasons for and dynamics of Russian peasant settlement in Siberia and the Russian Far East and replete with maps and tables, this work is a must for anyone interested in the question. However, it must be pointed out that much Soviet research has been done since Treadgold published his book. The time has now come for a serious update to be produced. There is no English investigation comparable to the masterly *La Sibérie: peuplement et immigration paysanne au XIX^e siècle* by François-Xavier Coquin (Paris: Institut d'Etudes Slaves, 1969. 789p. maps. bibliog. [Collection historique de l'Institut d'Etudes Slaves, 20]).

# The post-1917 period

546  **New Siberian towns: plans, motivations, problems, progress.**
Violet Conolly. *Sibirica* (Lancaster) no. 2 (1983), p. 5-17.
Violet Conolly (1900-88), a former researcher for the British Foreign Office, surveys new urban developments from the West Siberian oil fields to the hydro-electric power and diamond mining enterprises in the Soviet Far East. The Kremlin had by the late 1970s realized that decent living conditions were essential if workers were to be retained in the strategically important extractive and energy industries. Deficiencies abounded, however. The information is gleaned entirely from Soviet press and radio sources. See also another version of the same data in 'Notes on new Siberian towns' (*Asian Affairs*, vol. 14 [OS vol. 70], part 3 [Oct. 1983], p. 271-86. map).

547  **Spatial structure of consumer services in Primorskiy kray, Soviet Far East.**
T. P. Filicheva. *Soviet Geography*, vol. 31, no. 1 (Jan. 1990), p. 54-60. map. bibliog.
A researcher from the Soviet Far East Consumer Services Institute assesses factors which lead to inadequate provision of services in the region, and makes recommendations for improvements.

548  **Ways of improving settlement in West Siberia.**
L. P. Fuks, translated by Andrew R. Bond. *Soviet Geography*, vol. 28, no. 10 (Dec. 1987), p. 756-76. map.
Addressing the problem of rural population loss in western Siberia, the author, a member of the Siberian Experimental Design Unit, claims that forced resettlements to larger places are simplistic and counterproductive. He calls for a complex theory of settlement to be developed on the basis of which planning can be effective.

549  **Recent trends in Siberian urban growth.**
Gary Hausladen. *Soviet Geography*, vol. 28, no. 2 (Feb. 1987), p. 71-89. maps.
Provides a cumulation of data, much of it in tabular form, about changes in urban growth patterns in Siberia from 1959 to 1985. As the author indicates, the article provides a firm base from which investigations into the effects of new policies under Gorbachev can be gauged.

550 **Karl Marx Collective: economy, society and religion in a Siberian collective farm.**
Caroline Humphrey.   Cambridge: Cambridge University Press, 1983. 522p. maps. bibliog.

Based on fieldwork undertaken in the Barguzin District to the southeast of Lake Baikal, this social anthropologist's study of a collective farm in the Buryat Republic is a very valuable all-round investigation which not only contributes information on social and religious conditions in Buryatiya, but also casts considerable light on agrarian production methods and the level of life in rural Siberia in the 1960s and 1970s. The bibliography includes items on the Buryats, some written by Caroline Humphrey, which I have not included in this volume.

551 **Men of Siberia: sketch book from the Kuzbas.**
Hugo Huppert.   Moscow; Leningrad: Cooperative Publishing Society of Foreign Workers in the USSR; London: Lawrence, 1934. 325p. map.

This lively and unashamedly partisan study consists of a diary accompanied by sketches of daily life. It was written by a German who participated in 'compelling the earth to be rich', that is opening up Siberia industrially in the early five-year plan period. Building a new life in Novosibirsk, Prokopevsk, and at the Kuznetskstroi works are graphically depicted.

552 **A source on the far north east.**
Michael Kaser.   *Soviet Studies*, vol. 27, no. 4 (1975), p. 642-4.

Though brief, this précis of a book published in Magadan in 1969 provides rare information about the economic, administrative and social problems of the region in comparison to conditions in central Russia. The question of sewage disposal is but one item included.

553 **Magnetic mountain: city building and city life in the Soviet Union in the 1930s: a study of Magnitogorsk.**
Stephen Mark Kotkin.   PhD thesis, University of California, Berkeley, 1981. (Available from University Microfilms, Ann Arbor, Michigan, order no. NHF 89–16738).

Though strictly in the eastern Urals rather than Siberia, Magnitogorsk was closely linked to developments in the Kuznetsk Basin. This detailed study of civic, economic and social development would provide a good model for research into other cities in Siberia.

554 **The population of the Soviet Union: history and prospects.**
Frank Lorimer.   Geneva, Switzerland: League of Nations, 1946. 289p. maps. (Series of League of Nations Publications II. Economic and Financial 1946. II. A. 3).

Basing itself on the censuses of 1897 and 1926 this seminal study of population development in the USSR makes excursions into the eighteenth century and speculates about the later twentieth. Use of the index will show that a considerable amount of data concerns Siberia and the Soviet Far East. Recent changes in population figures may be found by looking at the indexes of two books which review censuses up to

**Population, Settlement and Urban Development.** The post-1917 period

1977: *Nationality and population change in Russia and the USSR* by Robert A. Lewis, Richard H. Rowland and Ralph S. Clem (New York: Praeger, 1976. 456p. bibliog.), and *Population redistribution in the USSR* by Robert A. Lewis and Richard H. Rowland (New York: Praeger, 1979. 485p. bibliog.). The 1979 figures for the north are included in *Polar Record*, vol. 19, no. 123 (Sept. 1979), p. 622-3 and vol. 20, no. 125 (May 1980), p. 169-70.

555 **Urban growth in Siberia and the Soviet Far East: multiplier effects of Japanese-supplied plants.**
R. S. Mathieson. *Soviet Geography*, vol. 21, no. 8 (Sept. 1980), p. 491-500. maps.

A researcher from the University of Sydney provides details of advanced industrial plants supplied to Siberia and the Soviet Far East from 1965 to 1977, and tries to work out the increase in each city's workforce stimulated by the presence of these high-technology industries.

556 **A study of population increases in the Greater Kuznetsk region, USSR, 1897-1966 as shown by growth of cities greater than 50,000 in 1966.**
Carl F. Ojala. *Professional Geographer*, vol. 20, no. 5 (Sept. 1968), p. 303-12. maps.

Demonstrates how rapid population increase has been in the area surrounding Kuznetsk in southwest Siberia, particularly since the development of the Ural–Kuznetsk Combine in the 1930s. In 1926 there were only three cities with 50,000 or more inhabitants; by 1966 there were 16.

557 **Population and labour supply in Siberia.**
V. I. Perevedentsev. *Soviet Sociology*, vol. 7, no. 3 (winter 1968-69), p. 33-56; vol. 7, no. 4 (spring 1969), p. 27-43; vol. 8, no. 1 (summer 1969), p. 24-67; vol. 8, no. 2 (fall 1969), p. 129-58; vol. 9, no. 3 (winter 1970-71), p. 424-74; vol. 11, no. 1 (summer 1972), p. 31-56; vol. 11, no. 2 (fall 1972), p. 107-25.

This is a complete translation, including tables, of *Migratsiya naseleniya i trudovye problemy Sibiri* (Population migration and Siberia's labour problem) (Novosibirsk: Nauka, Sibirskoe Otdelenie, 1966). Though in some respects dated, the data included are very valuable for assessing the problems associated with developing Siberia in the early Brezhnev period. Many of the conclusions remain valid now. A Western study completed at the same time is 'The manpower problem in Siberia' by Stephen G. Prociuk (*Soviet Studies*, vol. 19, no. 2 [1967], p. 190-210).

558 **The Soviet Far East: a report on urban and rural settlement and population change, 1966-1989.**
John Sallnow. *Soviet Geography*, vol. 30, no. 9 (Nov. 1989), p. 670-83. maps. bibliog.

The population of the Soviet Far East has grown from 5,435,000 in 1966 to 7,941,000 in 1989, 75 per cent of it urban. This overview of urban–rural population change and the evolution of settlement also provides details of cities whose populations will rise. A previous article, 'The population of Siberia and the Soviet Far East (1965-1976)' (*Soviet Geography*, vol. 18, no. 9 [Nov. 1977], p. 690-8), also basing its analysis on

Soviet figures, demonstrated that Siberia and the Soviet Far East were losing population in net terms, a condition particularly true in rural areas. Improvements to infrastructure might help people to stay.

559 **Behind the Urals: an American worker in Russia's city of steel.**
John C. Scott. Cambridge, Massachussetts: Riverside Press;
Boston, Massachusetts: Houghton Mifflin, 1942; London: Martin
Secker & Warburg in association with Herbert Joseph, 1943. 223p.
Reprinted, with an introduction by Stephen Mark Kotkin,
Bloomington, Indiana; London: Indiana University Press, 1973. 306p.

This memoir presents a graphic account of life and work in the Stalinist steel complex at Magnitogorsk in the 1930s. The reprint, apart from the introduction, also includes the texts of three depositions Scott made at the US Embassy in Moscow, and photographs of Magnitogorsk in the 1930s.

560 **Situations vacant in western Siberia.**
Kenneth Shaw. *Geographical Magazine*, vol. 51, no. 2 (Nov. 1978),
p. 154-8. map.

Discusses the difficulties experienced in the mid-1970s in persuading labour to move to, and more particularly, to stay in, western Siberia. The labour problem was threatening the success of the oil and gas production plans.

561 **Medical geography aspects of the design of the Ust-Ilimsk industrial node.**
L. I. Soboleva. *Soviet Geography*, vol. 15, no. 7 (Sept. 1974),
p. 422-8.

Discussing a rarely broached topic, namely the public health implications of new settlements in the Siberian taiga [the coniferous forest lying between tundra and steppe lands], the author points to several important factors. To prevent harm from pollution new settlements need to be away from industrial plants. To prevent tooth decay from mineral-deficient Angara river sources, water supplies need to have fluoride added to them. Reservoirs could lead to the proliferation of disease through mosquitoes breeding in shallows and small mammals going to drink could pass on leptospirosis. There are also endemic problems of tick-borne encephalitis, rabies and toxoplasmosis.

562 **The population dynamics of east Siberia and problems of production.**
V. V. Vorobëv. *Soviet Geographer*, vol. 16, no. 9 (Nov. 1975),
p. 584-93. bibliog.

This rather gloomy Soviet study of the manpower problem in the easterly sections of Siberia concluded that there would be no net inflow of population to the Far East before the year 2000, and that natural increase would be slow. Production could be improved only through automation and efficiency drives. For a Western view, see 'The nature of the manpower problem in the development of Siberia' by Peter de Souza (*Soviet Geography*, vol. 27, no. 10 [Dec. 1986], p. 689-715) which also assesses the importance of labour constrictions as a restrictive factor in economic growth.

563 **Permanent settlement of young people in the region of the Baikal–Amur trunk railway.**
V. V. Voronov, I. P. Smirnov. *Soviet Sociology*, vol. 21, no. 4 (1983), p. 20-31.

Translated from a Soviet sociological periodical, this article demonstrates how difficult it was to persuade young workers to settle for more than a short time along the course of the new main line railway linking the Lake Baikal region with the Amur river, because of the harsh climate and lack of amenities.

564 **Bratsk: pioneering city in the taiga.**
Norbert Wein. *Soviet Sociology*, vol. 28, no. 3 (March 1987), p. 171-94. maps.

A survey of impressions gained by a German expert on his third visit to Bratsk in 1986. Details of the hydro-electric dam, industrial pollution, food supply problems, the design of the city and the standard of life of the inhabitants are included. There are several photographs and diagrams.

565 **The builders of the Baikal–Amur railroad as a subject of sociological research.**
S. N. Zhelezko. *Soviet Sociology*, vol. 16, no. 3 (winter 1977), p. 3-17.

Frowned upon in the past as a bourgeois pseudo-science, sociology was later found to present useful research tools for the Soviet government. This article discusses the problem of retaining in the Soviet Far East the labour force persuaded to go there to build the new Baikal–Amur railway line. Statistical tables are included.

# Education and Science

566  **Talent school.**
Georgii Kiksman.  *Soviet Literature*, no. 4 (1975), p. 148-52.
Briefly encapsulates the search for hyper-intelligent schoolchildren to be trained up at Akademgorodok in western Siberia for possible entry in due course to the Siberian Section of the USSR Academy of Sciences.

567  **Siberian city of science (Akademgorodok).**
David M. Smith.  *Geographical Magazine*, vol. 51, no. 3 (Dec. 1978), p. 238-42. map.
This illustrated article gives an indication of the educational, scientific and social amentities in Akademgorodok, a settlement near Novosibirsk which was built in the late 1950s to house the members of the Siberian Section of the USSR Academy of Sciences and their families. At the time of writing it housed 50,000 people.

568  **Empire of knowledge: the Academy of Sciences of the USSR (1917-1970).**
Alexander Vucinich.   Berkeley, California; Los Angeles; London: University of California Press, 1984. 484p. bibliog.
Pages 285-9 provide one of the few Western accounts of the establishment of the Siberian Department of the USSR Academy of Sciences in 1957. See also the abstract of a paper 'Economics and social science in Siberia: the work of the Novosibirsk Centre' by E. Stuart Kirby (*Sibirica*, no. 3 [1987], p. 22-4). which provides insight into one part of the Academy's work.

# Political Developments

## Regionalism

569 **Afanasii Prokofevich Shchapov (1830-1876): Russian historian and social thinker.**
Gary Alan Hanson.   PhD thesis, University of Wisconsin, 1971.
(Available from University Microfilms, Ann Arbor, Michigan, order no. 71–24,462).
The first chapter highlights Shchapov's childhood in Siberia, his education at Irkutsk and Kazan. Chapter four concerns his exile in Siberia (1863-76) and chapter six his ideas on regionalism and federalism for the Russian Empire which lay behind much of Siberian *oblastnichestvo* [regionalism]. A survey of the early stages of the latter is developed positively, but all too briefly, in his 'Siberian regionalism in the 1860s' (*Topic*, no. 4 [spring 1974], p. 62-75).

570 **Regional consciousness in Siberia before and after October 1917.**
Norman G. O. Pereira.   *Canadian Slavonic Papers*, vol. 30, no. 1 (March 1988), p. 112-33.
Based partly on recent Soviet work and partly on archive materials at Columbia University, this article surveys the history of Siberian regionalism through its promising phase in the 1880s, when many of the early regionalists' dreams were realized, to the dismal period of revolution and civil war during which they failed to inspire the population with their vision and secure a clear public mandate for decentralized government. A weaker product by far is 'Siberian regionalism in revolution and civil war, 1917-1920' by Anthony P. Allison (*Siberica* [Portland, Oregon], vol. 1, no. 1 [summer 1990], p. 78-97).

571  **Siberian and Far Eastern publishing in late Imperial Russia.**
Patricia Polansky.  *Pacifica*, vol. 1, no. 2 (Sept. 1989), p. 77-100.

This extremely interesting study of publishing in eastern Siberia and the Russian Far East from 1880 to 1917 is included here because it emphasizes the role of journalism in developing an independent political mood in the region. Political exiles helped to make the printed media more radical than they would otherwise have been.

572  **The Siberian autonomous movement and its future.**
I. I. Serebrennikov.  *Pacific Historical Review*, vol. 3, no. 4 (1934), p. 400-15.

Written by a man with personal knowledge of the events described, this article concentrates on the development of Siberian regionalism from 1905 to its final outlawing by the Soviet government in 1923. The author believes that the eventual overthrow of Bolshevism is bound to lead to a resurgence of regionalism.

573  **Russian peasants and the elections to the fourth State Duma.**
Eugene D. Vinogradoff.  In: *The politics of rural Russia*, edited by Leopold H. Haimson.  Bloomington, Indiana; London: Indiana University Press, 1979, p. 219-60.

Part of this article contrasts the political mentality of the Siberian peasant with that of his European counterparts. Apart from this, however, Western historiography of Siberian political development in the Duma period is at a very primitive stage, there being but a few scattered references in studies of other issues.

574  **Towards a United States of Russia: plans and projects of federal reconstruction of Russia in the nineteenth century.**
Dimitrii S. von Mohrenschildt.  Rutherford, California: Fairleigh Dickinson University Press; London; Toronto, Canada: Associated Universities Presses, 1981. 309p. bibliog.

Several of the schemes for a decentralized Russian state outlined in this work include references to the place Siberia was to have in the new democratic order. Chapter six discusses the phenomenon of Siberian regionalism.

575  **Russia's land of the future: regionalism and the awakening of Siberia, 1819-1894.**
Stephen Digby Watrous.  PhD thesis, University of Washington, Seattle, Washington, 1970. (Available from University Microfilms, Ann Arbor, Michigan, order no. 71–17,009).

Far wider in content than its title suggests, this thesis covers the political, social and intellectual awakening of Siberian society in the nineteenth century. Beginning with a sketch of society in the early nineteenth century, it proceeds to discuss Mikhail Speranskii's contribution to developments, the period when Muravëv-Amurskii was governor-general in the Far East, the positive contribution of exiles to Siberian development, and then enters into a detailed study of the regionalist movement. It includes the first detailed English biographies of two noted regionalists: Grigorii Nikolaevich Potanin (1835-1920) and Nikolai Mikhailovich Yadrintsev (1842-94), and portrays the movement's achievements in the later nineteenth century as urbanization spread. It is a great pity that this dissertation was never published since much of its content is otherwise not available in English.

# Communist Party and Soviet administration

576　**The administration of northern peoples: the USSR.**
Terence Edward Armstrong.　In: *The arctic frontier*, edited by
R. St. J. Macdonald.　Toronto, Canada: Published in association with
the Canadian Institute of International Affairs and the Arctic Institute
of North America by the University of Toronto Press, 1966, p. 57-79.

Summarizes the administrative structure developed for the minorities of Siberia by the Soviet government. See also 'Administrative and constitutional changes in arctic territories: the USSR' by Neil C. Field (p. 160-93) which traces the evolution of administrative divisions of the Soviet northern territories from 1917 to 1960. The discussion also includes labour legislation, economic zones and planning systems.

# Economy

577 **Regional studies for planning and projecting: the Siberian experience.**
Edited by Abel Gazevich Aganbegyan. The Hague: Mouton, 1981.
312p. (United Nations Research Institute for Social Developments,
Geneva, Regional Planning, vol. 7).

A rare pre-*glasnost* insight into the Soviet planning process, this volume contains translations of articles by over twenty Soviet economists about their experiences in planning the future development of Siberia.

578 **Economic regionalization of the eastern zone of influence of the
Baikal–Amur mainline.**
P. Ya. Baklanov, V. N. Sevostyanov, I. E. Spektor. *Soviet
Geography*, vol. 20, no. 6 (June 1979), p. 335-53.

Soviet planners had conceived of the regional development of the zone round the Baikal–Amur railway (BAM) as a series of separate resource-based industrial complexes along the east–west axis of the railway. This article presents an alternative scheme: there could be several north–south links, each one joining an industrially developed centre on the old Trans-Siberian Railway with a new resource-based development on the BAM. Rail links would be built to join each one.

579 **Siberia today and tomorrow: a study of economic resources, problems
and achievements.**
Violet Conolly. London; Glasgow: Collins, 1975. 248p. maps. bibliog.

Wider in content than its title indicates, though still concentrating on economic factors, this work by a British Foreign Office researcher begins with a brief historical introduction and discusses the government and administration of Siberia. It proceeds to analyse economic issues (energy, mining, metallurgy, chemicals, agriculture, timber, transport), population and labour problems, and collaboration with foreign countries in development and trade projects. It also briefly alludes to the problems of the native peoples.

# Economy

580 **Soviet Asia: economic development and national policy choices.**
Leslie Dienes. Boulder, Colorado; London: Westview Press, 1987.
289p.

Part of this study is focused on Siberia. Chapter three investigates Soviet energy policy
and its effects on Siberian development. There is an unusual study entitled 'The
southern Ecumene from the Urals to Lake Baikal' which basically follows, but
updates, Hooson's analysis (q.v.). Chapter six covers population, employment and
settlement policy in Siberia and Kazakhstan. The economic and strategic significance of
the Soviet Far East are included.

581 **A new stage in the development of the Soviet Far East.**
Mikhail Sergeevich Gorbachëv. Moscow: Novosti, 1986. 39p.

Contains the text of Mikhail Gorbachev's Vladivostok speech of 28 July 1986 which set
out a new agenda for the Far East region both internally and in its relations with the
'Pacific Rim' countries. The speech and other relevant materials are translated in
*Current Digest of the Soviet Press* (vol. 38, no. 30 [27 Aug. 1986], p. 1-12, 31-2). See
also his *Toward a better world* (London: Hutchinson, 1987) which contains the text on
pages 329-59 and *Meaning of my life: perestroika*, English text edited and prepared by
Richard Alibegov and G. S. Bhargava (Edinburgh: Aspect Publications, in
cooperation with Progress Publishers, Moscow, and Arnold Publishers, New Delhi,
1990) which includes the text of his Krasnoyarsk speech.

582 **Siberia in the national economy.**
Aleksandr G. Granberg. *Soviet Review*, vol. 22, no. 2 (Feb. 1981),
p. 44-67.

This is a translation of an outspoken article by the Director of the Institute of
Economics and Organization of Industrial Production of the USSR Academy of
Sciences Siberian Section. Pro-Siberian in a manner reminiscent of the nineteenth-
century regionalists, Granberg argues that only the comprehensive development of
Siberia, hitherto neglected, can solve the USSR's economic problems.

583 **Soviet geography studies in our time. A Festschrift for Paul E. Lydolph.**
Edited by Lutz Holzner, Jeane M. Knapp. Milwaukee, Wisconsin:
College of Letters and Sciences and the American Geographical Society
Collection of the Golda Meir Library, University of Wisconsin, 1987.
376p. maps.

Scattered within this series of essays are three papers about Siberian economic
geography. Victor L. Mote's concerns development of the Soviet Far East and Eastern
Siberia; Philip Pryde's is about the formulation of environmental impact studies in
connection with Siberian development; and the late Theodore Shabad looks at Siberian
development under Gorbachev to 1987.

584 **A new Soviet heartland?**
David John Mahler Hooson. Princeton, New Jersey: Van Nostrand,
1964. 132p. maps. bibliog. (Van Nostrand Searchlight Books, no. 21).

In an unusual book containing conscious echoes of Halford J. Mackinder's 'heartland'
concept a professor of geography from the University of British Columbia detects a
swing of the centre of gravity of Soviet economic development to the Volga–Baikal

zone. A brief introduction to the natural habitat and Russian history leads into detailed surveys of population geography, energy, heavy industry and agriculture in the zone.

585 **Economics of Soviet regions.**
Edited by I. S. Koropecky, Gertrude E. Schroeder. New York: Praeger, 1981. 461p. bibliog.
Pages 235-66 of this technical investigation of the economics of regional development in the USSR refer to Siberia ('Asiatic RSFSR'). The conclusion is that scarcity of resources will lead to development being concentrated on a few territorial production complexes (TPCs).

586 **An appraisal of the Soviet concept of the territorial production complex.**
G. J. R. Linge, G. J. Karasaka, F. E. I Hamilton. *Soviet Geography*, vol. 19, no. 10 (Dec. 1979), p. 681-97.
Casts a critical eye over the Soviet plan to develop Siberia and the Soviet Far East through a series of isolated territorial [industrial] production complexes.

587 **Science and Siberia.**
Gurii Ivanovich Marchuk. Moscow: Novosti Press Agency Publishing House, 1983. 90p.
In a small format, with many colour illustrations, the author presents a glowing account of the potential of Siberia. His portrayal of the Kansk-Achinsk fuel and energy complex, of the Baikal–Amur railway and territorial production complexes is full of the official optimism of the high Brezhnev period, before the ecological disasters began to bite.

588 **Regional development in the USSR: trends and prospects. Colloquium 25-27 April 1979, Brussels.**
NATO Economics Directorate. Newtonville, Massachussetts: Oriental Research Partners, 1979. 294p. maps.
Though the contents of this volume refer to all regions of the USSR, considerable portions deal with Siberia and the Soviet Far East, particularly touching on energy, raw materials resources and the BAM Railway project. See also 'Pacific Siberian growth centers: a new Soviet commitment' by Victor L. Mote (*Soviet Union/Union Soviétique*, vol. 4, no. 2 [1977], p. 256-70) which addresses similar problems at the same period.

589 **Siberia: achievements, problems, solutions.**
Boris Pavlovich Orlov, translated from the Russian by David Marks. Moscow: Progress Publishers, 1977. 188p.
This pre-Gorbachev assessment of Siberia's economic development has naturally lost some of its original freshness. Yet it still bears looking at as a fairly candid official document reflecting the views current when it was compiled.

590 **The Soviet Far East: geographical perspectives on development.**
Edited by Allan Rodgers. London; New York: Routledge, 1990.
318p. maps. bibliog.

Consisting of twelve chapters by North American geographers, this work was stimulated by M. S. Gorbachev's promises in his 1986 Vladivostok speech to devote more resources to the Far East. An initial chapter by Gary Hausladen on settlement history (rather thin on recent Soviet research) is followed by a study of environmental constraints co-authored by Philip Pryde and Victor Mote, a study of population and labour by Ann C. Hegelson, and a general survey of resources by Craig ZumBrunnen. These are followed by accounts of the forest and fishing industries by Brenton Barr; the South Yakut TPC by Victor Mote; the transport system by Robert North; commodity movements and regional development by the editor; trade by Michael Bradshaw; and the prospects for development by Leslie Dienes. A final conclusion brings the discussion up to date. There are numerous statistical tables and maps.

591 **Soviet regional economic policy: the east–west debate over Pacific Siberian development.**
Jonathan R. Schiffer. London: Macmillan, 1989. 364p. maps.

Based on a PhD thesis prepared at the Centre for Russian and East European Studies of the University of Birmingham, this thorough work investigates the evolution of Soviet Far Eastern regional development policy.

592 **Summary of development in the Soviet north based on extracts from the Soviet press, 1974-1975.**
Walter Slipchenko, Catherine Dworschak, maps by Jim Bogart.
Ottawa: Department of Indian and Northern Affairs, 1976. 55p. maps.

This digest of information about developments in the north as reported in the Soviet press includes a great deal of information about matters south of the Arctic Circle, affecting most parts of Siberia and some of the Far East. Communications, land, air, rail and water transport, manufacturing, oil, gas and other extractive industries, power generation and transmission, forestry and fishing are all included, and there is a brief introduction on the minority peoples. The fourteen very useful maps each refer to one of the subjects outlined.

593 **Mathematical programming approaches to the planning of Siberian regional economic development: a non-mathematical survey.**
Mason H. Soule, Robert N. Taaffe. *Soviet Economy*, vol. 1, no. 1 (Jan.-March 1985), p. 75-98.

Mathematical programming models are applied by the Novosibirsk-based Institute of Economics and Organization of Industrial Production to derive and validate recommendations for development of the region. This is a non-specialist description, analysis and evaluation of the models and their role in Siberian economic planning. The models appear to be more useful for long-term than short-term use.

# Agriculture

594 **The economics of agriculture in the Yakut ASSR.**
Translated by the Department of the Secretary of State of Canada for
the Language Division, Bureau for Translations. *Extracts from the
Soviet Press on the Soviet North*, appendix B, part 1-2 (Nov.-Dec.
1960). 171p.

This rare technical paper on the economics of agriculture in Yakutiya was translated
from a work published in 1957 by the Yakut Section of the USSR Academy of
Sciences.

595 **Agro-industrial complexes and types of agriculture in eastern Siberia.**
V. P. Shotskii, translated by Béla Kecskés, translation edited by Paul
A. Compton. Budapest: Akadémiai Kiadó, 1979. 131p. maps.
bibliog. (Geography of World Agriculture, no. 8).

A general introduction to the natural history and socio-historical background of Siberia
and a summary of the methodology used leads into a survey of agricultural regions in
East Siberia. The Sayan, Irkutsk oblast and Irkutsk–Cheremkhovo territorial
production complexes and the Middle Angara, Transbaikal, Buryat and East
Transbaikal agro-industrial complexes are studied in depth.

596 **A deputy's inquiry.**
Anatolii Strelyanyi. *Soviet Sociology*, vol. 25, no. 3 (winter 1987-88),
p. 2-113.

A translation of 'Deputatskii voprosy' (*Novyi mir*, no. 2 [1986], p. 24-76), this is a
remarkable diary of events on a collective farm in southwest Siberia from 6 June to 27
July 1968. It provides a very rare insight into the actual workings of a collective from
the point of view of those directly involved in managing it, and to some extent depicts
the attitudes of peasant workers. Unusually for a Soviet publication, the emphasis is
laid on the individual rather than the collective.

597 **Agriculture in the pioneering regions of Siberia and the Far East:**
**present status, problems and prospects.**
Norbert Wein. *Soviet Geography*, vol. 25, no. 8 (Oct. 1984),
p. 592-625. maps. bibliog.
Reviews the extent to which marginal agricultural lands in Siberia and the Soviet Far
East can be expected to produce the meat, milk and vegetables needed. Extensive
modernization is needed. The last six pages include a translation of an article from
the Soviet government newspaper *Izvestiya* about problems of food supply.
Photographs, charts and tables are included in this thorough investigation.

# Herding and stockraising

598 **Notes on reindeer nomadism.**
Gudmund Hatt. *Memoirs of the American Anthropological*
*Association*, vol. 6, no. 2 (1949), p. 75-133.
Discusses the methods of reindeer husbandry used by the Chukchi, Koryak, Itelmen,
Yukagir and Nivkh in northeastern Siberia.

599 **Perestroika and the pastoralists.**
Caroline Humphrey. *Anthropology Today*, vol. 5, no. 3 (June 1989),
p. 6-10.
The author made two visits to Tuva during 1989 as adviser to a television crew making
a documentary. The present article surveys the apparent effects of Gorbachev's policy
of economic reform, in Kyzyl (the capital) and in the Mongum-Taiga district where the
livelihood is gained almost exclusively from herding yak and sheep. So far the results
seem contradictory and not very successful.

600 **Shepherds and reindeer nomads in the Soviet Union.**
Helmut Liely. *Soviet Studies*, vol. 31, no. 3 (1979), p. 401-16. bibliog.
This rare study of herders includes shepherds in the Altai mountains and Novosibirsk
oblast; the reindeer herders are Evenk, Even, Chukchi, Yukagir, Yakut and Koryak.
The detailed investigation of developments in the 1960s and 1970s includes sections on
the social effects on women of the herding life and attempts by the Soviet authorities to
settle nomads. 'Horse herding for meat in Yakutskaya ASSR' by V. N. Andreev
(*Polar Record*, vol. 15, no. 99 [Sept. 1971], p. 931-3). is an amended version of a paper
published in *Magadanskii olenovodnik* (Magadan Reindeerman), issue 22 (1970),
which briefly sets forth the economic and health benefits of horse ranching and outlines
the practical problems.

601 **Reindeer herders of northern Yakutiya: a report from the field.**
Piers Vitebsky. *Polar Record*, vol. 25, no. 154 (July 1989), p. 213-18.
map. bibliog.
Reports on the conditions facing Even herders in the contemporary era. The article, which is illustrated, is based on field observations. Other details may be found in his other articles including 'Perestroika reaches the reindeer herders of Siberia' (q.v.). Relevant papers which should be appearing in print soon are 'The crisis in Siberian reindeer herding today: a technical or social problem?' in *Siberia in the twentieth century: society and economic development*, edited by Alan Wood and Walter Joyce (London: Longman, 1991), and 'Landscape and self-determination among the Eveny: the political environment of Siberian reindeer herders today' in *Cultural understandings of the environment*, edited by David Parkin and Lisa Croll (London: Routledge, 1991).

602 **Tuvan reindeer husbandry in the early twentieth century.**
Ian Whitaker. *Polar Record*, vol. 20, no. 127 (Jan. 1981), p. 337-52.
map. bibliog.
Brief details of Tuvan history lead in to a discussion of reindeer herding among the Tuvinian before the Russian Revolution. The author also addresses the theory that reindeer husbandry originated in the Sayan mountains which lie in present-day Tuva.

603 **Reindeer husbandry.**
Edited by P. S. Zhigunov, translated from the Russian by
M. Fleischmann. Jerusalem: Israel Program for Scientific
Translations, 1968. 348p.
Translated from a standard Soviet textbook on the technicalities of the reindeer herding life, this is fundamental to an understanding of the methods employed in the USSR.

# Forestry

604 **Forest economy in the USSR: an analysis of Soviet competitive potentialities.**
Karl Viktor Algvere. Stockholm: Skogshögskolan Royal College of Forestry, 1966. 449p. maps. bibliog. (Studia Forestalia Suecica, 39).
Covering the natural conditions of the USSR, transport, the history of forestry since Peter the Great and the potentialities for exploitation of timber, the author also devotes sections to West Siberia, East Siberia and the Far East.

605 **The disappearing Russian forest: a dilemma in Soviet resource management.**
Brenton M. Barr, Kathleen E. Braden.   Totowa, New Jersey:
Rowman & Littlefield; London: Hutchinson, 1988. 252p. maps. bibliog.

As well as including a history of timber felling in the USSR and providing 'a reader's guide' to the technicalities of the industry, the authors discuss the constraints facing the Soviet government because of forest depletion, the international timber trade and the recreational and non-industrial uses of forests. Administrational problems still militate against optimum use of the forests as a sustainable renewable resource. The Siberian taiga (boreal forest) forms the basic Soviet timber resource.

606 **The forest sector of the Soviet Far East.**
Brenton M. Barr.   *Soviet Geography*, vol. 30, no. 4 (April 1989), p. 283-302.

Reviews a recently published book by Soviet forestry experts which gives new data on output totals, planned production targets, investment, age and species of stock, the structure of output for foreign and domestic markets and provides recommendations to improve the industry's performance. Since much of this material is unavailable elsewhere a detailed summary has been provided. Soviet experts are now proposing to increase the percentage of usage for every cubic metre cut and hope to perfect a finer end-product which can stand long transport hauls. This may usefully be compared with a far older study of the same region: 'The forest wealth of the Soviet Far East and its exploitation' by A. Tsymek (New York, 1936 [Institute of Pacific Relations. USSR Council Papers, 1936, no. 2]) and with item no. 607 below.

607 **The Soviet logging industry: a backward branch.**
W. Donald Bowles.   *American Slavic and East European Review*, vol. 17, no. 4 (1958), p. 426-38.

This article presents a summary of research findings. The period investigated is 1927-57. The problems of poor productivity, labour shortages, lack of adequately controlled investment and general inefficiency highlighted here have still not been eliminated from the Soviet forestry sector.

608 **The forest products industry: a specialized activity of the Sosva Valley section of the Ob Basin.**
S. T. Budkov.   *Soviet Geography*, vol. 11, no. 9 (Nov. 1970), p. 767-74. map. bibliog.

The construction of the Ivadel Railway from the Urals to the Ob river opened a new forest region for exploration. Fifteen logging centres are now in operation. The article describes the operations, proposes sound forest management and opposes hydroelectric power developments on the lower Ob because they would destroy this forest.

609   **The Eastern USSR: forest resources and forest exports to Japan.**
R. T. Fenton, F. M. Maplesden.   Rotorua, New Zealand: Forest
Research Institute, New Zealand Forest Service, 1986. [n.p.] (Forest
Research Institute Bulletin, no. 123).

I have not been able to see this study. It appears in the bibliography of item no. 605
above.

# Energy, Fuel and Mineral Resources

610   **Gas for the West from Siberia.**
Bill Baker.   *Geographical Magazine*, vol. 56, no. 2 (Feb. 1984),
p. 54-5. map.

Aided by coloured and monochrome illustrations, this brief article provides details of
the gas pipeline which was to go from Urengoi in western Siberia through Perm in the
Urals to Western Europe. Workers' temporary and permanent accommodation is
discussed. The negative side of such developments is highlighted in 'Gas, environmentalism and native anxieties in the Soviet Arctic: the case of Yamal peninsula' by Piers
Vitebsky (*Polar Record*, vol. 26, no. 156 [1990], p. 19-26. map. bibliog.).

611   **The electrical industry of central Siberia.**
Brenton M. Barr, James H. Bater.   *Economic Geography*, vol. 45,
no. 4 (Oct. 1969), p. 349-69. maps.

Investigates Soviet plans for hydro-electric and thermal power stations in central
Siberia and the use of ultra-high-voltage transmission lines. The authors have some
doubts as to whether the required quantity of electricity can be generated. Though
outdated the article is one of very few devoted to its subject, and it provides a clear
example of the grandiose plans put forward during the Brezhnev era.

612   **The Soviet energy system.**
Leslie Dienes, Theodore Shabad.   Washington, DC: V. H. Winston,
1979. 298p.

A well-researched and presented survey of all forms of energy in the USSR, this study
by two noted geographers contains numerous references to Asiatic sections of the
RSFSR. Pages 87-94 cover the West Siberia oil and gas field. 'The energy system and
economic imbalances in the USSR' by Leslie Dienes (*Soviet Economy*, vol. 1, no. 4
[Oct.-Dec. 1985], p. 340-72. bibliog.) claims that European Russia's energy deficiency
and 'voracious requirements' continue to distort Siberia's economic development.
Despite the BAM and oil and gas extraction, Siberia's economy has been stagnating. A

diversified economic base is required, but is sacrificed in favour of costly prestige projects.

613 **Tapping Siberian wealth: the Urengoi experience.**
Genrikh Gurkov, Valerii Evseev, translated from the Russian by Sergei Sosinskii. Moscow: Progress Publishers, 1984. 193p.

Recent economic and social history combine in this colourful popular account in which the authors relate the heroic development of the oil and gas field in northwest Siberia. 'The percentage of success' by Valerii Osipov, translated by Vladimir Talmyi (*Soviet Literature*, no. 10 [1977], p. 143-8) provides a brief biography of Yurii Ervier, one of the geologists most responsible for the discovery of the Tyumen oil field.

614 *West Siberian oil and natural gas: a study in Soviet regional development theory and practice.*
Augustine Idzelis. PhD thesis, Kent State University, 1978.
(Available from University Microfilms, Ann Arbor, Michigan, order no. 79–04802).

Investigates the territorial production complexes (TPCs) in the middle and northern Ob region whose function is to exploit gas and oil reserves. Detects an imbalance in the development of the specialized sector and support industries and services. This imbalance could become a serious hindrance to success of the enterprise. There is a very clear map of the region in 'West Siberia: the quest for energy' by John P. Hardt (*Problems of Communism*, vol. 22 [May-June 1973], p. 25-36) which raises questions about the attainability of Soviet plans for oil and gas production during the ninth five-year plan.

615 **Soviet natural resources in the world economy.**
Edited by Robert G. Jensen, Theodore Shabad, Arthur W. Wright. Chicago, Illinois; London: University of Chicago Press, 1983. 700p. maps. bibliogs.

An authoritative investigation of the Soviet Union's natural resources including timber, this volume assesses their importance in the world during a time of increasing raw material shortages. There are sections devoted to constraints facing economic exploitation of resources, territorial production complexes (TPCs), the BAM railway and foreign trade.

616 **Exploitation of Siberia's natural resources. Main findings of round table held 30th January–1st February 1974, in Brussels.**
Editor and chairman of round table, Yves Laulan. Brussels: NATO, Directorate of Economic Affairs, [1974]. 199p.

An international panel of fifteen economists discusses the state of Siberia's economy, with particular emphasis on the energy and fuel sector. The round table was convened in view of the oil price crisis arising from the 1973-74 hostilities between Israel and the Arab world. Many graphs and tables depict the reserves and production of fuel resources by the USSR.

617 **Western Siberia offers energy.**
N. Matrusov, translated by Judy Pallot. *Geographical Magazine*,
vol. 48, no. 9 (Jun. 1976), p. 548-52. map.

Illustrated in colour and monochrome, this article briefly summarizes the history of West Siberia, including a very rare colour photograph of the Kremlin hill at Tobolsk, showing why that spot became the early capital of Siberia. It proceeds to outline developments in oil and gas extraction which are laying the foundations for a productive economic region.

618 **Siberian diamonds.**
Valerii Dmitrievich Osipov, translated from the Russian by Xenia
Danko, edited by Percy Ludwick. Moscow: Foreign Languages
Publishing House, 1958. 74p.

This is a brief, illustrated publication relating to Soviet diamond production. See also 'Russia no. 2 in diamonds' by G. Switzer (*Lapidary Journal*, vol. 23, no. 11 [1970], p. 1516-19) which reviews the geology, problems and successes of the Sovet diamond industry and indicates that by 1972 the USSR might be the world's foremost producer of the gems.

619 **Economic-geographic assessment of oil resources in East Siberia and the Yakut ASSR.**
B. V. Robinson. *Soviet Geography*, vol. 26, no. 2 (1985), p. 91-7.
bibliog.

An expert from the Siberian Institute of Geology, Geophysics and Mineral Raw Materials in Novosibirsk states that the exploration of oil resources in eastern Siberia has largely been completed, but laments the difficulties of exploiting the deposits. Conditions are very harsh and financial constraints are severe. He proposes that a start be made with the Nepa-Botuobuya field in northern Irkutsk oblast.

620 **Minerals: a key to Soviet power.**
Demitri Boris Shimkin. Cambridge, Massachusetts: Harvard
University Press, 1953. 452p. bibliog. (Harvard Russian Research
Center Studies, no. 9).

This exhaustive study was one of the first Western monographs to investigate the whole range of minerals available in the Soviet Union. The index, if used creatively, guides the reader to a wealth of information about Siberia and the Soviet Far East.

621 **USSR energy atlas.**
United States Central Intelligence Agency (CIA). Washington, DC:
Superintendant of Documents, 1985. 79p. maps.

In a multiple presentation of maps, graphics, photographs and text the atlas presents an all-round survey of Soviet fuel and energy reserves. The CIA's low estimates of possible Soviet extraction capabilities were thought too low by David Wilson (q.v.).

622    **Gold: a world survey.**
Rae Weston.    New York: St. Martin's Press; London; Canberra:
Croom Helm, 1983. 406p. bibliog.

Pages 165-8 of this general survey cover Siberia, but one should also use the index for scattered references of relevance. Further data may be obtained from *A methodological study of the production of primary gold by the Soviet Union* by D. L. Dowle and M. Kaser (London: Consolidated Goldfields, 1974).

623    **The demand for energy in the Soviet Union.**
David Cameron Wilson.    Totowa, New Jersey: Rowman & Allanheld;
London, Canberra: Croom Helm, 1983. 310p. bibliog.

Based almost exclusively on Soviet sources, this general survey of energy consumption in the USSR contains considerable relevant material. The index can be helpful if used carefully. See also his fearfully overpriced *Soviet oil and gas to 1990* (London: Economist Intelligence Unit, 1980 [Economist Intelligence Unit Special Report, no. 90]).

# Industry

624 **T.P.C.s in the Soviet Union, with special focus on Siberia.**
Peter de Souza. Gothenburg: University of Gothenburg, 1989. 257p.
maps. bibliog. (Department of Human and Economic Geography,
School of Economics and Legal Science Publications. Edited by the
Department of Geography, Series B, no. 80).

A historical introduction to the territorial production complexes (TPCs) leads on to a
discussion of the theory behind their existence, a cost–benefit analysis, and a discussion
of their place in the Soviet economy. A gloomy picture of severe setbacks is relieved
by hopes for a bright future if the right decisions are taken. It is interesting to see how
relevant the following article on this subject still is. 'Industrial complexes in the
development of Siberia' by K. Warren (*Geography*, vol. 63 [July 1978], p. 167-78.
maps. bibliog.) provides summaries of seven attempted TPCs and the BAM railway
development and examines their strengths and the difficulties of planning for them.

625 **Current problems in the industrialization of Siberia.**
Boris Z. Rumer. Cologne, Germany: Bundesinstitut für
Ostwissenschaftliche und Internationale Studien, 1984. 43p. bibliog.
(Berichte des Bundesinstituts für Ostwissenschaftliche und
Internationale Studien, no. 48).

Apart from a few industrial sectors connected with resource extraction, Siberia has
been consistently deprived of investment funds. Consequently the manufacturing,
chemical and petrochemical sectors and infrastructure improvements lag well behind
those in European Russia, and do not conform to the region's growing needs. The
disproportion has been increasing, making Siberia more dependent on imports.
Development has not really been planned on a long-term basis, but attacked
spasmodically, ignoring the region's interests as an independent economic system. A
diversion of funds from military spending, increased Western credits and even the
granting of industrial concessions to foreigners are needed to overcome the problem.

626   **Progress report on the Kansk–Achinsk development.**
      Theodore Shabad.   *Soviet Geography*, vol. 24, no. 3 (March 1983),
      p. 249-56. maps.
A critical discussion of progress on the lignite-based electric power production zone in
south Siberia near Krasnoyarsk. An estimated 400 billion tons of reserves lie beneath
an area stretching from Kansk to Achinsk. The strip mining and plans to introduce new
technology to upgrade the fuel are assessed.

# Trade

627 **Soviet Asian–Pacific trade and the regional development of the Soviet Far East.**
Michael J. Bradshaw. *Soviet Geography*, vol. 29, no. 4 (April 1988), p. 367-93.
The title explains the contents of this article which reviews the possibilities for trade development eastwards from the Soviet Far East under conditions of *perestroika* [restructuring]. The pace of events is likely to make the conclusions dated fairly soon.

628 **Siberia and the Pacific: a study of economic developments and trade prospects.**
Paul Dibb. New York: Praeger, 1972. 289p. map.
Reviews the prospects for agricultural and industrial development in Siberia with trade in mind. Pre-Gorbachev, and published before the 1973-74 oil crisis, this work nevertheless supplies valuable information about conditions in the mid-Brezhnev era, when *détente* was leading Western industrialists and governments to postulate a great future for trade in Siberian products.

# Transport and Communications

629 **Transport in western Siberia: Tsarist and Soviet development.**
Robert Neville North. Vancouver, Canada: University of British
Columbia Press & Centre for Transportation Studies, 1979. 364p.
maps. bibliog.
Far more than an investigation of the Trans-Siberian Railway, this amounts virtually to
a history of road, river and rail transport and a broad study of economic development
in the region under Tsars and Soviets from well before the construction of the railway
up to 1975. There are numerous maps, diagrams and tables.

630 **Siberia: postmarks and postal history of the empire period.**
Philip E. Robinson. Sheffield, England: The author, 1990. 2nd ed.
184p. maps. bibliog.
A fascinating and very unusual publication, this book provides a short history of the
postal service in Siberia. It then lists all the post offices of the pre-revolutionary era,
including the travelling post offices aboard Trans-Siberian Railway trains, and
illustrates the vast variety of postmarks used on letters despatched from each of them.
See also 'Early T.P.O's of the Trans-Siberian Railway' (*The Stamp Lover* [Dec. 1989]).
His '"Wish I wasn't here": postcards from Siberia' (*British Journal of Russian
Philately*, 67 [Sept. 1989], p. 17-22), with its illustrations and list of publishers, reveals
a little of the variety of postcards produced in the late Tsarist period.

631 **Development of industry and transport in the north of the USSR.**
Samuil Venediktovich Slavin. Moscow: Izdatelstvo ekonomicheskoi
literatury, 1961. 301p. biliog.
This work by a famous Soviet investigator of the north has not been officially published
in English, but there is a typed translation from the book in the Scott Polar Research
Institute Library in Cambridge. It is a general survey of northern industry and
transport under the Bolsheviks. Naturally little is said about the slave-labour system,
though it was written in the freer atmosphere under N. S. Khrushchev.

632 **A history of Russian railways.**
John Norton Westwood. London: Allen & Unwin, 1964. 326p. maps.
This is included in the general section because of its broad account of pre- and post-revolutionary rail developments. Fairly brief surveys are given of all major developments from the Turksib [Turkestan–Siberian] to the Ussuri line. Chapter three is especially concerned with railways in Asia, but one should also look at the index.

# Air transport

633 **Aeroflot: Soviet air transport since 1923.**
Hugh MacDonald. London: Putnam, 1975. 323p. maps.
Provides an all-round survey of the operations of the Soviet airline up to the mid-1970s, including the vast region beyond the Urals. Demonstrates the vital nature of this form of transport in far-flung regions: in many places life would be virtually impossible without passenger and freight transport by plane or helicopter. A certain amount of extra information may be found in 'Soviet air-passenger transportation network' by Matthew Sagers and Thomas Maraffa (*Geographical Review*, vol. 80, no. 3 [July 1990], p. 266-78. maps).

# Rail transport to 1916

634 **The Siberian railway.**
Charles Raymond Beazley. *Scottish Geographical Magazine*, vol. 16, no. 1 (Nov. 1900), p. 617-30.
Considering the Siberian Railway to be 'the principal agent in a work of civilising and reclaiming a huge, but long-neglected country of no small capabilities', the author provides a history of the land with details of railway construction, settlement, industry, agriculture and trade.

635 **A biographical memorial of General Daniel Butterfield, including many addresses and military writings.**
Edited by Julia Lorrilard Butterfield. New York: Grafton Press, 1904. 379p.
Pages 294-301 of this biography concern the American soldier-businessman's visit to Moscow in 1893 to obtain concessions to help build the Trans-Siberian Railway.

## 636 Siberia and the Great Siberian Railway.

John Martin Crawford.   St. Petersburg: Departament torgovli i manufaktur, 1893. 265p.

The author of this informative propaganda by the Russian Department of Trade and Manufacturing, J. M. Crawford (1845-1917), published a companion pamphlet on Russian industry for the World's Columbia Exposition in Chicago, also in 1893. A similar publication is *The Great Siberian Railway*, edited by the Chancery of the Committee of Ministers (St. Petersburg: Government Printing Office, 1901. 16p.). It was intended for the Glasgow Universal Exhibition of that year.

## 637 Guide to the Great Siberian Railway.

Aleksandr Ippolitivich Dmitriev-Mamonov, A. F. Zdziarski, translated by Miss L. Kukol-Yasnopolsky, revised by John Marshall.
St. Petersburg: Typography of the Artistic Printing Society, 1900. 520p. maps. Reprinted Newton Abbot: David & Charles, 1971.

A richly illustrated and most informative book, this is an official Imperial Russian publication. There is information on history, geography, indigenous peoples, economic development, trade and water transport as well as details on the railway itself. Lists of timetables and fares are included. Unfortunately many of the illustrations are rather dark in the reprint.

## 638 The cosmopolitan railway, compacting and fusing together all the world's continents.

William Gilpin.   San Francisco, California: The History Co., 1890. 369p. maps.

William Gilpin (1822-94), one-time governor of the Colorado Territory, advocates a mind-boggling American scheme to link the continents by a rail route which would join Alaska to Siberia by a tunnel under the Bering Strait. A rival French scheme initiated in 1902 was equally unsuccessful, given the intransigence of Nicholas II's entourage against this foreign intrusion. See 'Lost opportunity: the Alaska–Siberia tunnel' by Benson Lee Grayson (*Asian Affairs*, vol. 8 [OS vol. 64], part 1 [Feb. 1977], p. 63-9). Harry de Windt pointed out the absurdity of the idea in his *From Paris to New York by land* (q.v.), pages 267-70.

## 639 The Obi railway.

Aleksandr Dmitrievich Golokhvastov.   London: McCorquodale & Co., 1881. 31p. map.

A Siberian entrepreneur proposes the construction of a railway to link the lower Ob region with the White Sea to ease communications with the interior. In the British Library there is a later prospectus by Golokhvastov, *A new trade route to connect Europe with western Siberia and China* (London, 1887) which is bound with *Report on the survey of the country between the mouth of the River Korotaika and Possl-Cort tents on the Obi River for the projected Obi railway. The survey was made by J. M. Voropay, esq., land surveyor and counsellor of state, at the request of A. D. Golokhvastov, and was completed in 1886* [n.d., n.p.].

### 640 The builders of the Trans-Siberian Railway.
Hilda Hookham.   *History Today*, vol. 16, no. 8 (1966), p. 528-37.
This illustrated article by a historian of China investigates the workers who built the Trans-Siberian Railway – some of whom were Chinese – and the construction methods used.

### 641 The Great Siberian Railway.
Petr Alekseevich Kropotkin.   *Geographical Journal*, vol. 5 (1895), p. 146-54.
Anarchist and geographer, Kropotkin (q.v.) had personal experience of Siberia as a soldier and had published a study in French *Orographie de la Sibérie* (Siberian orography) (Brussels, 1904. 119p.). The present article thus has an immediacy about it, being geographically accurate and presenting interesting information about the direction of the railway.

### 642 The Russian Empire and the Trans-Siberian Railway.
*Monthly Summary of Commerce and Finance* (Washington, DC), no. 6 (April 1899), p. 2501-99.
A survey of the economic prospects for Siberia, this article is intended to alert American businessmen to the possibilities of investment and trade in the region.

### 643 The Siberian Railway in war.
*World Today*, vol. 6 (May 1904), p. 607-15.
Presents a critical assessment of the performance of the new Trans-Siberian Railway during the Russo-Japanese war.

### 644 To the great ocean: Siberia and the Trans-Siberian Railway.
Harmon Tupper.   London: Secker & Warburg, 1965. 536p. maps. bibliog.
Based on extensive reading, some of which has not been mentiond in this present bibliography, Tupper's book is a thorough popular history of the genesis, construction and effects of the Trans-Siberian Railway. There are numerous monochrome illustrations and maps and helpful explanations of abstruse points in footnotes. This all adds up to an enjoyable read. A detailed investigation of the plans for building railways through Siberia from the original concept in 1857 to the beginning of construction in the 1890s is 'Plans for railway development in Siberia, 1857-1890 and Tsarist colonialism' by David Norman Collins, to be published in a forthcoming issue of *Siberica*. It examines arguments in favour of and against the concept in order to draw conclusions about the railway's place in Moscow's colonial development of Siberia.

# Rail transport from 1917

645   **The Baykal–Amur mainline: a major national construction project.**
V. Biryukov.   *Soviet Geography*, vol. 16, no. 4 (April 1975),
p. 225-30.

A Soviet planning official discusses the planning needed for the BAM project to succeed. Details about quantities of materials, sources of electricity and a special type of oil train to convey crude to the Far East for refining are included. See also 'Construction begins on Baykal–Amur mainline railroad' by Theodore Shabad (*Soviet Geography* [Nov. 1974], p. 587-90).

646   **BAM: road to new possibilities.**
Sergei Aleksandrovich Bogatko.   Moscow: Progress Publishers, 1981.
66p.

This is a small-format, racy, illustrated pamphlet by a Siberian hydraulic engineer-cum-journalist. Bogatko enthusiastically describes the progress of the BAM railway project, giving brief details about the regional TPCs which were being established to exploit the natural resources of the region northeast of Lake Baikal. See also 'Helicopter over BAM' by Olga Chaikovskaya, translated by John Gordon (*Soviet Literature*, no. 1 [1977], p. 129-42) – a journalistic account of a helicopter trip to various BAM construction sites during the early stages of the construction work.

647   **The railways of Siberia.**
M. V. Braikevich, I. R. Afonon.   *Russian Economist*, vol. 2, no. 5
(Oct.-Dec. 1921), p. 1490-1522. map.

The Honorary Secretary of the Russian Economic Association in London surveys the history, present state and future possibilities of Siberian railways with a view to trade being established with the Bolshevik régime under the New Economic Policy.

648   **The BAM and the economic development of the Soviet Far East.**
P. G. Bunich.   *Soviet Geography*, vol. 16, no. 10 (Dec. 1975),
p. 643-52.

Blithely and without any doubts, the author explains the BAM railway's future contribution towards the economic development of the Soviet Far East. New industries will be fostered such as coal, oil, gas, steel, hydro-electric power installations, metalworking and chemicals. Fishing, forestry and trade with the Pacific region will also be increased.

649   **The Trans-Siberian Railway.**
Paul E. Garbutt.   *Journal of Transport History*, vol. 1 (1953-54),
p. 238-49. map.

A professional British railwayman who had published a book on Russian railways in 1949 presents a short historical survey of the construction and use of the Trans-Siberian Railway up to the post-World War II period.

650 **The BAM: labor, migration and prospects of settlement.**
Deborah A. Kaple. *Soviet Geography*, vol. 27, no. 10 (Dec. 1986),
p. 716-40.
Considering the BAM scheme an excellent opportunity to study labour management
and organization in a centrally planned economy, the author has carried out research
into the subject. There is a complex interaction between official government and Party
coaxing of people to move into and settle the region and the relatively free and
unhindered migration of workers. Young people working on the BAM are of an age to
settle down and start families; the problem is that they do not want to do this anywhere
near the railway.

651 **Case study of transport in the Urals–West Siberia–North Kazakhstan
region.**
Vladimir Kontorovich. In: *Soviet transportation project*, edited by
H. Hunter. Washington, DC: Wharton Econometric Forecasting
Associates, 1982. [n.p.].
This publication, which I have not seen, also includes *Case study of the BAM and East
Siberian transport capacity problems* by Victor L. Mote.

652 **The great Baikal–Amur railway.**
Compiled by V. I. Malashenko. Moscow: Progress Publishers, 1977.
171p.
This is a mediocre literary compendium in poetry and prose about the construction of
the Baikal–Amur railway and the possibilities for development in the far-flung region
through which it was heroically being pushed. I have included it as a curiosity of the
Brezhnev era.

653 **The Amur–Yakutsk mainline: a soviet concept or reality?**
Victor L. Mote. *Professional Geographer*, vol. 39, no. 1 (1987),
p. 13-23.
This northwards continuation of the 'Little BAM', first surveyed in the late 1930s, was
approved for construction only in March 1985 and just before Gorbachev took over. It
was supposed to reach Tommot by 1990 and Yakutsk by 1995. There have been
problems with funding and the harsh environment. Even if completed, will this single
line with low-grade rails be adequate to the task?

654 **Containerization and the Trans-Siberian land bridge.**
Victor L. Mote. *Geographical Review*, vol. 74, no. 3 (Jul. 1984),
p. 304-14.
Reviews the probabilities of success for the Soviet plan to establish a transcontinental
rail transit route for containerized traffic between Japan and Europe.

655 **BAM, boom, bust: analysis of a railway's past, present and future.**
Victor L. Mote. *Soviet Geography*, vol. 31, no. 5 (May. 1990),
p. 321-31. bibliog.
Graphically depicts the problems encountered in constructing the Baikal–Amur railway
and the financial implications of the scheme. A 'nestling' of Brezhnev, the project was
'well-meant but misguided'. Returns on the outlay will come, but they will be very
modest and will not be evident for years to come.

656 **Railway built in the Tyumen taiga.**
Valerii Povolaev. *Soviet Literature*, no. 7 (1974), p. 138-40.
Included, despite its brevity, because there is very little in English on the railway in
question, this article depicts the construction of the Tyumen–Surgut railway for the
West Siberian oil and gas fields. The Soviet Writers' Union were spurring on the young
Communist volunteers. See also 'Knights of the silver spike' by Aleksei Frolov,
translated by Elisabeth Waters (*Soviet Literature*, no. 10 [1974], p. 146-51).

657 **The Baikal–Amur mainline and its TPCs.**
Henry Ratnieks. *Sibirica*, no. 2 (1986), p. 28-40. maps.
Succinctly summarizes the development of over ten territorial production complexes
associated with the BAM railway, but sees no very rapid expansion of production in
the area. Considers the project to have been motivated by military-strategic rationale
rather than real economic needs.

658 **Gateway to Siberian resources: the BAM.**
Theodore Shabad, Victor L. Mote.   New York; London: Wiley, 1977.
189p. maps. bibliog.
Presents a detailed and optimistic account of the economic development prospects of
the region through which the Baikal–Amur railway is to pass. Item no. 655 (above)
presents an update to the data in this book.

659 **John F. Stevens: American assistance to Russian and Siberian railroads.**
Jacqueline D. St. John.   PhD thesis, University of Oklahoma, 1969.
(Available from University Microfilms, Ann Arbor, Michigan, order
no. 69-21992).
Head of the Advisory Commission of American Experts to Russia, John F. Stevens
was actively involved with helping to revive the railways in Siberia from 1917 to 1922.
This thesis claims that his success was limited partly by administrative confusion within
the American command structure, but partly by the civil war and complications with
the Japanese and British.

660 **TURKSIB: on the opening of the Turkestan–Siberian railway, May 1,
1930.**
Moscow: [n.p.], 1930. 64p.
Included in Kerner's bibliography (q.v.), this pamphlet issued in connection with the
opening of the Turkestan–Siberia railway in 1930 has proved difficult to consult.

661   **A second Trans-Siberian.**
Vladimir Zhuravlëv, translated from the Russian by Yurii Shirokov.
Moscow: Progress Publishers, 1980. 151p.
I have not seen this, but it is probably a translation of his 1976 *Skazanie o BAMe*
(Tale of the BAM), a fairly solid popular work about the new railway.

# Road transport

662   **Problems of passenger mobility and road transport in the southern Far
East region.**
R. V. Vakhnenko. *Soviet Geography*, vol. 31, no. 1 (Jan. 1990),
p. 61-3.
A researcher from the Pacific Geographical Institute claims that the whole of the
Soviet Maritime Region needs to improve its road infrastructure, particularly as the
number of cars is increasing.

# Water transport

663   **Reference and guide book for the Irtysh and lower Ob.**
V. V. Degtyarev, M. E. Budarin.   Washington, DC: US Department
of Commerce, Office of Technical Services, Joint Publications
Research Service, 1963. 122p. (JPRS 17,339).
Translated from a Soviet work issued in Omsk in 1966, this reference guide to
navigation on the Irtysh and lower Ob river systems provides very rare information
about steamship services within the USSR.

664   **The northern sea route and the economy of the Soviet north.**
Constantine Krypton.   London: Methuen, 1956. 219p. map. bibliog.
Broader in scope than its title suggests, this work discusses many aspects of the
economic development of Siberia, including southern Siberian grain and industry, the
main and lesser Siberian rivers.

665   **The northern sea route: its place in Russian economic history before
1917.**
Constantine Krypton.   New York: Research Program on the
USSR, 1953. 193p. map. bibliog. (Studies on the USSR, no. 2).
Like the previous volume and Robert North's work on West Siberian transport (q.v.),
this book covers an amazing amount of ground. There is a very helpful section on the
Trans-Siberian Railway, on internal river traffic along the Ob and Enisei systems and a

general survey of the growth of the economy of central Siberia. The bibliography is extensive.

666 **Soviet waterways: the development of the inland navigation system in the USSR.**
Andrei Lebed, Boris Yakovlev, English-language edition edited by Olive J. Frederiksen. Munich, Germany: Institute for the Study of the USSR, 1956. 161p. maps. (Institute for the Study of the USSR, Series 1, no. 36).

Sections of this work relate to Siberia. There is a study of the Enisei system before 1914 and in chapter eight information about the Enisei, Irtysh and other rivers in the Soviet era.

667 **A visit to Yakutiya.**
Robert N. North. *Soviet Geography*, vol. 31, no. 2 (Feb. 1990), p. 134-9.

A Western expert on Siberian transport, the author spent ten days in 1989 in Yakutiya investigating transport on the Lena river. Details are provided of port activities at Yakutsk and Osetrovo. Local officials give their views about developments under Gorbachev.

# Literary Works about Siberia

### 668 Queer fish.
Viktor Petrovich Astafev. Moscow: Progress Publishers, 1982. 444p.

Astafev (1924- ), one of a new breed of native Siberian writers, was born in central Siberia near Krasnoyarsk where he now lives. Inmate of an orphanage, railwayman and soldier he now writes pungent and hard-hitting short stories about his native Siberia including those in the above translated collection. See also *The horse with the pink mane and other stories* (Moscow: Progress Publishers, 1975); 'Six short stories', translated by Alice Ingham (*Soviet Literature*, no. 5 [1984], p. 96-116); 'To live your life' (*Soviet Literature*, no. 1 [1988], p. 3-44) – full of slang, river boats and war memories – and 'Lyudochka', translated by David Gillespie (*Soviet Literature*, no. 8 [1990], p. 3-39).

### 669 The third truth.
Leonid I. Borodin, translated from the Russian by Catriona Kelly.
London: Collins Harvill Press, 1989. 189p.

This novel set in the taiga forest is ostensibly about the relationships between a game warden, a poacher, a White officer and his daughter. The deeper themes intertwined within it are the Gulag experience, the deflowering of the virgin forest by industry and the search for spiritual values (the game warden becomes a Christian). Borodin (1938- ), a writer from Irkutsk, received prison sentences from 1967-77 and 1982-87 for participation in the Social Christian Union and publishing his collection of short stories, *Story of a strange time*, outside the USSR.

### 670 The year of miracle and grief.
Leonid I. Borodin, translated from the Russian by J. Bradshaw.
London; New York: Quartet Books, 1984. 186p.

Lake Baikal is one of the principal heroes of this sad, lyrical tale of first love. The lake's changing moods are painted in the imagination through the boy's responses to them. Atmospheric accounts of exciting days fishing for grayling, swimming and pine-nut gathering are interspersed with an enchanting mystery wherein the boy becomes

168

part of the living legend of Baikal and the heroic ancestors after whom the region's locations were named. He falls in love with a curse-entrapped princess.

671 **Valentin Rasputin: a general view.**
Deming Brown. In: *Russian literature and criticism: selected papers from the Second World Congress for Soviet and East European Studies*, edited by Evelyn Bristol. Berkeley, California: Berkeley Slavic Specialties, 1982.

Provides an overview of the work of the famous Siberian writer and ecology activist. A joint American–Russian evaluation of Rasputin is to be found in 'Two points of view' (*Soviet Literature*, no. 3 [1987], p. 148-68) in which Elizabeth Rich and Nikolai Kotenko participate. A round-table discussion about similar issues, also involving Rich, is in *Soviet Literature*, no. 5 (1989), p. 150-60.

672 **The ferry: sketches of the struggle for socialism in the Altai mountains.**
Mark Egart. Moscow: Cooperative Publishing Society of Foreign Workers in the USSR; London: Martin Lawrence, 1932. 151p.

The six short stories in this collection basically consist of propaganda designed to show that the Altaian people and poor Russian settlers were engaged in a joint struggle to get rid of priests and bourgeois exploiters. The coming of collective, mechanized agriculture is lauded. Unfortunately there are serious errors in the preface, both in spellings and in facts. There are some unusual photographs of life in the 1920s.

673 **A garden in Siberia.**
John Elsom. *Contemporary Review*, vol. 246 (Jan. 1985), p. 27-31.

This brief study is included because it is virtually the only thing in English on the famous Soviet writer Afanasii Lazarevich Koptëlov (1903- ), a Siberian who now lives in the country near Novosibirsk and has written a good deal about the Altai. The article takes the form of a lively report on an interview with the author, who proudly showed his carefully hybridized Siberian apples: a great achievement of the new order, but spoke little about his trilogy on Lenin in Siberia. As far as I know, none of Koptëlov's works have been published in English, probably because he could in no way be classed as a dissident.

674 **National attitudes in the far north east: the Chukchi writer Rytkheu.**
James Forsyth. *Sibirica*, no. 4 (1988), p. 20-7.

Briefly outlining the history and numbers of the Siberian Eskimos and Chukchi from the first Russian contact to the Soviet era, Forsyth shows how Rytkheu has a dual attitude towards the Russians: praising them for the achievements brought about since 1917, he is still aware of arrogance and racist attitudes. His recent works show a growing respect for northeastern traditions including the shamans whom he previously lambasted.

675 **Valentin Rasputin and Soviet Russian village prose.**
David Charles Gillespie. London: Modern Humanities Research
Association, 1986. 98p. bibliog. (MHRA Texts and Dissertations,
vol. 22).

An author of the 'village' school, Rasputin (1937- ) is concerned to fight a last-ditch
battle to preserve what he regards as valid in old Russia. This study shows his use of
Siberian themes as a critique of Soviet values. The doomed village of Matëra near the
Angara river, about to be flooded by the Bratsk dam, is a symbol of the extermination
of the pristine and pure by modernity, just as the attitude of Andrei towards nature in
*Live and remember*, translated by Antonina W. Bouis (New York: Macmillan, 1978)
symbolizes Russia's denial of her rural roots.

676 **Siberian gold.**
Theodore Acland Harper, in collaboration with Winifred Harper.
London: Hutchinson, 1937. 288p.

This adventure yarn about European gold-miners up against thugs in deepest Siberia is
notable for a curious attempt to make the characters speak in a russified vocabulary.
I have included it not because of any great literary merit, but because it represents
something of a European view of what Siberia is like.

677 **They found their voice: stories from Soviet nationalities with no written
language before the 1917 October revolution.**
Compiled by Evgenia Imbovits. Moscow: Progress Publishers, 1977.
255p.

Contains English translations of short literary works by Chukchi, Udegei, Buryat,
Mansi, Yukagir, Nivkh and Tuvinian authors.

678 **Armoured train 14-69: a play in eight scenes.**
Vsevolod Vyacheslavovich Ivanov, translated by Gibson Cowan,
A. J. K. Grant. London: Martin Lawrence; New York: International
Publishers, 1933. 59p.

The dramatized version of a story which appeared in his untranslated *Partizanskie
rasskazy* (Partisan stories), this play deals with episodes in the civil war in Siberia in a
thoroughly pro-Bolshevik manner, as one might expect from a committed Siberian
writer in the Stalin years. A critique of Ivanov (1895-1963) is 'Somewhere in Siberia'
by Evsei Tseitlin (*Soviet Literature*, no. 7 [1980], p. 128-33).

679 **Vassilii Shukshin: painter of everyday life in contemporary Siberia.**
Rosemarie Kieffer, translated from the French by W. Riggan. *Books
Abroad*, vol. 50 (spring 1976), p. 349-51.

Provides a rare and all too brief study of literary works by the esteemed and popular
Siberian writer, film maker and actor, Vasilii Makarovich Shukshin (1929-74). Within a
text restricted in size like the country of Luxembourg from which she writes, Kieffer
manages to encapsulate the essence of Shukshin's genius. A master of dialogue, he
depicted rough diamonds from Siberia in a tragi-comic vein. Eloquently painting with
words he also conveyed much of the strange beauty of Siberia.

680 **A stride across a thousand years. Prose, poetry and essays by writers of the Soviet north and Far East.**
Compiled by Svetlana Kovalenko, translated from the Russian.
Moscow: Progress Publishers, 1986. 244p.

A foreword by Vladimir Sanghi, the first Nivkh writer, explaining how the Soviet régime has enabled the Siberian minority peoples to develop indigenous literatures leads into twenty-three items by writers from the following nationalities: Nanai, Yakut, Chukchi, Nenets, Dolgan, Nivkh, Eskimo, Mansi, Khanty, Yukagir, Even, Evenk and Itelmen. There is a brief biographical sketch and photograph of each author, five of whom are women.

681 **Vasili and Vasilissa: Siberian stories.**
Compiled by Nina Kupreyanova. Moscow: Progress Publishers, 1981. 389p.

This is another selection of recent literary offerings from Siberia. It includes seven stories by contemporary Soviet authors including Yurii Ritkheyu, whose 'When the whales leave' is on pages 109-99. The collection's title comes from Valentin Rasputin's 'Vasili and Vasilissa' which is on pages 322-51.

682 **Korolenko's stories of Siberia.**
Lauren G. Leighton. *Slavonic and East European Review*, vol. 49, no. 115 (April 1971), p. 200-13.

Vladimir Grigorevich Korolenko (1853-1921) spent years in Siberian exile, and in 1880-1915 wrote a cycle of sixteen stories about Siberia. The stories admirably balance social concern with literary achievement, and gained the admiration of Chekhov. They include scenes of exile life, kindly peasant characters, mystical tramps and encounters with robbers. Only one has been translated into English in *Makar's dream and other stories* (London: T. Fisher Unwin, 1892 [Pseudonym Library, vol. 13, Russian Stories, vol. 1], p. 1-47). Makar's dream describes the brutish, short life of a descendant of early Russian settlers who has become Yakutized, and proceeds to depict his journey to judgement in allegorical terms which fuse folkloristic and pseudo-Christian themes.

683 **On the edge of the world.**
Nikolai Semënovich Leskov, translated by A. E. Chamot. In: *The sentry and other stories* by Nicolai Lyeskov. London: John Lane the Bodley Head, 1922, p. 189-320.

'The conditions of Russian missionary work in northeast Siberia in the nineteenth century are intimately described in Lyeskov's deeply imaginative story *On the edge of the world* (1876)' [quoted from *Survey of Russian History* by Bernard H. Sumner (London: Gerald Duckworth, 1944, p. 24)]. Based on the life of Bishop Nil of Yaroslavl, a missionary in the 1850s, the story contrasts the simple living faith of a native guide with the sterile rigidities of official Orthodoxy. The hero finds the old missionary Father Kiriak rather cynical, and discovers that he has much to learn from the native people he meets. A sensitive literary criticism of this tale and its deeper meaning in Leskov's non-institutional, semi-Protestant and rather mystical view of Christianity is found in 'Leskov's "At the edge of the world": the search for an image of Christ' by K. A. Lantz (*Slavic and East European Journal*, vol. 25, no. 1 [spring 1981], p. 34-43).

684 **Father and son.**
Georgii Mokeevich Markov, translated by Vladimir Talmyi. *Soviet Literature*, no. 8 (1966), p. 3-96; no. 9 (1966), p. 3-89.
Born in Novaya Kuskova, Tomsk Province in 1911, the son of a hunter/farmer, Markov graduated from Tomsk University, supported the Bolsheviks and became a prominent writer in the socialist realism genre. He rose to become secretary of the Soviet Writers' Union Board and a member of the Supreme Soviet. See 'Georgii Markov and his novels' by Solomon Smolyanitskii (*Soviet Literature*, no. 4 [1974], p. 105-9) and the interview with him in no. 8 (1966), p. 4. *Father and son*, a semi-autobiographical novel, tells of the establishment of a farming commune on the Vasyugan river near the Ob in 1921, which Markov's father actually did. The Bistrykov family developed for this novel featured also in later publications.

685 **Salt of the earth.**
Georgii Mokeevich Markov, translated by Ralph Parker. *Soviet Literature*, no. 2 (1961), p. 3-123; no. 3 (1961), p. 27-98.
Consists of the second part of a long novel about the transformation of Siberia from a land of exile and misery to one of socialist construction. A brief autobiography and photograph of the author are included on pages 4-5. A later novel based on the fictional town of Sinegorsk and partly concerned with Siberian revolutionary history is 'For the coming century', translated by Monica Whyte (*Soviet Literature*, no. 4 [1982], p. 9-96) and translated by Tracy Kuehn in no. 3 (1986), p. 3-80.

686 **Siberia.**
Georgii Mokeevich Markov, translated by Vladimir Leonov, Eve Manning. *Soviet Literature*, no. 2 (1970), p. 4-109; no. 10 (1971), p. 8-136; no. 4 (1974), p. 7-105.
Translates parts of a long novel about Ivan Akimov, a Bolshevik exile in Siberia, who helps to arrange the escape to Stockholm of a noted expert in Siberian natural resources. The escape is arranged so that the resources cannot be exploited by capitalists, but will eventually be worked for the people's benefit.

687 **Siberian garrison.**
Rodion Markovits, translated from the Hungarian by George Halasz. London: Peter Davies, 1929. 387p.
This detailed semi-autobiographical novel realistically evokes the life of a Hungarian caught up in World War I who ends up as a prisoner-of-war in Siberia.

688 **Snow people.**
Taeki Odulok, translated by James Cleugh. London: Methuen, 1934. 152p. Also published New Haven, Connecticut: Human Relations Area Files, 1954. 73p.
Written by a pro-Communist Yukagir author who was also known as Nikolai I. Spiridonov, this poignant evocation of life among the Chukchi before the 1917 Revolution may be seen as propaganda at one level, but it supplies a human dimension to investigations of the relations between the native people and Russian interlopers.

689 **[Peoples of the north: their arts and handicrafts.]**
*Soviet Literature*, no. 1 (1976), p. 1-191. map.
The whole of this issue of the journal is devoted to the fiction, poetry, legends and fine arts of the minority peoples of Siberia. There is no title; the heading in square brackets is from the label on the introductory map. The twenty-two items of literature are by Dolgan, Yukagir, Yakut, Nanai, Koryak, Chukchi, Nenets, Even, Evenk, Selkup, Nivkh, Mansi, Khanty and Ulchi authors. There are also short traditional tales from the Chukchi, Eskimo, Koryak, Itelmen, Even, Kerek, Oroch and Ket respectively. Articles on dance, decorative arts and painting are accompanied by monochrome and coloured illustrations. There is an ethnographical note and a biographical paragraph on each author. A further item, a brief travelogue by the Mansi author Yuvan Shestalov 'You too will have wings' (about a helicopter trip over the Vasyugane region of northwest Siberia where oil has been found) is in *Soviet Literature*, no. 3 (1976), p. 136-44.

690 **Is it far to Chukotka?**
Irina Raksha, translated by Helen Tate. *Soviet Literature*, no. 3 (1981), p. 71-104.
Born in the Altai region not far from Shukshin's birthplace, Irina Raksha grew up beside the mighty Katun river. She worked as a tractor driver on the Urozhainyi State Farm and later moved to Chukotka. Her literary efforts have earned her the title 'poetic ambassador of Siberia and the polar expanses'. The above story about Russian experiences in that distant region is introduced by Vsevolod Surganov. 'The whole wide world', translated by Susan Henderson (*Soviet Literature*, no. 3 [1979], p. 3-132) evokes the Altai. The heroes are old revolutionary peasants and the mountains themselves.

691 **Farewell to Matyora: a novel.**
Valentin Grigorevich Rasputin, translated by Antonina W. Bouis.
New York: Macmillan, 1979. 227p.
Construction of the Bratsk dam on the Angara river in East Siberia threatens the survival and disrupts the traditional lives of the inhabitants of Rasputin's fictional village of Matëra. His intention in writing this work was to attack the effects of industrialization and rapid social change on a small, isolated Siberian community. In contrast, the villagers' folklore traditions and pantheism are depicted positively. They are fragile in face of the bureaucratic monolith called 'progress'. A new translation by David Gillespie (Bedminster, England: Bristol Press) has been announced and will be published in 1991.

692 **Siberia on fire, stories and essays.**
Valentin Grigorevich Rasputin, selected, translated and with an introduction by Gerald Mikkelson, Margaret Winchell. DeKalb, Illinois: Northern Illinois University Press, 1989. 230p. maps. bibliog.
A brief literary and biographical introduction leads in to the publication of an Americanized version of six short stories and six essays on Siberian history, literature and environmental issues. Rasputin evokes the mysterious joy of tramping deep in the taiga to collect berries; he uses a motor-boat trip across Baikal in a storm to create a psychological mood of introspection, deepened by the lake's brooding presence. He expresses profound regret at the passing of village Russia (see also items 671, 691). In

the last essay he evaluates the work of Aleksandr Vampilov (q.v.), another author from Irkutsk. Two stories in this collection have also appeared separately in *Soviet Literature*: 'The fire', translated by Alex Muller (no. 7 [1986], p. 3-55) and 'What shall I tell the crow?', translated by Valentina Jacque (no. 2 [1987], p. 30-47).

### 693   Old Memyl laughs last: short stories.

Yurii Sergeevich Rytkheu, translated by D. Rottenberg.   Moscow:
Foreign Languages Publishing House, [*c*. 1955]. 197p.

The son of a Chukchi hunter and an Eskimo mother, Rytkheu (1930- ) was the first of his nation to become an established literary figure. He even became secretary of the Leningrad Union of Writers. This publication contains four of his early short stories which, whilst obviously very pro-Soviet, give an authentic whiff of the impact of rapid social change in the post-revolutionary era. The culture shock of air travel or seeing trees and hearing the wind in their branches, the coming of film shows to the villages, and the tension as a hunter has to adapt to collective farm life are simply but effectively depicted. A brief essay about how he felt when back in Chukotka hearing a school teacher teaching about him is 'The unusual lesson' (*Soviet Literature*, no. 8 [1974], p. 141-4). See also 'The death of Atyk', translated by John Russell (*Soviet Literature*, no. 7 [1980], p. 120-7) and 'Your native country's distant shores', translated by Sergei Ess (*Soviet Literature*, no. 12 [1982], p. 118-31).

### 694   Stories from Chukotka.

Yurii Sergeevich Rytkheu, translated by David Fry.   London:
Lawrence & Wishart, 1956. 268p.

A brief autobiographical sketch introduces this publication of thirteen short stories by the Chukchi writer, two of which are duplicates of the ones in item no. 693. The stories are basically concerned with the changes brought to Chukchi life by the Soviet régime and occasionally with the rapacious activities of foreigners like Captain Sime. The heroes do not regret the passing of seal-oil lamps when Soviet electricity comes. They consider the good of the collective farm hunters before their own well-being. Another story in the same vein, 'When the whales leave' (*Soviet Literature*, no. 12 [1977], p. 3-73), was also published in item no. 681 (above). Rytkheu, like many others in the USSR, has begun to utter more critical sentiments since the onset of *glasnost*. An example of this may be found in 'Arctic silence', in *The best of Ogonyok: the new journalism of glasnost*, edited by Vitalii Korotich, translated by Cathy Porter (London: Heinemann, 1990. p. 169-73) which attacks past Russian and Soviet ethnic policies.

### 695   Last tribute to custom.

Vladimir Sanghi, translated by Tamara Barrett.   *Soviet Literature*,
no. 4 (1975), p. 91-100.

Sanghi is a Nivkh. He was born in northern Sakhalin and is the first professional writer of his nation. This tale is about tribal life in the Soviet period. 'The man of Ykhmif', translated by S. Rot (*Soviet Literature*, no. 4 [1986], p. 133-40) is a fragment of an epic poem about the Nivkh.

696 **Coaster captain.**
Sergei Sartakov, translated by Michelle King. *Soviet Literature*, no. 2
(1978), p. 3-35.
A tale about boatmen on the Surgut river saving people from drowning in the rapids,
this is representative of the work of another official Soviet writer (1908- ). A literary
study of Sartakov's works by Aleksandr Borshchagovskii is included on pages 3-8,
along with a photograph of the author.

697 **Children of the Soviet Arctic.**
Tikhon Zakharovich Sëmushkin. London: Hutchinson, 1944. 256p;
London: Travel Book Club, 1947. 251p.
Impressed by Chukotka and its people when he came on official assignments in the
mid-1920s, the author returned to organize a boarding school and cultural service base
(kultbaza) in the early Stalin years. He wanted to present an authentic fictionalized
account of how education was brought to the Chukchi from 1928 onwards. The result
was this story, possessing a warm human element and some humour. The excerpts
from the teacher's diary which are included could well be Sëmushkin's own.

698 **Alitet goes to the hills: a novel.**
Tikhon Zakharovich Sëmushkin, translated from the Russian by
B. Isaacs. Moscow: Foreign Languages Publishing House, 1952.
2nd ed. 594p.
Winner of a Stalin prize, this illustrated novel portrays the cruel colonialists (Russian
and American) who exploited the Chukchi for profits. It also attacks the shaman, who
is seen as deceiver of the people. The first few pages of the book consist of an
explanatory author's introduction. The novel was later made into a film. See also his
*Peoples regenerated* (Moscow: Foreign Languages Publishing House, 1953. 30p.) which
consists of two articles reprinted from the magazine *Soviet Union*.

699 **Kolyma tales.**
Varlam Tikhonovich Shalamov, translated from the Russian by John
Glad. New York; London: W. W. Norton, 1980. 222p.
Born in 1907, Shalamov was sent to the camps in Siberia on two separate occasions for
a total of seventeen years, spending much of the time in the Kolyma system. These
stories are a powerful evocation of the horrors of the Stalin era.

700 **Viktor Astafev: the Soviet bard of Siberia.**
N. N. Shneidman. *Russian Language Journal*, no. 114 (1979),
p. 99-107.
Presents a critique of the writings and neo-religious ecological concerns of a Russian
writer whose canvas depicts the spoliation of Siberia. See also 'Man, nature and the
roots in recent Soviet Russian prose' in *Studies in honour of Louis Shein*, edited by
S. D. Cioran (Hamilton, Ontario: McMaster University, 1983, p. 125-33). Soviet
appreciations of Astafev's work include 'An eternal festival of light: on the prose of
Victor Astafyev' by Igor Dedkov (*Soviet Literature*, no. 5 [1984], p. 131-8), and an
interview by Aleksandr Fëdorov which appeared in the same publication (no. 10
[1985], p. 134-43), along with a photograph of Astafev.

## Literary Works about Siberia

701 **I want to live: short stories.**
Vasilii Makarovich Shukshin, translated by Robert Daglish. Moscow:
Progress Publishers, 1973. 257p.

Consists of sixteen short stories by a noted Soviet film maker and writer (1929-74) who originated in the Altai in southwest Siberia. The stories were published in the USSR in two separate collections in 1968 and 1970. They deal with events in the lives of simple village folk from the Altai. Young men try their luck with girls, finding problems especially when the girls are sophisticated outsiders holding a fashion show in the village hall. Children face the trauma of exams; a driver sees wolves kill his sleigh horse in front of his eyes; men pick up dutch courage by quaffing home-made mead before trying match making. Though set in the modern era with trappings such as internal combustion engines, they have a certain folksy air about them. The subjects tackled are universal, not specifically Soviet, hence their appeal.

702 **The white shaman.**
Nikolai Shundik, translated by Susan Henderson. *Soviet Literature*,
no. 3 (1981), p. 3-69.

An introductory article about the author by Irina Bogatko reveals that he is a Russian (1920- ) who has taught in Chukotka. He chronicles the birth of the new order in Chukotka in his novels and stories. This one concerns the ever-growing friendship between the Russian and Chukchi peoples.

703 **[Siberia.]**
*Soviet Literature*, no. 3 (1980), p. 1-207. map.

There is no overall title to this issue of *Soviet Literature* which is all devoted to the literature and arts of Soviet Siberia. There are twenty-five short stories and poems by Russian and native writers including Yuvan Shestalov, Georgii Markov, Sergei Sartakov, Valentin Rasputin, Sergei Zalygin, Vasilii Shukshin and Aleksandr Vampilov. There are snappy journalistic items about Mirnyi, Surgut and Tayura on the Baikal–Amur railway, and two articles of literary criticism. There is a brief explanation about how a film about oil exploration, *Siberian saga*, was made. Pavel Muratov writes about Siberia's museum collections, and Valerii Cherepanov gives tantalizing illustrations about wooden architecture in Siberia. At the rear are photographs and biographies of all the writers.

704 **Duck hunting.**
Aleksandr Valentinovich Vampilov, translated and adapted by Alma
H. Law. New York: Dramatists' Play Service, [c. 1980]. 81p.

Vampilov was a dramatist from Irkutsk. In his short life (1937-72) before he was drowned in Lake Baikal he wrote promising plays and sketches, reminiscent of Chekhov. This play investigates the psychological make-up of a weak-willed man who comes to grief in his personal and professional life. Negligent and dishonest, he always takes the line of least resistance.

705  **Michael Strogoff, the courier of the Czar.**
Jules Verne, translated from the French by W. H. G. Kingston.
London: Sampson, Low & Co, 1877. 377p. Also published London:
Thomas Nelson, 1912. 372p.

A swashbuckling romp through the 'wild east' to Irkutsk, this offering by the famous French fantasy novelist concerns the attempts of a Tsarist messenger to get his important information through to Irkutsk despite attacks by rebellious Tatars, the weather and wild animals.

# Bibliographies

706 **Soviet Asia: bibliographies. A compilation of social science and humanities sources on the Iranian, Mongolian and Turkic nationalities, with an essay on the Soviet-Asian controversy.**
Compiled by Edward Allworth. New York; Washington, DC; London: Praeger, 1975. 686p.

This is an extremely erudite work, part five of which is devoted to Siberia and Mongolia. Chapters thirty-one onwards refer to the Altaian, Buryat, Dolgan, Khakass, Tuvinian and Yakut peoples. Chapter thirty-six is about Siberia. The entries are either scholarly works in Russian or bibliographies from which more information may be obtained.

707 **Research catalogue.**
American Geographical Society. Boston: G. K. Hall, 1962. vol. 12.

Section thirty-eight (pages 08745-08820) is on Siberia and contains a great deal of material. The problem is that items in Russian are included in English translation on the cards.

708 **How we lost the Civil War: bibliography of Russian emigre memoirs on the Russian Revolution, 1917-1921.**
David Arans. Newtonville, Massachussetts: Oriental Research Partners, 1988. 200p. (ORP Bibliographical Series, no. 6).

This well-annotated list of émigré memoirs about the 1917 Revolution and civil war includes quite a few items relevant to Siberia and the Soviet Far East. There are good author and subject indexes.

709 **The Yudin library, Krasnoiarsk (eastern Siberia).**
Alexis Vasilevich Babine. Washington, DC: Press of Judd & Detweiler, 1905. 40p.

Compiled by a Russian author (1866-1930) whose two-volume history of the USA was published in St. Petersburg, this pamphlet describes the library belonging to a Siberian merchant Yudin which was housed in a special building in Krasnoyarsk, until it was purchased by the Americans in 1907. It has largely been incorporated into the Library of Congress as the Yudin Collection.

710 **Materialy k ukazatelyu literatury o Sibiri na evropeiskikh yazykakh s 1917g. po 1930g.** (Materials for an index of literature about Siberia in European languages from 1917 to 1930).
Compiled by Aleksei Mikhailovich Belov. Leningrad: Izdatelstvo Akademii nauk SSSR, 1931. 35p.

Contains references to publications including short book reviews published from 1917 to 1930 in any European language and on any subject providing Siberia is included. The very brief annotations are in Russian. There are interesting items in it about natural history, minerals and mining which have not been incorporated in the present bibliography. Abstruse but very interesting periodicals such as *Mining and Scientific Press* (San Francisco) were searched in the preparation of this work.

711 **Bibliography of Asian studies.**
Ann Arbor, Michigan: Association for Asian Studies, 1969- .

Originally included in the journal *Asian Studies*, this list has been published separately annually from 1969 onwards. There is a section about the Soviet Far East. Works in Russian and other languages are included.

712 **Arctic bibliography.**
Prepared for and in cooperation with the Department of Defense under the direction of the Arctic Institute of North America. Washington, DC: Department of Defense; Montreal, Canada; London: McGill-Queen's University Press, 1953-75. 16 vols.

This massive, exhaustive work on the Arctic regions, containing in total 108,723 entries, has immense numbers of items relating to Siberia. Predominantly they concentrate on the area to the north of that stressed in this bibliography, but there are some relevant English works which I have not been able to include.

713 **Books on Soviet Russia, 1917-1942. A bibliography and a guide to reading.**
Philip Grierson. London: Methuen, 1943. 354p.

Though most of the works on Siberia mentioned by Grierson have been included in this present bibliography, his annotations have their own flavour and readers might wish to consult them.

714 **Guide to geographical bibliographies and reference works in Russian or on the Soviet Union.**
Chauncy D. Harris. Chicago, Illinois: University of Chicago Press, 1975. 477p. maps. (University of Chicago Department of Geography, Research Paper, no. 164).

This annotated list of 2,660 bibliographies and reference aids covers all aspects of Soviet geography (physical, transport, economic and regional). Siberia and the Soviet Far East are naturally included. See the detailed contents pages.

715 **Guide to documents and mss. in the United Kingdom relating to Russia and the Soviet Union.**
Compiled by Janet M. Hartley. London: Mansell, 1987. 560p.

The first systematic record of documents relating to Russia and the Soviet Union in British repositories, this work covers every conceivable area. It should be read in tandem with *The study of Russian history from British archival sources*, edited by Janet M. Hartley (London: Mansell, 1987. 208p.) which has several articles of interest to Siberian studies.

716 **Guide to the study of the Soviet nationalities: non-Russian peoples of the USSR.**
Edited by Stephen M. Horak. Littleton, Colorado: Libraries Unlimited, 1982. 265p.

Particularly important in this volume is the section by Marjorie Mandelstam Balzer about the peoples of Siberia (pages 239-52). There is a useful brief introduction and a select annotated bibliography.

717 **Russia and the Soviet Union: a bibliographic guide to western language publications.**
Edited by Paul L. Horecky. Chicago, Illinois; London: Chicago University Press, 1965. 473p.

Siberian items are included on pages 69-73 of this work. Other relevant items do occur in the text, but unfortunately there is no subject index.

718 **Paleosiberian peoples and languages: a bibliographical guide.**
Roman O. Jakobson, Gerta Hüttl-Worth, John Fred Beebe. New Haven: Human Area Relations Files Press, 1957. 222p.

A very thorough cross-referenced bibliography containing items published from the beginning to the mid-1950s, with annotations limited to the particular subject under review, this work has been of great help in compiling the present bibliography. There are many specialized items in it which I have not been able to include.

719 **Books in English on the Soviet Union, 1917-73: a bibliography.**
Compiled by David Lewis Jones. New York; London: Garland Publishing, 1975. 331p.

This bibliography contains a short section (p. 252-4) of direct relevance. Many other entries are of tangential significance.

720   **Northeast Asia: a selected bibliography. Contributions to the
      bibliography of the relations of China, Russia and Japan, with special
      reference to Korea, Manchuria, Mongolia and eastern Siberia, in
      oriental and European languages.**
      Robert J. Kerner.   Berkeley, California: University of California
      Press, 1939. 2 vols. (Publications of the Northeast Asia Seminar of the
      University of California).

Part four in volume two is on Siberia. Many of the references, which were mainly
published between 1900 and 1937, are in Russian, though there are some in English;
they are not annotated.

721   **Arctic and subarctic regions.**
      H. G. R. King.   Oxford; Santa Barbara, California: Clio Press, 1989.
      293p. (World Bibliographical Series, vol. 99).

Since this work, like the *Arctic bibliography* (q.v.), concentrates on the polar regions,
only some of the items refer to the more southerly sectors of Siberia and the Soviet Far
East. The annotations are thorough and helpful.

722   **The Uralic and Altaic series: an analytical index.**
      John R. Krueger.   Bloomington, Indiana: Indiana University Press;
      The Hague: Mouton, 1970. 81p. (Indiana University Publications,
      Uralic and Altaic Series, no. 100).

Contains a very helpful index to the complete run of the fundamentally important
Uralic and Altaic Series published by Indiana University Press throughout the 1960s,
several of whose volumes are included in the present bibliography.

723   **To Russia and return. An annotated bibliography of travellers' English-
      language accounts of Russia from the ninth century to the present.**
      Harry W. Nerhood.   Columbus, Ohio: Ohio State University Press,
      1968. 367p.

An essential aid to anyone investigating travel literature about Russia, this work has
been of great benefit in preparing the present bibliography. Some items in it have not
been included.

724   **Linguistic bibliography for the year.**
      Published by the Permanent International Committee of Linguistics.
      Cambridge: Heffers, 1939- ; currently The Hague; Boston,
      Massachussetts; London: Martinus Nijhoff.

This annual bibliograpy of linguistic publications is a massive work containing sections
on all the world's languages. Used selectively it can provide detailed information on
the specific language groups of relevance to this work.

725  **An annotated bibliography on Soviet northern transport, 1975-86.**
Robert Neville North.   Vancouver, Canada: University of British
Columbia Department of Geography, 1987. 163p. (Departmental
Paper, no. 38).

Although the 1400 entries in this work are mainly relevant to the area to the north of
the region covered by the present bibliography, some items relating to regions farther
south are included. There are subject and geographical indexes. The majority of the
references are to works in Russian.


726  **The bibliographic work of the State Public Scientific Technical Library
of the Siberian Section of the USSR Academy of Sciences.**
Patricia Polansky.   *Libri*, vol. 33, no. 4 (1983), p. 274-88.

Reveals a little-known but vital activity of the main academic library in Siberia, the
State Public Scientific Technical Library in Novosibirsk, namely the preparation of
bibliographical guides to everything published in or about Siberia. This work results in
the publication of bimonthly and quarterly periodicals including *Istoriya Sibiri:
tekushchii ukazatel literatury* (History of Siberia: periodical index to literature);
*Narodnoe khozyaistvo Sibiri i Dalnego Vostoka: tekushchii ukazatel literatury* (The
economy of Siberia and the Far East: periodical index to literature); and *Nauka,
literatura, iskusstvo Sibiri: tekushchii ukazatel literatury* (Science, literature, the arts in
Siberia: periodical index of literature). They include publications in foreign languages
as well as in Russian. See also Pat Polansky's 'Recent studies of Siberian books and
reading: a review essay' (*Journal of Library History*, vol. 22, no. 1 [1987], p. 58-69).


727  **Russia/USSR: a selective, annotated bibliography of books in English.**
Anthony Thompson.   Oxford; Santa Barbara, California: Clio Press,
1979. 302p. map. (World Bibliographical Series, vol. 6).

Items 337, 339, 686 and 1209-12 of this companion volume to the present one and to
King (q.v.) are of interest.

# Encyclopaedias and Reference Works

**728 Great Soviet encyclopaedia: a translation of the third edition.**
New York: Macmillan; London: Collier Macmillan, 1973-83. 32 vols.
The editors claim that this is 'a faithful translation of the Soviet national encyclopaedia, unannotated and as true as possible to the content and meaning intended'. This indicates that it contains all the ideological distortions of the original. It also means that any article about Siberia will give an official Brezhnev-era view of developments. Nevertheless, it would be wrong to dismiss everything in the work. Used judiciously it can provide a good deal of information about many aspects of Siberia from physical geography to ethnic minorities, from city locations to flora.

**729 Modern encyclopaedia of Russian and Soviet history.**
Edited by Joseph L. Wieczynski. Gulf Breeze, Florida: Academic International Press, 1975-90. 53 vols.
This monumental work contains several items on Siberian history. Examples are as follows: 'Siberia, the conquest and colonization of' (vol. 35 [1983], p. 92-7); 'Shchapov' (vol. 34 [1983], p. 168-71); 'Potanin' (vol. 29 [1982], p. 119-20); 'Yadrintsev' (vol. 44 [1987], p. 134-6); 'Siberian oblastniki' (vol. 35 [1983], p. 108); 'The exile system in Russia' (vol. 11 [1979], p. 27-31); 'Badmaev, P. A.' (vol. 2 [1976], p. 234-7); 'Revolution of 1905 in Siberia' (vol. 31 [1983], p. 71); 'Siberian Social-Democratic Union' (vol. 35 [1983], p. 110-13); and 'Siberian oblast duma' (vol. 35 [1983], p. 107-8).

**730 New Encyclopaedia Britannica.**
Chicago: Encyclopaedia Britannica, 1979. 15th ed. 30 vols.
The Micropaedia has several short entries about Siberia. For instance there is an entry in volume nine entitled 'Siberia', with cross references to entries in both the Micropaedia and the Macropaedia. The latter has several significant entries, such as 'Altaic languages' and 'Altai mountains' (vol. 1, p. 635-41) or 'Amur' (ibid., p. 716-17), or 'Siberian cultures' (vol. 16, p. 724-7). The entries often have bibliographies and coloured illustrations or maps.

## Encyclopaedias and Reference Works

731 **Russian Yearbook.**
Edited by Howard Percy Kennard [and Netta Peacock]. London:
Eyre & Spottiswoode, 1911. 387p. maps.

This directory was intended to assist Anglo-American business interests in their
contacts with the Russian market. There is a good deal of information about Siberia
and about British firms operating there (use the helpful index). The *Yearbooks* were
issued yearly until 1916. Netta Peacock edited a Russian almanac once during the
Allied intervention period (London: Published for the Anglo-Russian Trust by Eyre &
Spottiswoode, 1919. 209p.). There was also *Russian–American Annual for 1916*
(Moscow: Russian–American Chamber of Commerce, 1916. 152p.). An equivalent for
the Soviet period was *Soviet Union yearbook*, which in 1928 was edited by A. A.
Santalov and Louis Segal (London: George Allen & Unwin, 1928. 587p.) but this had
very little directly about Siberia in it.

732 **Sibirskaya sovetskaya entsiklopediya.** (Siberian Soviet encyclopaedia.)
Edited by Mark K. Azadovskii (et al.). Novosibirsk: Novosibirskoe
kraeveoe izdatelstvo, 1929-30. 2 vols. Reprinted Zug, Switzerland:
IDC, 1970.

Written in Russian, this encyclopaedia gives invaluable details about very varied
aspects of Siberian studies, including biographies. Unfortunately, owing to the
changing political situation as Stalin's dictatorship was installed, only the first two
volumes of a projected four were ever published, reaching the letter K. The reprint is
in microfiche form. It is earnestly to be hoped that a new version of this work may be
undertaken and completed.

# Periodicals

733 **Siberian/ questions/ sibériennes.**
Edited by Boris Chichlo.   Paris: Institut d'Etudes Slaves, 1990- .
This very new periodical began publication in 1990. It is issued in French, Russian and English by the Centre d'études sibériennes de l'Institut du monde soviétique et de l'Europe centrale et orientale. The first issue was devoted to the indigenous peoples of Siberia, particularly concentrating on the Evenk, Shor, Chukchi and Eskimo.

734 **Siberica: a journal of North Pacific studies.**
Edited by Thomas Vaughan, Elizabeth A. P. Crownhart-Vaughan.
Portland, Oregon: Oregon Historical Society, 1990- .
Another new journal, this time devoted to the whole North Pacific area, this publication replaces *Sibirica*, the occasional publication of the British Universities Siberian Studies Seminar, edited by Alan Wood and published at Lancaster. Four issues of *Sibirica* were issued from no. 1 (1983) to no. 4 (1989) before publication was transferred to Oregon.

735 **SUPAR report.**
Edited by Robert B. Vaillant.   Honolulu, Hawaii: Center for the Soviet Union in the Pacific–Asian Region, School of Hawaiian, Asian & Pacific Studies, University of Hawai'i at Manoa, 1987- .
Valuable because it is so specialized, this publication presents brief information about events, publications and press coverage of the Soviet Far East. Data are included on Soviet trade and relations with countries on the Pacific Rim.

# Indexes

There follow three separate indexes: authors (personal and corporate), editors and translators; titles; and subjects. Title entries are italicized and refer either to the main titles, or to other works cited in the annotations. The numbers refer to bibliographical entry rather than page numbers. Individual index entries are arranged in alphabetical sequence.

# Index of Authors

## A

Ablitt, G. 448
Abramova, Z. 191
Ackerman, C. 265
Afonon, I. 647
Aganbegyan, A. 577
Agee, J. 535
Agreli, J. 153
Aipin, Y. 379
Aizman, N. 155
Akiner, S. 314
Alec-Tweedie, E. 112
Aleksandrov, V. 227
Alekseev, N. 471
Alekseev, V. N. 209
Alekseev, V. P. 326
Algvere, K. 604
Alibegov, P. 581
Allison, A. 570
Allworth, E. 706
Amalrik, A. 514
American Geographical
    Society 707
Anderson, M. 228
Andreev, V. 600
Andrusz, G. 486
Appleby, J. 172
Aramilev, I. 83
Arans, D. 708
Arctic Institute of North
    America 712
Argunov, I. 315
Armstrong, T. 15, 32,
    124-5, 171, 229, 339,
    538. 576

Aronson, G. 372
Arsenev, V. 33
Arutyunov, S. 192
Asai, T. 336
Astafev, V. 668
Atkins, T. 152
Atkinson, L. 34
Atkinson, T. 35-6
Austerlitz, R. 440
Auty, R. 32
Avakumović, I. 63, 470
Avvakum 16
Azadovskii, M. 429, 732

## B

Babakov, V. 315
Babine, A. 709
Babó, A. 322
Baedeker, K. 117
Baerlein, H. 265
Bagrow, L. 132-4, 140
Baievsky, B. 303
Baikalov, A. 1, 230, 252
Baker, B. 610
Baklanov, P. 578
Balzer, M. 379-80, 472,
    716
Baranov, E. 539
Barber, N. 92
Barlow, P. 43
Barr, B. 590, 605-6, 611
Barr, W. 174, 345
Barratt, G. 492

Barrett, T. 695
Barrett-Hamilton, G. 37
Bartels, A. 316
Bartels, D. 316
Bartlett, R. 487, 511-12
Bassin, M. 231, 253
Batalden, S. 450
Bater, J. 15, 218, 611
Bauer, J. 107
Bawden, C. 451
Baxter, J. 152
Beable, W. 118
Beazley, C. 223, 634
Bečvar, G. 265
Beebe, J. 718
Bell, J. 17, 267
Belov, A. 710
Belov, M. 238
Beniowski, M. 18
Beresford, B. 24
Berg, L. 145, 173
Berger, J. 515
Bergman, S. 84
Berk, S. 268
Bess, D. 312
Beveridge, A. 38
Bezborodov, S. 304
Bhargava, G. 581
Birdwood, G. 78
Birkett, K. 499
Birron, A. 176, 180
Biryukov, V. 645
Black, J. L. 13, 19, 221
Black, L. 389
Blair, A. 527
Blanchard, I. 232

Bobrova, R. 503
Bogart, J. 592
Bogatko, I. 702
Bogatko, S. 646
Bogoras-Tan, W. 317, 357,
    363, 418-19, 430-2, 473
Boiko, V. 318-19, 384
Boland, I. 519
Bolshakoff, S. 452
Bond, A. 146, 548
Bookwalter, J. 39
Borisov, A. 141
Borodin, G. 85
Borodin, L. 669-70
Borshchagovskii, A. 696
Bosson, J. 406
Botting, D. 86
Bouis, A. 675, 691
Bourdeaux, M. 456
Bowles, W. 607
Braden, K. 605
Bradshaw, J. 670
Bradshaw, M. 11, 590, 627
Braikevich, M. 647
Braithwaite, A. 290
Bräker, H. 448
Bramont, J. 497
Brand, A. 20
Brändström, E. 40
Bridge, R. 125
Bristol, E. 671
British and Foreign Bible
    Society 450
British Museum 207
Brockett, E. 526
Broekmeyer, M. 125
Broido, E. 493
Broido, M. 493
Broido, V. 493
Brostrom, K. 16
Brower, H. 27
Brown, A. 105
Brown, D. 671
Brown, J. 459
Bryce, J. 77
Budarin, M. 663
Budkov, S. 608
Budnikov, G. 87
Buel, J. 494
Bugaenko, E. 155
Bunich, P. 648
Burnham, J. 88

Burr, M. 33, 89
Burton, A. 233
Bury, H. 41
Buse, D. 19
Bush, R. 42
Butler, J. 121
Butterfield, D. 635
Butterfield, J. 635
Buxhoeveden, S. 269

C

Campbell, D. 125
Campbell, M. 509
Canada, Department of
    Northern Affairs 174
Canada, Department of
    the Secretary of State
    165, 594
Canada, Department of
    Trade and Commerce
    270
Carr, E. 495
Casanowicz, I. 476
Cash, A. 520
Chaikovskaya, O. 646
Chamot, A. 683
Channing, C. 305
Channon, J. 221, 288, 487
Chaput, D. 312
Chard, C. 193, 371, 387
Chater, A. 66
Chekhov, A. 43
Chemezov, V. 300
Cherepanov, V. 703
Cherkasov, A. 320
Chernetsov, V. 194
Chernov, Y. 175
Cherry, S. 142
Chichlo, B. 125, 474, 733
Chisholm, H. 496
Chivilikhin, V. 90
Chulaki, S. 129, 169
Ciliga, A. 516
Cioran, S. 700
Ciszek, W. 453
Clem, R. 554
Cleugh, J. 688
Cliffe, A. 516
Clough, G. 520
Cochrane, J. 44
Cohn, N. 436

Cole, J. 127
Cole, Z. 176, 180
Coleman, F. 271
Colenso, M. 394
Collinder, B. 416
Collins, D. 13, 210, 221,
    272, 454-5, 540, 644
Collins, P. 45
Colquhoun, A. 46
Compton, P. 595
Comrie, B. 398
Conger, D. 91, 126, 338
Connaughton, R. 273
Conolly, V. 12, 91, 546,
    579
Conquest, R. 113, 306,
    517, 528
Constantin, G. 21
Cooley, W. D. 52
Coquin, F. 545
Cottrell, C. 47
Cowan, G. 678
Coxe, W. 234
Coxwell, C. 433
Cravath, P. 92
Crawford, J. 636
Croll, L. 601
Cross, A. 34
Crowell, A. 327
Crownhart-Vaughan, E.
    164, 236, 734
Crystal, D. 405
Csanyi, A. 329
Culin, S. 30
Curtin, J. 353
Curtis, D. 48
Czaplicka, M. 48, 321, 445

D

Daglish, R. 701
Dall, W. 360
Dallin, D. 517
Dalton, J. 257
Danemaris, D. 9
Daniels, G. 514
Danik, R. 391
Danko, X. 618
Darel, S. 518
Darst, R. 146
Davies, R. 2
Dedkov, I. 700

Degtyarev, V. 663
Dehn, M. 40
Deich, L. 496
Delisle, J. N. 132
Dellenbrant, J. 125
Dementev, G. 176
Demidov, E. 49
Demidov, P. 163
Dewar, H. 516
Dewar, M. 516
Dewdney, J. 135
Deyneka, A. 456
Deyneka, P. 456
Dibb, P. 628
Dicks, E. 217
Dienes, L. 125, 162, 580,
    590, 612
Digby, B. 82, 93, 177
Dioneo (*pseud.*) *see*
    Shklovskii, I.
Diószegi, V. 322, 367, 434,
    475
Dmitriev-Mamonov, A.
    637
Dmytryshyn, B. 221,
    235-6, 246
Dobell, P. 51
Dolgikh, B. 195
Dominique, P. 89
Donne, J. le 249
Donner, K. 323, 376
Dostoevsky, F. 497
Dotsenko, P. 274
Dowle, D. 622
Downing, R. 107
Drew, R. 237
Duff, C. 6
Dunn, E. 212, 324-5
Dunn, S. 204, 212, 325,
    335
Dwinger, E. 275
Dworschak, C. 592
Dyrenkova, N. 474

E

Edelman, M. 307
Eden, C. 3
Edwards, H. 497
Edwards, L. 74
Edwards, M. 94
Egart, M. 672

Ellis, J. 468
Ellison, H. 541
Elsom, J. 673
Elvin, H. 95
Emiot, I. 372
Epstein, V. 129
Erickson, J. 12
Erlich, E. 154
Erman, A. 52
Eshtokin, A. 155
Ess, S. 693
Esztergar, M. 329
Etter, C. 435
Evseev, V. 613
Ewing, T. 169

F

Falkov 304
Fëdorov, A. 399
Fedoseev, G. 96
Fedotov, S. 153
Felinska, E. 498
Fenton, R. 609
Fernier, F. 516
Fic, V. 276
Fidlon, D. 129
Field, H. 326
Field, N. 576
Filicheva, T. 547
Fisher, C. 214
Fisher, H. 301
Fisher, R. 238-9
Fithian, F. 308
Fitzhugh, W. 327
Flaherty, D. 453
Fleischmann, M. 603
Fleming, P. 92, 277
Florovsky, A. 136
Florovsky, G. 457
Fodor's 119
Footman, D. 277-8
Forrer, L. 232
Forsyth, J. 13, 221, 674
Foster, J. 217
Foust, C. 240-1
Fowler, M. 523
Fox, H. 106
Frank, A. 535
Frank, J. 497
Fraser, J. 53
Frederiksen, O. 666

Freidberg, A. 186
French, R. 13, 15, 218
Friend, M. 368
Fries, H. 22
Friis, H. 166
Frolov, A. 656
Fry, D. 694
Fuks, L. 548
Fullard, J. 135
Furneaux, R. 152

G

Galazii, G. 187
Galton, D. 279
Gapanovich, J. 242
Garbutt, P. 649
Garnett, C. 497
Garrett, P. 458
Garrett, W. 364
Gay, J. 280
Gelman, H. 11
Georgi, J. 328
Gerrare, W. (*pseud.*) *see*
    Greener, W.
Gershevsky, N. 151
Gibson, J. 132, 211, 227,
    243-4, 542
Gilbert, M. 137
Gillespie, D. 668, 675, 691
Gilmour, J. 459
Gilpin, W. 638
Ginsburg, M. 528
Ginzburg, E. 514
Glad, J. 699
Gladkov, N. 176
Gmelin, J. 22
Goldenberg, L. 138
Goldman, B. 97
Goldman, M. 186
Goldstein, D. 497
Golokhvastov, A. 639
Goodlet, R. 78
Gorbachëv, M. 581
Gorban, N. 244
Gorbatov, A. 520
Gordon, J. 646
Gorishina, Z. 232
Gorshenin, K. 150
Gorshkov, G. 154
Goryushkin, L. 221
Gourevitch, A. 150

Gourko, D. 55
Gowing, L. 56
Graham, H. 229
Graham, S. 57
Granberg, A. 582
Grant, A. 678
Graves, W. 281
Grayson, B. 638
Great Britain, Admiralty,
    Naval Intelligence
    Section 5
Great Britain, Foreign
    Office, Historical
    Section 157, 167
Greener, W. 54
Greey, E. 474
Gregory, J. 127
Grierson, P. 713
Griffin, H. 98
Grim, J. 476
Grossman, L. 497
Grousset, R. 222
Grubbs, C. 283
Gryaznov, M. 196
Guillemard, F. 76
Gurev, I. 315
Gurkov, G. 613
Gurvich, I. 400
Gusev, O. 186
Gustafson, T. 11

H

Hadow, M. 521
Haigh, A. 275
Haimson, L. 573
Hajdú, P. 329
Halasz, G. 687
Hale, C. 458
Hall, H. 321
Hallowell, A. 474
Halstead, C. 141
Hamilton, F. 586
Hanna, G. 96
Hansen, J. 509
Hanson, G. 569
Hara, T. 381
Harari, M. 514, 519
Hardt, J. 614
Harper, A. 326
Harper, T. 676
Harper, W. 676

Harris, A. 97
Harris, C. 714
Harrison, J. 245, 347
Harrison, M. 100
Hartley, J. 450, 715
Harva, U. see
    Holmberg, U.
Haskett, J. 499
Hastings, J. 445
Hatt, G. 598
Hauner, M. 214
Hausladen, G. 128, 549,
    590
Hautzig, E. 522
Haviland, M. 48
Hawes, C. 58
Hayward, M. 514, 519
Heeper, W. 360
Hegelson, A. 590
Hellie, R. 488
Henderson, D. 217
Henderson, S. 690, 702
Heron, M. 83
Hilger, M. 352
Hill, S. 59
Hirszowicz, L. 374
Hodges, A. 282
Hogarth, J. 196
Holland, W. 161
Hollander, J. 188
Holmberg, U. 437
Holmes, K. 28
Holt, T. 142
Holubnychy, L. 359
Holzman, F. 309
Holzner, L. 583
Hookham, H. 640
Hooson, D. 584
Hopkins, D. 197
Hoppál, M. 475
Horak, S. 716
Horder, M. 44
Horecky, P. 717
Howard, B. 60, 494
Hughes, J. 310
Hulbert, H. 79
Hultén, E. 178
Humphrey, C. 13, 339,
    356, 394, 550, 599
Hunczak, T. 212
Hunt, F. 283
Hunter, H. 651
Huppert, H. 551
Hur, S. 381

Hüttl-Worth, G. 718

I

Ides, E. 23, 132
Idzelis, A. 614
Imbovits, E. 677
Ingham, A. 668
Isaacs, B. 698
Ischboldin al Bakri, B. 392
Isaev, M. 401
Ivanov, B. 449
Ivanov, V. 122, 678
Ivanova, E. 150
Ivanov-Mujiev 108

J

Jacobson, S. 420
Jacoby, S. 514
Jacque, V. 692
Jaensch, F. 28
Jakobson, R. 421, 718
Janik, M. 391
Jefferson, R. 61
Jensen, R. 615
Jochelson, W. 198, 330,
    382, 395-6, 422, 427,
    477
Jones, D. 719
Jones, H. 37
Jones, W. 99
Jordan, R. 170
Joyce, W. 601

K

Kalesnik, S. 129
Kantorovich, V. 168
Kaple, D. 650
Karasaka, G. 586
Kaser, M. 552, 622
Katkov, G. 252
Katser, J. 368
Kazmer, D. 254
Kecskés, B. 595
Kep, J. 279

190

Kelly, C. 669
Kelly, P. 125, 142, 146
Kennan, G. 62, 500
Kennan, G. F. 500
Kennard, H. 731
Kerner, R. 213, 720
Kieffer, R. 679
Kiksman, G. 566
Kindall, S. 283
King, H. 721
King, M. 696
Kingston, W. 705
Kirby, E. S. 12, 130, 159, 239, 311, 568
Kirchner, W. 22, 228
Kiš, D. 535
Kisaku, T. 30
Klements, D. 445
Klippenstein, L. 467
Knapp, J. 583
Knox, A. 284
Knox, T. 42
Knystautas, A. 179
Kobtzeff, O. 460
Kochan, L. 375
Koerber, L. von 523
Kojeuroff, G. 354
Kolarz, W. 331
Kolchak, A. 301
Kolz, A. 285
Komarov, B. 188
Komissarov, B. 349
Kontorovich, V. 651
Kontzevich, I. 461
Korolenko, V. 682
Koropecky, I. 585
Korotich, V. 694
Korsakov, G. 423
Kostikov, V. 155
Kotenko, N. 671
Kotkin, S. 553, 559
Kotzebue, A. von 24
Kovalenko, S. 680
Kovalëv, R. 150
Krader, L. 355, 478
Krasheninnikov, S. 164
Kraus, D. 194
Kravchinskii-Stepnyak, S. 501
Kreicbergs, V. 532
Kreinovich, E. 397
Krishkin, V. 87
Kristof, L. 214
Krivoshchekov, V. 386

Križanić, J. 246
Kroeger, C. 216
Kröger, T. 502
Kropotkin, L. 63, 139, 641
Krueger, J. 29, 407, 423, 722
Krypton, C. 664-5
Kuehn, T. 685
Kukol-Yasnopolsky, L. 637
Kuoijok, K. 332
Kupreyanova, N. 681
Kyler, R. 323

L

Lamplugh, B. 101
Landor, A. 348
Lansdell, H. 64
Lantz, K. 683
Lantzeff, G. 223, 247-8
Latham, R. 333
Latimer, R. 64
Lattimore, O. 113, 311, 385, 517
Laufer, B. 334
Laughlin, W. 326
Laulan, Y. 616
Lauterbach, R. 113
Law, A. 704
Lebed, A. 666
Ledward, R. 141
Ledyard, J. 25
Lee, P. 377
Lehrman, E. 438
Leighton, L. 682
Lengyel, E. 6
Lensen, G. 215
Leonov, V. 686
Leskov, N. 683
Lesseps, J. de 26
Lethbridge, A. 57
Letiche, J. 246
Levenstern, E. 349
Levin, M. 195, 335, 369
Levin, N. 374
Levine, I. 513
Lewis, E. 402
Lewis, R. 554
Lewitter, L. 32
Libby, D. 359
Lied, J. 65
Liely, H. 600

Linge, G. 586
Lipper, E. 524
Littlepage, J. 312
Lobanov-Rostovsky, A. 216
London, E. 505
Long, J. 284
Longworth, P. 362
Lonsdale, R. 255
Lopatin, I. 408, 479
Lorimer, F. 554
Löve, D. 175
Luckett, R. 299
Ludolf, H. 20
Ludwick, P. 618
Lydolph, P. 127, 143
Lyons, E. 283

M

MacAndrew, A. 497
McCullah, F. 286
MacCulloch, J. 437
MacDonald, H. 633
Macdonald, R. 576
McGraw, P. 22
Mackler, M. 497
MacLaren, R. 287
McNeal, R. 362
Magarshak, D. 43
Magnarella, P. 383
Majewicz, A. 13, 336, 390, 410-11, 424
Majewicz, E. 410-11, 425
Malashenko, V. 652
Mandel, W. 332
Manning, E. 686
Maplesden, F. 609
Maraffa, T. 633
Marchuk, G. 587
Markhinin, E. 153
Markov, G. 684-6, 703
Markovits, R. 687
Marks, D. 589
Marsden, K. 462
Marsh, C. 102
Marshall, J. 637
Marshall, Jr, R. 446
Martin, J. 224
Martynov, A. I. 199
Martynov, A. V. 190
Masakazu, Y. 208

191

Massey, R. 267
Massey-Stewart, J. 15, 154, 190, 512
Masterson, J. 27
Mathieson, R. 555
Matrusov, N. 617
Matthews, W. 403
Maurin, V. 203
Mawdsley, E. 288
Mazour, A. 504
Meakin, A. 54
Medov, P. 401
Medow, I. 111
Meisak, N. 4, 120
Menges, K. 409
Merck, C. 28
Meyerhoff, A. 147
Michael, H. 200-2, 204, 225, 480
Michael, M. 31
Michie, A. 56
Micklin, P. 146
Mihalisko, K. 335
Mikhailov, T. 481
Mikhailovskii, V. 482
Mikkelson, G. 692
Mildmay, E. 492
Milescu see Spathary, N.
Miller, M. 63
Minenko, N. 489
Minorsky, T. 229
Mitchell, E. 112
Mitchell, K. 161
Mochanov, Y. 200
Moessner, V. 19
Mohrenschildt, D. von 574
Moore, F. 102
Mora, S. 525
Morley, J. 289
Morray, J. 309
Morrison, J. 145
Morrow, I. 275
Moszyńska, W. 194
Mote, V. 11, 125, 256, 583, 588, 590, 651, 653-5, 658
Mowat, F. 103
Muller, A. 692
Müller, G. 250
Munich, Institute for the Study of the USSR 666
Muratov, P. 703
Murby, R. 290

Myckoff, W. 128

N

Nadarov, I. 257
Nagishkin, D. 438
Nalivkin, D. 148
Nansen, F. 66
NATO see North Atlantic Treaty Organization
Nazarov, A. 174
Nekrich, A. 306
Nerhood, H. 723
Newby, E. 104, 462
Nicolaievsky, B. 517
Nielsen, P. 404
Nikiforoff, C. 145
Nikolaev, S. 163
Noble, A. 67
Nork, K. 526
Norman, B. 518
Norman, H. 68
North, R. 12-13, 125, 590, 629, 667, 725
North Atlantic Treaty Organization, Economics Directorate 588, 616
Norton, H. 160
Novik, E. 483
Novitskii, V. 291
Novomeysky, M. 105
Nuttonson, M. 144

O

Odulok, T. 688
Ognëv, S. 180
Ohnuki-Tierney, E. 351
Oinas, F. 429
Ojala, C. 556
Okladnikov, A. 191, 199, 203-4, 225-6
Olcott, M. 146
Oliver, P. 18
Omelchuk, A. 401
Orlov, B. 589
Osers, E. 106
Osipov, V. 613, 618
Ossendowski, F. 69, 292
Otter-Barry, R. 70

Ovchinnikov, A. 301

P

Paderin, G. 168
Palen, L. 69
Pallas, P. 27, 250
Pallot, J. 617
Papmehl, K. 228
Parker, R. 685
Parkin, D. 601
Partanen, J. 481
Parvilahti, U. 527
Pavlenko, V. 129
Pavlov, P. 239
Peacock, N. 731
Pereira, N. 293, 570
Perelman, W. 108
Perevedentsev, V. 557
Permanent International Committee of Linguists 724
Perry-Ayscough, H. 70
Peshchurov, M. 259
Petrov, V. 528
Pfizenmayer, E. 181
Philips, L. 185
Phillips, E. 205
Phillips, G. 356
Pierce, R. 28, 248
Pieroth, D. 287
Piip, B. 154
Pika, A. 316
Piłsudski, B. 336, 391, 410-11, 424-5, 439-40
Pinkus, B. 373
Piotrowski, R. 505
Pokshishevskii, V. 129, 543
Polansky, P. 11, 571, 726
Polevoi, B. 132
Pollock, J. 463
Polovtsoff, A. 55
Popov, A. 388
Poppe, K. 412
Poppe, N. 252, 406, 413, 449
Porter, K. 694
Portisch, H. 106
Potapov, L. 335
Povolaev, V. 656
Powers, W. 206
Preiss, A. 529

Price, H. 294
Price, J. 71
Price, M. 72
Prociuk, S. 557
Prokhorov, B. 316, 386
Pryde, P. 182, 187, 583, 590

Q

Quimby, G. 198

R

Rachlin, I. 530
Rachlin, R. 530
Radloff, F. 441
Raeff, M. 258
Ragozin, L. 203
Raikhman, E. 161, 183
Raksha, I. 690
Randall, F. 506
Rasputin, V. 186, 675, 681, 691-2, 703
Rast, N. 148
Ratnieks, H. 125, 657
Ratushinskaya, I. 43
Ravenstein, E. 259
Rawicz, S. 107
Ray, D. 365
Rayner, S. 94, 364
Reichman, H. 260
Remezov, S. 132, 134, 140
Render, W. 24
Rerikh, N. see Roerich, N.
Resnick, A. 8
Rich, E. 671
Ridley, J. 73
Riggan, W. 679
Ristenen, E. 388
Rittman, M. 397
Robinson, B. 619
Robinson, G. 544
Robinson, P. 630
Rodgers, A. 590
Rodgers, G. 124
Rodney, W. 290
Roerich, N. 442
Rondière, P. 6
Ronen, O. 173
Rookwood, A. 159

Rookwood, R. 159
Rosenberg, W. 295
Rosenfeld, M. 372
Rot, S. 695
Rottenberg, D. 693
Rowell, M. 172
Rowland, R. 554
Rowley, G. 124
Rozwadowski, J. 425
Rudenko, S. 207
Ruhlen, M. 405
Rumer, B. 625
Rumyantsev, B. 337
Russell, J. 693
Russia, Committee of Ministers 636
Russian–American Chamber of Commerce 731
Ryazanovskii, V. 337
Rytkheu, Y. 338, 693-4
Rywkin, M. 248
Ryzhkov, A. 108

S

Safronov, S. 490
Sagers, M. 633
St. George, G. 7
St. John, J. 659
Sallnow, J. 13, 156, 558
Sample, L. 388
Sanarov, V. 370
Sanghi, V. 695
Sano, C. 352
Santalov, A. 731
Sartakov, S. 696, 703
Sarychev, G. 28
Sauer, M. 28
Saul, N. 261
Saunders, G. 306
Saunders, M. 275
Savoskul, S. 13, 339, 442
Schiffer, J. 591
Schneierson, V. 90
Schottenstein, I. 251
Schroeder, G. 585
Schütt, P. 106
Schuttz, A. 399
Schwarz, S. 375
Scott, J. C. 559
Scott, J. S 179

Seaton, A. 362
Seebohm, H. 184
Segal, L. 731
Sei, W. 340
Sëmushkin, T. 697-8
Semyonov, Y. 217
Serebrennikov, I. 572
Sergeev, M. 121, 186
Servadio, G. 104
Sevostyanov, V. 578
Shabad, T. 12-13, 127, 583, 612, 615, 626, 645, 658
Shafranovskaya, T. 349
Shalamov, V. 699
Shaw, D. 12
Shaw, K. 560
Shcherbovich, S. 345
Sheepshanks, J. 41
Shestalov, Y. 689, 703
Shifrin, A. 531
Shimkin, D. 341, 378, 620
Shimkin, E. 341
Shinkarëv, L. 8
Shirokogorov, S. 342-3, 484
Shirokov, Y. 661
Shklovskii, I. 74
Shklovskii, Z. 74
Shoemaker, M. 38
Shoolbraid, G. 443
Shotskii, V. 595
Shneidman, N. 700
Shternberg, L. 350
Shukshin, V. 701, 703
Shundik, N. 702
Siikala, A. 485
Šilde, A. 532
Simchenko, Y. 386
Simmons, E. 43
Simon, S. 475
Simpson, C. 414
Simpson, G. 47
Simpson, J. 75
Simpson, M. 191
Singleton, F. 188
Sinor, D. 226, 415, 417, 441
Skrynnikov, R. 229
Skvirskii, D. 96
Slavin, S. 9, 631
Slezkine, Y. 316
Slipchenko, W. 131, 592
Smele, J. 272, 285
Smirnoff, E. 464

Smirnov, I. 563
Smirnov, M. 296
Smirnov, V. 149
Smith, C. 297
Smith, D. 567
Smith, E. 509
Smith, G. 356
Smolyanitskii, S. 684
Snow, R. 298
Soboleva, L. 561
Sochurek, H. 10
Sokolov, A. 150
Solomon, M. 533
Solzhenitsyn, A. 534
Soudakoff, S. 429
Sosinskii, S. 613
Soule, M. 593
Souza, P. de 125, 562, 624
Sovkina, R. 154
Spalding, Captain 80
Sparks, J. 25
Sparvenfeldt, J. 134
Spasskii, I. 232
Spathary, N. 134
Spektor, I. 578
Stadling, J. 76
Staf, K. 108
Stajner, K. 535
Stallybrass, E. 459
Stamoolis, J. 465
Stanford, D. 109
Stanislawski, M. 372
Starr, S. 211
Stebelsky, I. 218, 544
Stebnitskii, S. 423
Steeves, P. 447
Steiger, A. 2, 113
Stein, H. 532
Stejneger, L. 178
Stephan, J. 12, 219, 264, 381
Stevenson, J. 17
Stevenson, P. 514
Stewart, G. 299
Strahlenberg, P. von 29
Strauss, R. 122
Strelyanyi, A. 596
Strod, I. 300
Stroganov, S. 180
Struve, N. 46
Suh, D. 381
Suklova, M. 507
Sullivan, J. 262, 508
Summer, S. 344

Sumner, B. 216, 683
Suslov, S. 151
Sutherland, C. 504
Sutton, F. 110
Sverdrup, H. 361
Sverdrup, M. 361
Swan, Mrs 459
Swayne, H. 70
Swearingen, R. 11
Switzer, G. 618
Symmons-Symonolewicz,
    K. 314
Szyrma, L. 498

T

Taaffe, R. 593
Taft, M. 71
Taksami, C. 319, 400
Talmyi, V. 613, 684
Tate, H. 690
Taylor, P. 260
Tchernavin, T. 491
Terpak, L. 43
Terpak, M. 43
Terry, S. 535
Thiel, E. 159
Thomas, A. 132, 136
Thomas, B. 123
Thompson, A. 727
Thompson, B. 550
Thompson, M. 207
Thompstone, S. 263
Thornton 132
Tierney, E. see Ohnuki-
    Tierney, E.
Titelbaum, O. 145
Tkachëv, V. 163
Toews, J. 467
Tolmachëv, A. 185
Tolmachoff, I. 181
Tomilin, A. 180
Tomilov, N. 320, 393
Tomkeieff, S. 148
Tompkins, S. 287
Tooke, W. 328
Toru, A. 336
Travis, F. 500
Treadgold, D. 216, 545
Tripolskii, L. 111
Trofimov, S. 150
Trotsky, L. 509

Tseitlin, E. 678
Tsymek, A. 606
Tulynina, L. 154
Tupper, H. 644
Turner, S. 77
Tyurin, I. 150

U

Ukhtomskii, E. 78
United States, Central
    Intelligence Agency
    621
United States, Department
    of Commerce 663
United States, Department
    of Defense 712
United States, War
    Department 157
Urness, C. 27
Uvachan, V. 345

V

Vaillant, R. 735
Vainshtein, S. 394
Vakhnenko, R. 662
Vale, M. 188
Vampilov, A. 703-4
Vanderlip, W. 79
Varneck, E. 301, 346
Vasilevich, G. 444
Vasilevskii, R. 199, 202
Vaughan, T. 236, 734
Vdovin, I. 345
Venyukov, M. 80
Vereshchagin, N. 177
Verne, J. 705
Vevier, C. 44
Vining, L. 286
Vinogradoff, E. 573
Vinogradov, V. 16
Vins, G. 468
Visser, J. de 10
Vitebsky, P. 366, 601, 610
Vlasto, A. 32
Vlodavetz, V. 154
Vorobëv, V. 189-90, 562
Voronov, V. 563
Voropai, J. 639
Vucinich, A. 568

Vucinich, W. 212
Vvedenskii, B. 161, 183

### W

Waal, A. de 537
Wada, H. 381
Wada, S. 340
Walford, N. 222
Walker, M. 119
Wallace, A. 359
Wallace, H. 113, 517
Ward, J. 302
Wardrop, O. 482
Warren, K. 624
Wasilewska, E. 536
Waters, E. 527
Watrous, S. 25, 575
Waxell, S. 31
Weille, B. 530
Wein, N. 564, 597
Wells, W. 89
Wenyon, C. 81
Westgarth, J. 313
Westoll, T. 148
Weston, R. 622
Westwood, J. 632
Wheatcroft, S. 517
Whitaker, I. 199, 602

Whittingham, B. 264
Whyte, F. 84
Whyte, M. 685
Wieczynski, J. 220, 729
Wigmans, J. 537
Wild, M. 275
Wileman, D. 229
Wilgress, L. 114
Willetts, H. 534
Williams, D. 469
Williams, J. 151
Williams, P. 532
Wilson, D. 13, 125, 623
Wilson, H. 112
Wilson, L. 107
Winchell, M. 692
Windt, H. de 50, 358, 638
Winius, A. 133
Winston, C. 524
Winston, R. 524
Witney, T. 534
Wixman, R. 314
Woehrlin, W. 506
Wolfson, Z. 125
Wood, A. 12-13, 15, 221,
    510-12, 601, 734
Wood, G. 169
Wood, J. 115, 160
Woodcock, G. 63, 470
Woodroffe, C. 80
Worth, D. 426-7

Wright, A. 615
Wright, G. 14
Wright, R. 82
Wyman, W. 216

### Y

Yakovlev, B. 666
Yakovlev, N. 352
Yamaha, M. 352
Yanovskii, N. 4
Yarmolinsky, A. 43, 428
Yarros, G. 507
Yoshizaki, M. 208
Yurlova, M. 116

### Z

Zalygin, S. 703
Zaslavskaya, T. 13
Zdziarski, A. 637
Zenzinov, V. 513
Zhelezko, S. 565
Zhigunov, P. 603
Zhuravlëv, V. 661
Zlobin, A. 108
Zubkov, P. 169
ZumBrunnen, C. 590

# Index of Titles

## A

Aboriginal Siberia: a study
  in social anthropology
  48, 321
Account of a geographical
  and astronomical
  expedition to the
  northern parts of
  Russia 28
Account of a voyage of
  discovery to the north-
  east of Siberia, the
  frozen ocean and the
  north-east sea 28
Account of the Russian
  discoveries between
  Asia and America 234
Across Siberia in the
  dragon year of 1796 30
Across Siberia on the great
  post road 81
Adventurous journey
  (Russia–Siberia–
  China) 112
Aeroflot: Soviet air
  transport since 1923
  633
Afanasii Prokofevich
  Shchapov (1830-1876)
  historian and social
  thinker 569
After wild sheep in the
  Altai and Mongolia 49
Agricultural climatology of
  Siberia: natural belts
  and agro-climatic
  analogues in north
  America 144
Agrochemistry of the soils
  of the USSR 150
Agro-industrial complexes
  and types of
  agriculture in eastern
  Siberia 595
Ainu–English index
  dictionary to B.
  Piłsudski's
  'Materials for the study

of the Ainu language
  and folklore' of 1912
  425
Ainu folklore: traditions
  and culture of the
  vanishing aborigines of
  Japan 435
Ainu of the northwest coast
  of southern Sakhalin
  351
Ainu prayer texts 424
Alitet goes to the hills 698
All the Russias 68
Alone with the hairy Ainu
  348
Altai–Himalaya 442
American expedition 31
American soldiers in
  Siberia 283
America's Siberian
  adventure 281
Among prisoners of war in
  Russia and Siberia 40
Among the Mongols 459
Among the Samoyed in
  Siberia 323
Among the tundra people
  361
Anarchist prince 63
Ancient art of the Amur
  region 191
Ancient population of
  Siberia and its culture
  203
Annotated bibliography on
  Soviet northern
  transport, 1975-1986
  725
Archaeological
  investigations in
  Kamchatka 198
Archaeology and
  geomorphology of
  northern Asia 201
Arctic and subarctic regions
  721
Arctic bibliography 712
Arctic frontier 576
Argonauts of Siberia: the
  diary of a prospector
  99

Armoured train 14-69: a
  play in eight scenes 678
Army behind barbed wire:
  a Siberian diary 275
As far as my feet will carry
  me 107
Asiatic Russia 14
Aspects of Church history
  457
Aspects of religion in the
  Soviet Union, 1917-
  1967 446
Atlas of Siberia. Facsimile
  edition 140

## B

Baedeker's Russia, 1914
  117
Baikal 186
Baikal meridian 107
BAM: road to new
  possibilities 646
Bear worshippers of Yezo
  and the island of
  Karafuto (Saghalien)
  474
Beasts, men and gods 292
Behind the Urals: an
  American workman in
  Russia's city of steel
  559
Beria's gardens: ten years'
  captivity in Russia and
  Siberia 527
Bering land bridge 197
Best of Ogonyok: the new
  journalism of glasnost
  694
Between White and Red
  275
Beyond the Ural
  mountains: the
  adventures of a
  Siberian hunter 83
Bibliography of Asian
  studies 711
Big red train ride 104
Biographical memorial of

General Daniel
    Butterfield 635
Birds of Siberia 184
Birds of the Soviet Union
    176
Birobidzhan affair: a
    Yiddish writer in
    Siberia 372
Boche and Bolshevik 294
Bolsheviks and the Czech
    legion 276
Bolsheviks discover Siberia
    304
Bolsheviks in Siberia, 1917-
    1918 298
Books in English on the
    Soviet Union, 1917-73
    719
Books on Soviet Russia,
    1917-1942 713
Brief remarks on the
    structure of the
    Nymlyan (Koryak)
    language and its
    dialects 423
Britmis: a great adventure
    of the war 282
Bukharans in trade and
    diplomacy, 1558-1702
    233
Buriat grammar 413
Buriat reader 406


C

Cambridge encyclopaedia
    of language 405
Cambridge history of early
    inner Asia 226
Canadians in Russia, 1918-
    1919 287
Canadian's road to Russia
    287
Carnivorous mammals of
    Siberia 180
Catalogue of the active
    volcanoes of
    Kamchatka and the
    continental parts of
    Asia 154
Chekhov: a biography 43
Chekhov: a life 43

Chernyshevskii the
    journalist 506
Children of the Soviet
    Arctic 697
Christians from Siberia 463
Chukchee mythology 473
Church, nation and state in
    Russia and Ukraine
    455
Circumpolar north: a
    political and economic
    geography 124
Civil rights in Imperial
    Russia 512
Civil war in Russia 277
Civil war in the taiga 300
Climates of the Soviet
    Union 143
Climates of the USSR 141
Collected works of
    Bronisław
    Piłsudski 336
Commercial Russia 118,
    266
Conquest of Siberia 217
Conquest of Siberia and the
    history of the
    transactions, wars,
    commerce, etc. carried
    on between Russia and
    China 250
Conservation in the Soviet
    Union 187
Cosmopolitan railway,
    compacting and fusing
    together all the world's
    continents 638
Cossack girl 116
Cossacks 362
Count Benyowsky, or the
    conspiracy of
    Kamtschatka 24
Count N. N. Muraviev-
    Amursky 262
Coup d'état of Admiral
    Kolchak 268
Crossroads of continents:
    cultures of Siberia and
    Alaska 327
Cult of the dead among the
    natives of the Amur
    basin 479
Current problems in the
    industrialization of
    Siberia 625

Customary laws of the
    nomadic tribes of
    Siberia 337
Czars, Soviets and
    Mennonites 467


D

Dana Wilgress memoirs
    114
Dawn in Siberia: the
    Mongols of Lake
    Baikal 356
Death can wait 96
Decembrists in Siberian
    exile 499
Decorative art of the Amur
    tribes 334
Demand for energy in the
    Soviet Union 623
Dersu the trapper 33
Dersu Uzala 33
Destruction of nature in the
    Soviet Union 188
Development of industry
    and transport in the
    north of the USSR 631
Development of Siberia:
    people and resources
    13, 221, 454
Dictionary of western
    Kamchadal 426
Disappearing Russian
    forest: a dilemma in
    Soviet resource
    management 605
Dr. Baedeker and his
    apostolic work in
    Russia 64
Dostoevsky: a biography
    497
Dostoevsky: the years of
    ordeal 497
Doukhobors 470
Duck hunting 704
Dzieje Polaków na Syberi
    391


E

Eastern Orthodox mission
    theology today 465

Eastern Siberia 157
Eastern USSR: forest
    resources and forest
    exports to Japan 609
Eastern vistas 97
Eastwards to empire:
    exploration and
    conquest on the
    Russian open frontier
    to 1750 248
Economic development of
    the Soviet Far East 161
Economics of Soviet
    regions 585
Eleven years in Soviet
    prison camps 524
Elsa Brändström, der
    Engel von Sibirien 40
Empire of knowledge: the
    Academy of Sciences
    of the USSR 568
Empire of the steppes 222
Encyclopaedia of religion
    and ethics 445
Endless steppe 522
Environmental misuse in
    the Soviet Union 188
Essays in political
    geography 214
Essays on Tatar history 392
Ethnic origins of the
    peoples of northeast
    Asia 195
Exiled to Siberia 529
Explorations of
    Kamchatka, north
    Pacific scimitar 164
Exploitation of Siberia's
    natural resources 616


F

Faith on trial in Russia 456
Far Eastern Republic: its
    natural resources,
    trade and industries
    158
Far Eastern Republic of
    Siberia 160
Farewell to Matyora 691
Fate of Admiral Kolchak
    277

Feeding the Russian fur
    trade 542
Ferry: sketches of the
    struggle for socialism
    in the Altaian
    mountains 672
Fire came by: the riddle of
    the great Siberian
    explosion 152
First Americans: origins,
    affinities, adaptations
    326
First-fruits of a mission to
    Siberia 459
First guidebook to prisons
    and concentration
    camps of the Soviet
    Union 531
Five thousand miles in a
    sledge 56
Flora of Kamchatka and
    the adjacent islands
    178
Fodor's 91: Soviet Union
    119
Folktales of the Amur:
    stories from the
    Russian Far East 438
Forced labor in the Soviet
    Union 517
Foreign missions of the
    Russian Orthodox
    Church 452
Forest economy in the
    USSR 604
Forgotten journey 92
Forgotten village: four
    years in Siberia 502
Founding of the Russian
    empire in Asia and
    America 245
Four thousand miles across
    Siberia 81
Freshwater fishes of the
    USSR and adjacent
    countries 173
From Paris to New York
    by land 638
From Pekin to Calais by
    land 50
From president to prison 69
From Siberia to Kuibyshev:
    reflections on Russia,
    1919-43 114

From the Arctic Ocean to
    the Yellow Sea 71
From the Volga to the
    Yukon: the story of the
    Russian march to
    Alaska and California
    217
Frontier in perspective 216
Frozen Asia: a sketch of
    modern Siberia 3
Frozen tombs of Siberia
    207
Frozen tombs: the culture
    and art of the ancient
    tribes of Siberia 207


G

Gateway to Siberian
    resources: the BAM
    658
Genesis of the soils of
    western Siberia 150
Geography of the Soviet
    Union 127
Geography of the Soviet
    Union: physical
    background,
    population, economy
    129
Geography of the USSR
    127
Geography of the USSR: a
    regional survey 127
Geology of the USSR 148
Geology of the USSR: a
    short outline 148
George Kennan and
    Russia, 1865-1905 500
G.-F. Müller and Siberia,
    1733-43 19
G.-F. Müller and the
    Imperial Russian
    Academy 19
G.-F. Müller and the
    Russian Academy of
    sciences contingent in
    the second Kamchatka
    expedition 19
Glimpses of Siberia 4
Gold: a world survey 622
Gold Khan 436

*Gorski viyenats: a garland of essays offered to Professor Elizabeth Mary Hill* 32
*Grammatical sketch of Yupik Eskimo* 420
*Great Baikal–Amur railway* 652
*Great Siberian migration: government and peasant in resettlement* 545
*Great Siberian Railway* 636
*Great Siberian Railway from St. Petersburg to Pekin* 38
*Great Soviet encyclopaedia* 728
*Great Tolbachik Fissure eruption: geological and geophysical data* 153
*Greater Russia* 54
*Guide to documents and mss. in the United Kingdom relating to Russia and the Soviet Union* 715
*Guide to geographical bibliographies and reference works in Russian or on the Soviet Union* 714
*Guide to the Great Siberian Railway* 637
*Guide to the study of the Soviet nationalities* 716
*Guide to the world's languages* 405
*Gulag archipelago, 1918-1956: an experiment in literary analysis* 535

## H

*Handbook of Siberia and Arctic Russia* 5
*Held by the Bolsheviks: the diary of a British officer in Russia* 286
*Hell in Siberia* 526
*Historico-geographical description of the north and eastern parts of Europe and Asia* 29
*History of Russian railways* 632
*History of Siberia from Russian conquest to revolution* 221, 540
*Horse with the pink mane and other stories* 668
*Horseman of the steppes* 362
*House of the dead, or prison life in Siberia* 497
*How Russia prepared: USSR beyond the Urals* 307
*How we lost the Civil War: bibliography of Russian emigre memoirs on the Russian Revolution, 1917-1921* 708

## I

*Illness and healing among the Sakhalin Ainu: a symbolic interpretation* 351
*In Bolshevik Siberia, the land of ice and exile* 89
*Incredible mile: Siberia, Mongolia, Uzbekistan* 95
*Incredible Siberia* 115
*Indigenous peoples of the Soviet north* 316
*In far north-east Siberia* 74
*In search of a Siberian klondike* 79
*In search of Soviet gold* 312
*In the uttermost east* 58
*Into the whirlwind* 519
*Introduction to Altaic linguistics* 412
*Innocent of Moscow: the apostle of Kamchatka and Alaska* 458
*Involuntary journey to Siberia* 514

*Irkutsk: a guide* 121
*I saw Siberia* 106
*I want to live* 701
*Islamic peoples of the Soviet Union* 314
*Island: a journey to Sakhalin* 43
*It happens in Russia: seven years' forced labour in the Siberian gold field* 528

## J

*Japan moves north: the inside story of the struggle for Siberia* 271
*Japanese intervention in the Russian Far East* 271
*Jewish autonomous region: photo album* 155
*Jews in the Soviet Union* 375
*Jews in the Soviet Union since 1917* 375
*Jews in the Soviet Union since 1917: paradox of survival* 374
*Jews of the Soviet Union: the history of a national minority* 373
*John F. Stevens: American assistance to Russian and Siberian railroads* 659
*John Ledyard's journey through Russia and Siberia, 1787-1788* 25
*Journal of the embassy from their majesties John and Peter Alexievits, emperors of Muscovy, &c, over land into China* 20
*Journey from St. Petersburg to Pekin, 1719-22, by John Bell of Antermony* 17
*Journey in southern Siberia: the Mongols, their religion and myths* 353

200

*Journey to Siberia* 106

### K

*Kamchadal culture and its relationships in the old and new worlds* 371
*Kamchadal texts collected by W. Jochelson* 427
*Karl Marx collective: economy, society and religion in a Siberian collective farm* 550
*Ket: a contribution to the ethnography of a central Siberian tribe* 377
*King stork and king log: at the dawn of a new reign. A study of modern Russia* 501
*Kolchak and Siberia: documents and studies, 1919-1926* 272
*Kolyma* 113
*Kolyma: gold and forced labor in the USSR* 525
*Kolyma tales* 699
*Kolyma: the arctic death camps* 517, 528
*Koreans in the Soviet Union* 381
*Kropotkin* 63
*Kuril islands: Russo-Japanese frontier in the Pacific* 219

### L

*Lake Baikal, Baikal nature reserve areas* 186
*Land beyond the mountains: Siberia and its people today* 8
*Land commune and peasant community in Russia: communal forms in Imperial and early Soviet society* 512
*Languages of the Soviet Union* 398

*Languages of the USSR* 403
*Left behind: fourteen months in Siberia during the Revolution* 269
*Lenin in Siberia: records, documents and recollections* 503
*Letters home from the Far East and Russia, 1931* 92
*Letters of Anton Chekhov* 43
*Liberals in the Russian Revolution* 295
*Life and labors of the schema monk Zosima* 461
*Life of a Russian exile: the remarkable experiences of a young girl* 507
*Life with trans-Siberian savages* 60
*Life written by himself. With the study of V. V. Vinogradov* 16
*Linguistic bibliography for the year* 724
*Living tundra* 175
*Long walk* 107
*Lost legion: a Czech epic* 265

### M

*Magadan* 533
*Magnetic mountain: city building and city life in the Soviet Union in the 1930s: a study of Magnitogorsk* 553
*Makar's dream and other stories* 682
*Mammals of eastern Europe and northern Asia* 180
*Mammoth and mammoth hunting in north-east Siberia* 177
*Man and cultures* 359

*Man and mystery in Asia* 69
*Mangazeya* 238
*March of the 50,000* 265
*Material on the Orochee language, the Gold (Nanai) language and the Olchi (Nani) language* 408
*Materials for the study of the Ainu language and folklore* 425
*Materials for the study of the Olcha (Ulča/Mangun/Năni) language and folklore* 411
*Materials for the study of the Orok (Uilta) language and folklore* 410
*Materialy k ukazatelyu literatury o Sibiri* 710
*Meaning of my life: perestroika* 581
*Medicinal plants in Russia in the eighteenth and early nineteenth centuries* 172
*Memoir of Mrs. Stallybrass* 459
*Memoirs and travels of Mauritius Augustus count de Benyowsky in Siberia, Kamchatka, the Liukiu islands and Formosa* 18
*Memoirs of a revolutionary* 493
*Memoirs of a revolutionist* 63
*Memories of travel* 77
*Men of Siberia: sketch book from the Kuzbas* 551
*Mennonite encyclopaedia* 467
*Methodological study of the production of primary gold by the Soviet Union* 622
*Michael Bakunin* 495
*Michael Speransky: statesman of imperial Russia* 258

*Michael Strogoff: the courier of the Czar* 705

*Military monograph on Siberia* 157

*Minerals: a key to Soviet power* 620

*Modern encyclopaedia of religions in Russia and the Soviet Union* 447

*Modern encyclopaedia of Russian and Soviet history* 729

*Most remarkable year in the life of Augustus von Kotzebue, containing an account of his exile into Siberia* 24

*Mountain trails* 96

*Mutilingualism in the Soviet Union* 402

*Muscovite and mandarin: Russia's trade with China and its setting, 1727-1805* 240

*My childhood in Siberia* 491

*My escape from Siberia* 505

*My exile to Siberia and escape* 493

*My flight from Siberia* 509

*My life: an attempt at an autobiography* 509

*My life in Mongolia and Siberia* 41

*My mission to Siberia: a vindication* 462

*My Siberian life* 105

*My Siberian year* 48

*Mythology of all races* 437


N

*Narrative of a journey round the world during the years 1841 and 1842* 47

*Narrative of a pedestrian journey through Russia and Siberian Tartary* 44

*Nation killers* 306

*National languages in the USSR: problems and solutions* 401

*Nationalities question in the Soviet Union* 356

*Nationality and population change in Russia and the USSR* 554

*Native races of the Russian Empire* 333

*Natural history of the USSR* 179

*Natural regions of the USSR* 145

*Naturalist in Russia: letters from Peter Simon Pallas to Thomas Pennant* 27

*Nature and natural resources of the Soviet Far East* 183

*New Encyclopaedia Britannica* 730

*New Russia: from the White Sea to the Siberian steppe* 57

*New Siberia* 10

*New Siberia, being an account of a visit to the penal island of Sakhalin* 50

*New Soviet heartland?* 584

*New stage in the development of the Soviet Far East* 581

*New trade route to connect Europe with western Siberia and China* 639

*Nganasan: material culture of the Tavgi Samoyeds* 388

*N. G. Chernyshevskii* 506

*Nomads of southern Siberia: the pastoral economies of Tuva* 394

*Non-Slavic peoples of the Soviet Union* 314

*Northeast Asia: a selected bibliography* 720

*Northeast Asia in prehistory* 193

*Northern thebaid: monastic saints of the Russian north* 461

*Northern sea route and the economy of the Soviet north* 664

*Northern sea route: its place in Russian economic history before 1917* 665

*Notes of a Russian revolutionary* 514

*Notes on the late expedition against the Russian settlements in eastern Siberia* 264

*Novosibirsk* 120


O

*Obi railway* 639

*Oil and gas potential of the Soviet Far East* 147

*Old Memyl laughs last: short stories* 693

*On sledge and horseback to outcast Siberian lepers* 462

*One-arm Sutton* 110

*One chilly Siberian morning* 86

*Oral epic of Siberia and central Asia* 443

*Ore deposits of the USSR* 149

*Oriental and western Siberia: a narrative of seven years' explorations* 35

*Overland through Asia* 42

*Overland to China* 46


P

*Paleosiberian peoples and languages: a bibliographical guide* 718

*Paris to New York overland* 50

*Partizanskie rasskazy* 678

*Paying guest in Siberia* 521

*Peasant colonisation of Siberia* 541

People and land of
Birobidzhan 155
People I know in
Birobidzhan 155
Peoples of asiatic Russia
330
Peoples of Siberia 335
Peoples of the north: their
arts and handicrafts
689
Peoples of the Soviet Far
East 331
Peoples of the Soviet north
345
Peoples of the Soviet north
and their road to
socialism 345
Peoples of the USSR: an
ethnographic
handbook 314
Peoples regenerated 698
Physical geography of
Asiatic Russia 151
Politics of rural Russia 573
Popular beliefs and
folklore tradition in
Siberia 434
Population of the Soviet
Union: history and
prospects 554
Population redistribution in
the USSR 554
Prehistory of western
Siberia 194
Princess of Siberia: the
story of Maria
Volkonsky and the
Decembrist exiles 504
Prison life in Siberia 497
Prisoner of the Reds: the
story of a British
officer captured in
Siberia 286
Prisoners of Russia: a
personal study of
convict life in Sakhalin
and Siberia 494
Problems of the Pacific,
1936 161
Proceedings of the
Permanent
International Altaistic
Conference 415
Profits of slavery: Baltic

forced laborers and
deportees under Stalin
and Khrushchev 532
Project Kuzbas: American
workers in Siberia,
1921-1926 309
Prospector in Siberia 65
Psychomental complex of
the Tungus 343
Punished peoples: the
deportation and fate of
Soviet minorities at the
end of the Second
World War 306

Q

Queer fish 668

R

Real Siberia 53
Rebel on the bridge: a life
of the Decembrist
Baron Andrey Rozen
492
Recollections of Siberia in
the years 1840 and
1841 47
Recollections of the Tartar
steppes and their
inhabitants 34
Red bear or yellow dragon
100
Red road through Asia: a
journey by the Arctic
Ocean to Siberia,
Central Asia and
America 97
Rediscovered country 168
Reference and guide book
for the Irtysh and
lower Ob 663
Regional developments in
the USSR: trends and
prospects 588
Regional studies for
planning and
projecting: the Siberian
experience 577

Reindeer husbandry 603
Reise durch Sibirien von
dem Jahre 1733 bis
1743 22
Reindeers, dogs and
snowshoes 42
Religion in the USSR 449
Reminiscences of Russia 73
Report of the British and
Foreign Bible Society
450
Report of the Canadian
Economic
Commission (Siberia)
270
Republic in the heart of
Asia: fortieth
anniversary of Soviet
Tuva 169
Republic of Ushakovka.
Admiral Kolchak and
the allied intervention
in Siberia, 1918-1920
273
Research catalogue [of the
American
Geographical Society]
707
Results of ornithological
explorations in the
Commander islands
and Kamtschatka 178
Return to happiness 65
Reminiscences of the
mission to Siberia 459
Revelations of Siberia by a
banished lady 498
Revolution in the north:
Soviet ethnography
and nationality policy
332
Ribbon of iron 54
Rim of mystery: a hunter's
wanderings in
unknown Siberian
Asia 88
Rite techniques of the
Siberian shaman 485
Road to oblivion 513
Roughing it in Siberia 61
Royal hordes: nomad
peoples of the steppes
205
Ruling Russia: politics and

administration in the age of absolutism 249
Russia, a compleat historical account of all the nations which compose that empire 328
Russia and Asia 216
Russia and Asia: essays on the influence of Russia on the Asian peoples 212
Russia and her colonies 331
Russia and the Soviet Union: a bibliographical guide to western language publications 717
Russia as I know it 50
Russia enters the twentieth century 252
Russia/USSR: a selective, annotated bibliography of books in English 727
Russia, with Teheran, Port Arthur and Peking 117
Russian advance 38
Russian almanac 731
Russian–American annual for 1916 731
Russian civil war 288
Russian colonial expansion to 1917 248
Russian conquest of Kamchatka 251
Russian conspirators in Siberia 492
Russian engineer 313
Russian enigma 516
Russian frontier: the impact of borderlands upon the course of early Russian history 220
Russian fur trade 239
Russian gazetteer and guide 118
Russian history atlas 137
Russian imperialism from Ivan the Great to the Revolution 212
Russian land, Soviet people 127
Russian life today 41

Russian literature and criticism: selected papers from the second World Congress for Soviet and East European Studies 671
Russian Mississippi? 253
Russian monetary system: a historico-numismatic survey 232
Russian nihilism and exile life in Siberia 494
Russian settlement in the north 538
Russian statecraft: the Politika of Iurii Krizhanich 246
Russian thought and society, 1800-1917. Essays in honour of Eugene Lampert 511
Russian Yearbook 731
Russians on the Amur: its discovery, conquest and colonization 259
Russia's 'age of silver': precious metal production and economic growth in the eighteenth century 232
Russia's eastward expansion 215, 223
Russia's land of the future: regionalism and the awakening of Siberia, 1819-1894 575
Russia's small peoples: the policies and attitudes towards the native northerners, seventeenth century to 1938 316

S

St. Innocent: apostle to America 458
Sakhalin 167, 219
Samoyed peoples and languages 329
Science and Siberia 587

Second Trans-Siberian 661
Secret service on the Russian front 275
Secret Siberia 6
Secrets of Siberia 89
Selected letters of Fedor Dostoevsky 497
Selective index to Siberian, Far Eastern and Central Asian materia medica 172
Sentry and other stories 683
Seven thousand days in Siberia 535
Shaman: patterns of Siberian and Ojibway healing 476
Shamanism in Siberia 475
Shamans, lamas and evangelicals: the English missionaries in Siberia 451
Shipwreck of a generation 515
Shooting trip to Kamchatka 49
Short account of the historical development and present position of Russian Orthodox missions 464
Short outline history of the Far Eastern Republic 271
Siberia 6, 72, 703
Siberia: achievements, problems, solutions 589
Siberia and Central Asia 39
Siberia and northwest America, 1788-1792: the journal of Carl Heinrich Merck 28
Siberia and the exile system 500
Siberia and the Great Siberian Railway 636
Siberia and the Pacific: a study of economic developments and trade prospects 628
Siberia and the reforms of 1822 258
Siberia and the Soviet Far East 130

*Siberia and the Soviet Far East: strategic dimensions in multinational perspective* 11

*Siberia: an experiment in colonialism* 237

*Siberia: a record of travel, climbing and exploration* 77

*Siberia as it is* 50

*Siberia in Asia: a visit to the valley of the Yenesay in east Siberia* 184

*Siberia in the seventeenth century* 247

*Siberia: its conquest and development* 217

*Siberia: its resources and possibilities* 303

*Siberia: land of great prospects* 4

*Siberia 1971: a report on the visit of the honourable Jean Chrétien* 131

*Siberia 1: Siberian questions: economy, ecology, strategy* 125

*Siberia on fire: stories and essays* 692

*Siberia: postmarks and postal history of the Empire period* 630

*Siberia: problems and prospects for regional development* 12

*Siberia: Russia's frozen frontier* 126

*Siberia, sixty-five degrees east of Greenwich: oil and people* 87

*Siberia: the new frontier* 7

*Siberia today and tomorrow* 579

*Siberia: two historical perspectives* 15, 512

*Siberian and other folk tales: primitive literature of the empire of the Tsars* 433

*Siberian Arctic* 65

*Siberian days* 67

*Siberian diamonds* 618

*Siberian diary of Aron P. Toews* 467

*Siberian encounter* 104

*Siberian garrison* 687

*Siberian gold* 676

*Siberian journey down the Amur* 45

*Siberian journey: the journal of Hans Jakob Fries, 1774-1776* 22

*Siberian man and mammoth* 181

*Siberian overland route from Peking to Petersburg* 56

*Siberian passage: an explorer's search into the Russian Arctic* 181

*Siberian/ questions/ sibériennes* 733

*Siberian seven* 463

*Siberians* 103

*Siberia's untouched treasure* 305

*Siberica: a journal of north Pacific studies* 734

*La Sibérie: peuplement et immigration paysanne au XIX$^e$ siècle* 545

*Sibirica* 12, 734

*Sibir: my discovery of Siberia* 103

*Sibirskaya sovetskaya entsiklopediya* 732

*Sibirskie ogni* 4

*Side-lights on Siberia* 75

*Sidelights on the Siberian campaign* 267

*Silver madonna, or the odyssey of Eugenia Wasilewska* 536

*Sixteen years in Siberia* 496

*Sixteen years in Siberia: memoirs* 530

*Sketch of the life and literary career of Augustus von Kotzebue* 24

*Slavery in Russia* 488

*Snow people* 688

*Social organisation of the Mongol-Turkic pastoral nomads* 355

*Social organization of the northern Tungus* 342

*Soils of eastern Siberia* 150

*Soils of southern Siberia from the Urals to the Baikal* 150

*Some features of the morphology of the Oirot, Gorno-Altai, language* 414

*Sonechka: a life in Siberia* 535

*Song in Siberia* 456

*South Siberia* 196

*South Siberian oral literature: Turkic texts* 441

*Southern Ussurian district at the present time* 257

*Soviet and Tsarist Siberia* 85

*Soviet Asia* 2

*Soviet Asia: bibliographies* 706

*Soviet Asia: economic development and national policy choices* 580

*Soviet Asia mission* 113

*Soviet, but not Russian: the 'other' peoples of the Soviet Union* 732

*Soviet deportation of nationalities* 306

*Soviet energy system* 612

*Soviet Far East* 159, 163, 219

*Soviet Far East: a survey of its physical and economic geography* 159

*Soviet Far East: a tour of Primorye Territory* 163

*Soviet Far East: a tour of Sakhalin* 108

*Soviet Far East: geographical perspectives on development* 590

*Soviet Far East in antiquity* 204

*Soviet Far East: questions and answers* 162

*Soviet frontiers of tomorrow* 98

Soviet geography studies in our time: a Festschrift for Paul E. Lydolph 583

Soviet gold: my life as a slave laborer in the Siberian mines 528

Soviet government and the Jews, 1948-1967 373

Soviet natural resources in the world economy 615

Soviet north: present development and prospects 9

Soviet oil and gas to 1990 623

Soviet regional economic policy: the east–west debate over Pacific Siberian development 591

Soviet Russia fights crime 523

Soviet Sakhalin 168

Soviet transportation project 651

Soviet Union 119

Soviet Union: a geographical survey 129

Soviet Union in maps 135

Soviet Union yearbook 731

Soviet waterways: the development of the inland navigation syatem in the USSR 666

Sparrow in the snow 518

Spoils of progress: environmental pollution in the Soviet Union 186

Sport and exploration in the Far East: a naturalist's experiences in and around the Kurile islands 84

Stories from Chukotka 694

Story of a Siberian exile 505

Strange Siberia along the Trans-Siberian Railway 71

Stride across a thousand years. Prose, poetry and essays by writers of the Soviet north and Far East 680

Strod 300

Struggle for democracy in Siberia, 1917-1920: eyewitness account of a contemporary 274

Studies in frontier history 311, 385

Studies in honour of Louis Shein 700

Studies in Russian historical geography 15, 218

Studies in Siberian ethnogenesis 202

Studies in Siberian shamanism 480

Study of Russian folklore 429

Study of Russian history from British archival sources 450, 715

Summary of development in the Soviet north based on extracts from the Soviet press, 1974-1975 592

Summer on the Yenesei 48

Sun and snow: a Siberian adventure 109

SUPAR report 735

Survey of Russian history 683

Survey of the Uralic languages 416


T

Tapping Siberian wealth: the Urengoi experience 613

Ten months among the tents of the Tuski 360

Ten years in Russia and Siberia 537

Tent life in Siberia 62

Testimony of Kolchak and other materials 301

They found their voice: stories from Soviet nationalities 677

Third truth 669

This warm Siberia 4

Three generations of suffering 468

Three years travels from Moscow over-land to China thro' Great Ustiga, Siriania, Permia, Sibiria, Daour, Great Tartary etc. to Pekin 23

Through Kamchatka by dog sled and skis 84

Through Russian Central Asia 57

Through Russia's back door 113

Through Siberia 64, 76

Through Siberia, an empire in the making 82

Through Siberia, the land of the future 66

Through the gold fields of Alaska to the Bering Strait 358

Through the highlands of Siberia 70

Tigers, gold and witch doctors 93

Times atlas of the world 135

Together with the Ainu, a vanishing people 352

To Russia and return 723

To Siberia and Russian America 236

To the great ocean: Siberia and the Trans-Siberian Railway 644

Toward a better world 581

Towards a united states of Russia 574

T.P.C.s in the Soviet Union, with special focus on Siberia 624

Tracing shamans in Siberia: the story of an ethnographical expedition 322

Trailing the Bolsheviks 265

Trans-Siberia by rail and a month in Japan 101

206

Trans-Siberian 92
Trans-Siberian and urban change in Siberia in a space-time framework, 1885-1913 539
Trans-Siberian express 122
Trans-Siberian handbook 123
Trans-Siberian rail guide 122
Trans-Siberian railroad and the Russian revolution of 1905 260
Translations of Russian game reports 174
Transport in western Siberia: tsarist and Soviet development 629
Travels and adventures of John Ledyard 25
Travels from St. Petersburg in Russia to diverse parts of Asia 17
Travels in Kamtchatka and Siberia 51
Travels in Kamtschatka during the years 1787 and 1788 26
Travels in Siberia 59
Travels in Siberia, including excursions northwards down the Ob 52
Travels in the east of Nicholas II 70
Travels in the regions of the upper and lower Amoor 36
Treasure of the land of darkness: the fur trade and its significance for mediaeval Russia 224
Tsar and Cossack, 1855-1914 362
Tungus event: the great Siberian catastrophe of 1908 152
Turkic languages and peoples: an introduction to Turkic studies 409
TURKSIB: on the opening of the Turkestan–Siberian railway 660

U

Unknown Chekhov: stories and other writings 43
Uralic and Altaic series: an analytical index 722
Uralic languages: description, history and foreign influences 417
Urge to the sea: the course of Russian history 213
USSR energy atlas 621
USSR in maps 135

V

Vagabonding at fifty: from Siberia to Turkestan 112
Valentin Rasputin and Soviet Russian village prose 675
Vascular plants of the Siberian north and the northern Far East 185
Vasilii and Vasilissa: Siberian stories 681
Vladivostok under Red and White rule 297

W

West Siberian oil and natural gas: a study in Soviet regional development theory and practice 614

What is Asia to us? Russia's heartland yesterday and today 214
When I was young 267
White armies of Russia 299
White generals 299
Wilderness survey: true story of a taiga tragedy 90
Winds of wanderlust: hiking and tourist trails of the Soviet Union 111
Winter trek 386
With God in Russia. My 23 years as a priest in Soviet prison and labour camps in Siberia 453
With the 'die-hards' in Siberia 302
With the Russians in Mongolia 70
Within the whirlwind 519
Women in exile: wives of the Decembrists 504
Wyna: adventures in eastern Siberia 55

Y

Yakut manual 407
Yakutiya as I saw it 108
Yakutiya before its incorporation into the Russian state 225
Year of miracle and grief 670
Years off my life 520
Yermak's campaign in Siberia 229
Young Stalin: the early years of an elusive revolutionary 509
Yudin library, Krasnoiarsk (eastern Siberia) 709

# Index of Subjects

## A

Abakan 453
Administration 5, 46, 221, 241, 247, 249, 258, 262, 316, 318, 325, 331, 345, 368, 460, 552, 576, 579, 650
Agriculture 2, 5, 14, 39, 68, 77, 89, 98, 113-14, 144, 150, 171, 221, 237, 252, 254, 256, 304, 310, 514, 521-2, 550, 579, 584, 594-7, 664, 672-3, 684, 690
Ainu 208, 330-1, 333, 335, 347-53, 424, 435, 439, 445, 483
Air transport 159, 592, 633, 689, 693
Akademgorodok 6, 566-7
Alaska 27, 197, 211, 215, 234, 327, 364, 371, 420, 458
Alcoholism 79
Alexander I
*see* History
Altai region and mountains 35, 49, 57, 70, 77, 97, 111-12, 145, 157, 196, 203, 207, 228, 232, 320, 326, 355, 442, 452, 454-6, 540, 600, 672-3, 690, 701, 730
*see also* Barnaul; Biisk
Altaian people 202, 314, 331, 333, 335, 337, 394, 409, 414, 433-4, 441, 447, 454-5, 471, 672, 706
*see also* Teleut
Altaic languages 1, 385, 395, 398, 406-15, 441, 722
America and Siberia
*see* United States and Siberia
Amur region 14, 36, 45, 63, 159, 191, 201, 203, 211, 242, 248, 252, 259, 261-2, 289, 334, 336, 347, 362, 438, 458, 470, 543
*see also*
Blagoveshchensk;
Dauriya;
Komsomolsk;
Maritime region;
Nivkh; Oroch; Orok;
Ussuri region;
Vladivostok
Amur river 48, 64, 82, 117, 201, 259, 730
Anadyr river 280
Angara river 561
Anglicanism 41
Archaeography 209
Archaeology 238
*see also* Prehistory
Architecture 52, 57, 138, 703
Armstrong, T. 32
Arsenev, V. K. 33, 169
Artëm 163
Arts 162, 703
*see also* Architecture;
Illustrations;
Literature; Prehistoric
and ethnic art
Association of the Small
Peoples of the Soviet
North 316
Astafev, V. P. 668, 700
Atkinson, L. 34
Atkinson, T. W. 35
Avvakum, priest
*see* History

## B

Baikal, lake 6, 95, 105, 121, 145, 186, 189-90, 670, 692
Baikal–Amur railway
(BAM) 12, 94, 106, 318, 563, 565, 578, 587-8, 615, 624, 645-6,
648, 650-2, 655, 657-8, 661, 703
Bakunin, M. 495
Barnaul 456
Beijing 20, 23, 117, 282
Bentham, S. 228
Benyowsky, M. A.
*see* History
Bering, V.
*see* History
Bering Sea tunnel scheme 638
Bering Strait 25, 197, 200
Bestuzhev, N. A.
*see* History
Biisk 47, 530
Billings, J. 28
Birobidzhan 6, 105, 155, 372-5
*see also* Jews
Blagoveshchensk 117, 496
Bolsheviks
*see* Communist Party
Bookwalter, J. W. 39
Borodin, L. 669-70
Borodin, P. A. 85
Botany
*see* Flora
Brändström, E. 40
Bratsk 6, 86, 121, 564
Brezhnev, L. I. 655
Britain and Siberia 3, 5, 12, 15, 32, 34, 47, 53, 57, 71, 86, 98, 109, 118, 224-6, 273, 277, 282, 285-6, 288, 297, 302, 311-13, 450-1, 459, 462, 659, 731
British and Foreign Bible
Society 450
British Museum 207
British Universities
Siberian Studies
Seminar 12-13, 390
Buddhism 52, 446, 448-9, 451, 550
*see also* Buryat Mongols
Bukhara 233
Burkhanism 335, 447

Buryatiya 2, 52, 59,
64, 74, 113, 248, 298,
459, 469
*see also* Buryat Mongols;
Transbaikalia
Buryat Mongols 6, 13, 52,
93, 202, 322, 330-3,
335, 337, 353-6, 406,
409, 413, 433, 445,
451, 459, 469, 475,
478, 481, 483, 550,
677, 706

## C

Canada and Siberia 53, 57,
103, 114, 144, 165,
267, 270, 287, 290,
470, 592, 594
Catherine II
*see* History
Catholicism 453
Central Asia 35, 57, 68, 97,
112, 146, 222, 252
*see also* Bukhara;
Dzhungaria
Chekhov, A. P. 43
Chernyshevskii, N. G.
*see* History
China 17, 20-1, 23, 36,
41-2, 45-6, 100, 113,
136, 169, 219, 237,
240, 250, 262, 331,
347, 385, 496
*see also* Amur river;
Beijing; Kyakhta;
Manchuria; Macao
Chita 45, 107, 117
Christianity
*see* Anglicanism;
Catholicism; Non-
conformism; Old
Believers; Orthodoxy;
Skoptsy
Chukchi 62, 88, 156, 330-1,
335, 338-9, 345,
357-61, 418, 430, 433,
445, 473, 475, 598,
600, 674, 677, 688-9,
693-4, 697, 702, 733
Chukotka 9, 44, 63, 74, 86,
107, 124, 145, 156,
159, 181, 192-3, 201,

248, 280, 513-14,
552, 690
*see also* Anadyr; Bering
Sea tunnel scheme;
Chukchi; Indigirka;
Kolyma; Magadan
Climate 14, 52, 125, 129,
141-5
Colloque international sur
la Sibérie, 1983 125
Colonialism 210-12, 215,
221, 229-31, 236-7,
242, 245, 247-8, 250,
259, 314, 316, 320,
324-5, 327, 331-2, 335,
339, 345, 356-7, 359,
362, 382, 395, 400-2,
404, 454, 460, 540,
644, 674, 688, 694-5,
698, 702
*see also* Imperialism;
History: settlement
Communications 11-12, 14,
592
*see also* Mail; Telegraph;
Transport
Communist Party 265, 267,
271-2, 274, 276, 278,
283, 286, 298, 300,
310, 729
*see also* Brezhnev;
Gorbachev; Stalin
Constitutional Democratic
Party 295
Consumers 547
*see also* Food supply
problems
Cook, J.
*see* History
Cooperatives 268, 270
Cossacks 63, 116, 229, 236,
239, 241-5, 247-8,
250-1, 362, 526
Crime 221, 258, 512, 523
Crimean War 264
Czechoslovak legion 265,
276, 291

## D

Dauriya 16, 20, 23
Decembrists

*see* History
Denbigh, Mr 43
Dersu Uzala 33, 169
Dobell, P. 51
Dolgan people 184, 314,
335, 339, 475, 483,
680, 689, 706
Dolgikh, M. P. 196
Dostoevsky, F. M. 497
Dudinka 527, 535
Dzhugdzhur mountains 96
Dzhungaria 244

## E

Economic geography 2, 4,
127, 129, 159, 167,
583-4, 590, 710, 714
*see also* History:
economic
Economy 4, 6, 113, 125-6,
157, 159, 161-2, 266,
270, 552, 577-93, 612,
625, 629, 728, 731-2
*see also* Agriculture;
Cooperatives; Energy
and fuel; Electricity;
Oil and gas; Fisheries;
Forestry; Fur trade;
Herding and
stockraising; High
technology; Industry;
Labour; Minerals and
mining; Planning;
Resources; Territorial
production complexes;
Trade
Education 7, 228, 252,
315-16, 320, 324, 339,
344, 359, 384, 400,
451, 491, 522, 566-8,
575, 693, 697
*see also* Akademgorodok
Electricity 6, 304, 546, 564,
587, 592, 608, 611,
626, 694
Energy and fuel 11, 69, 94,
131, 163, 309, 579-80,
584, 587-8, 611, 616,
621, 623, 626
*see also* Electricity; Oil
and gas

Enets people 329, 335, 434, 475, 480
Enisei region 9, 515, 527
Enisei river 48, 52, 61, 64-5, 97, 111, 184, 201, 238, 664-6
Eniseisk 71, 516
Environmental problems 94, 125, 146, 175, 179, 182, 186-90, 315, 318, 379, 386, 389, 564, 583, 601, 605, 608, 610, 669, 671, 675, 691-2, 700
  see also Baikal, lake; Fauna; Flora; Forestry; Fur trade; Khanka, lake
Ermak Timofeev
  see History
Erman, A. 52
Eskimo 330, 335, 339, 345, 363-5, 420, 434, 445, 680, 689, 733
Eurasia 214
Even people 315, 318, 331, 335, 339, 344, 366, 432-3, 483, 600-1, 680, 689
Evenk people 36, 52, 93, 315, 318, 333, 335, 339, 342-4, 367-9, 433-4, 444-5, 480, 483-4, 513, 600, 680, 689, 733
Exile system
  see History: political: exile system

F

Family 486
Far Eastern Republic 100, 158, 160, 271
Fauna 3, 5, 14, 16, 28, 37, 42, 48-9, 52, 57, 70, 83-4, 88, 123, 145, 151, 164, 172-6, 178-80, 182-4, 187, 513, 561, 710, 728
  see also Fur trade; Fisheries; Herding and

stockraising; Mammoths
Fisheries 158, 184, 187, 270, 590, 592
Flora 3, 5, 14, 16, 28, 37, 42, 48-9, 52, 70, 83-4, 102, 145, 151, 164, 172, 175, 178-9, 184-5, 710, 728
Folklore 321, 327, 329, 335-6, 343, 351, 353, 357, 363, 368, 371, 377-8, 380, 382-3, 385-6, 395-7, 410-11, 419, 425, 427-44, 689
  see also Shamanism
Food supply problems 28, 52, 564, 597, 600
Forestry 5, 114, 131, 158, 184, 187, 270, 527, 579, 590, 592, 604-9, 615
France and Siberia 264-5, 272-3, 277, 284, 638
Frontier
  see Colonialism; History; Imperialism; Turner, F. J.
Frost, G. 500
Fur trade 23, 83, 158, 174, 211, 213, 224, 237-9, 247, 251, 542

G

Geographical discovery
  see History: exploration; Travel
Geography 3-6, 12, 14, 124-71, 219, 230, 259, 637, 707, 710, 720, 728, 730, 732
  see also Climate; Economic geography; History: economic; Environmental problems; Geopolitics; Physical geography; Rivers; Water transfers
Geopolitics 214
  see also Eurasia; Imperialism

Germans 528
  see also World War I; World War II
Gmelin, J.-G.
  see History
Godunov, B.
  see History
Golchikha 48
Golden Horde 224
  see also Tatars
Gorbachev, M. S. 13, 130, 219, 366, 581, 583, 590, 667
Great Tartary 20, 23, 28, 35, 44
Gypsies 370

H

Herding and stockraising 366, 384, 386, 395-6, 598-603, 693-4
  see also Altaian; Buryat Mongols; Chukchi; Enets; Evenk; Kazakhs; Koryak; Nenets; Nganasan; Shor; Tatars; Tuvinian; Yakut; Yukagir
High technology 11, 555, 587, 590, 610, 613, 625-6
Hill, E. M. 32
Historiography 210, 235, 260, 276, 561
  see also Turner, F. J.
History 5-7, 12, 14, 93, 98, 102, 105, 109, 110, 114, 116, 119, 137, 160, 162, 164, 167, 169, 209-313, 316, 331, 345-6, 362, 392, 492-538, 542, 551, 553, 556, 575, 617, 637, 672, 678, 684-6, 708, 720, 728-32
Alexander I 258
Avvakum Petrovich 13, 16, 510
Benyowsky, M. A. 18, 24

History *cont.*
 Bering, V. 15, 31, 243
 Bestuzhev, N. A. 499
 Catherine II 249
 Chernyshevskii, N. G.
  506, 511
 Chronicles 229
 Cook, J. 28
 Decembrists 490, 492,
  499, 504, 508
  *see also* History:
  Bestuzhev, Rozen
 Economic history 46,
  53-4, 65-7, 71-2, 79,
  98, 109, 114, 127,
  156-61, 167-8, 227,
  232-3, 237-41, 243,
  246, 252, 254-6, 259,
  263, 266, 270, 272,
  285, 290-1, 303-5, 629,
  632, 634-44, 647, 649,
  659, 664-5
  *see also* Agriculture;
  Fur trade; History:
  fairs; Industry;
  Minerals; Railways
 Ermak 229, 248
 Exile sytem 6, 14, 24,
  41-3, 47, 50, 58, 60,
  63-4, 69, 75-6, 79, 107,
  219, 391, 453, 490,
  492-537, 575, 640, 669,
  682, 699, 729
  *see also* Kolyma
 Exploration 6-8, 13,
  15-31, 164, 221, 234,
  243, 248, 259
  *see also* History:
  Bering, Cook,
  Gmelin, Müller
 Fairs 227, 237
 Fortifications 20, 138,
  213, 218, 238, 244, 248
 Gmelin, J.-G. 13
 Godunov, B. 248
 Ivan IV, the Terrible 248
 Ivan III, the Great 248
 Kolchak, A. V. 65, 268,
  272-3, 277, 291, 296,
  299, 301
 Križanić, J. 246
 Kropotkin, P. A. 63
 Kuchum, khan 133
 Lenin, V. I. 503
 Müller, G.-F. 13, 19

Muravëv-Amurskii, N.
 N. 45, 262, 495, 575
Name of Siberia 1, 229,
 392
Nicholas II 41, 78, 269
1905 Revolution 69, 260,
 729
Peter the Great 23, 237,
 604
Political history 3, 14,
 157, 247, 573
 *see also*
 Administration;
 Communist Party;
 Constitutional
 Democratic Party;
 Decembrists;
 History: Speranskii;
 Regionalism;
 Mensheviks;
 Socialist
 Revolutionary Party
Potanin, G. N. 575, 729
Regionalism 76, 268,
 295, 511, 569-75, 582,
 591, 729
 *see also* History:
 Potanin, Shchapov,
 Yadrintsev
Remezov, S. U. 132-4,
 138, 140
Rozen, A. 492
Shchapov, A. P. 569,
 729
Settlement 6, 8, 42, 46,
 73, 221, 230, 243, 259,
 278, 453, 487, 538-65,
 590, 634, 682, 729
 *see also* Urbanization
Spathary, N. 21, 134
Speranskii, M. 258
Stalin, I. V. 2, 6, 113,
 202, 304, 306, 310,
 312, 509, 697-9, 732
Trotsky, L. D. 509
Ungern-Sternberg,
 baron 292, 297
Witte, S. Y. 69
Yadrintsev, N. M. 575,
 729
Housing 156, 171, 486,
 522, 546
Hudson's Bay Company 47
Huns 205

I

Illustrations 10, 14, 17, 35,
 37-9, 49, 54, 57-8, 64,
 68, 70-2, 78, 88-9, 91,
 97, 100, 111, 113,
 115-16, 120-1, 123,
 126, 129, 131, 155, 157,
 160, 162, 166, 169-70,
 179, 186, 190, 196,
 199, 204-5, 207, 229,
 236, 304, 327, 338,
 349, 364, 366, 462,
 587, 617, 637, 689, 703
Imperialism 210, 212,
 214-16, 231, 236, 245,
 248, 252
 *see also* Colonialism;
 Mercantilism
Indigirka river 181, 664
Industry 2, 5-6, 8, 61, 64,
 98, 114, 158, 237, 252,
 255, 267, 270, 304-5,
 307, 309, 313, 522,
 551, 578-9, 584, 592,
 631, 664-5, 710
Institute of Pacific
 Relations, Hawaii 183
International Association
 for Quaternary
 Research 197
International Work Group
 for Indigenous Affairs
 316, 386
Irbit 227
Irkutsk 6-7, 17, 30, 47, 52,
 56, 59, 64, 68, 71,
 85-6, 117, 121, 123,
 157, 294, 310, 458,
 524, 528, 669, 692
Irtysh river 57, 244, 663,
 666
Islam 314
Itelmen 31, 37, 62, 164,
 198, 251, 330-1, 333,
 335, 339, 371, 426-8,
 445, 598, 680, 689
Ivan IV, the Terrible
 *see* History
Ivan III, the Great
 *see* History
Ivanov, V. V. 678

J

Janin, C. 312

212

Janin, M. 284
Japan 18, 30, 80, 100, 166,
 219, 235, 264, 270,
 273, 283, 297, 301,
 331, 336, 347, 352,
 555, 609, 654, 659
 *see also* Ainu; Russo-
 Japanese War
Jesup North Pacific
 Expedition 317, 327,
 334, 357, 363, 382,
 395-6, 418-19, 422,
 430, 473, 477
Jews 372-5, 522, 530, 533
 *see also* Birobidzhan
Jochelson, W. 198
Journalism in Siberia 571


K

Kamchatka 9, 15, 18-19,
 24-6, 28, 31, 37, 49,
 51, 59, 62, 64, 79, 84,
 124, 145, 153-4, 164-5,
 193, 198, 201, 243,
 248, 251, 264, 280, 458
Karagas people 322, 335
Kazakhs 326, 335, 337, 355
Kazakhstan 35, 67, 146,
 306, 580
Kemerovo 199
Kennan, G. 50, 62, 500,
 523
Ket people 48, 323, 330,
 335, 339, 376-8, 434,
 475, 483, 689
Khabarovsk 117, 123, 159
Khakass people 314, 326,
 331, 335, 409, 436,
 471, 706
Khakass Autonomous
 Region 453
 *see also* Minusinsk
Khanka, lake 182
Khanty people 184, 194,
 202, 315, 335, 337,
 339, 379-80, 416-17,
 434, 445, 472, 480,
 680, 689
Khrushchev, N. S. 168,
 306, 631
Kirgiz people 202, 335, 337
Knox, A. 284

Kolchak, A. V.
 *see* History
Kolyma region 517, 519,
 524-5, 528, 699
Kolyma river 74, 200, 664
Komsomolsk-na-Amure
 113
Koptëlov, A. L. 673
Korean people 331, 335,
 381
Korolenko, V. G. 682
Koryak people 62, 74, 202,
 330-1, 333, 335, 339,
 382-3, 419, 423, 433,
 445, 475, 477, 598,
 600, 689
Kotzebue, A. von 24
Krasnoyarsk 18, 51, 59, 61,
 64-5, 71-2, 97, 113,
 117, 286, 292, 453,
 516, 535, 581, 668, 709
Križanić, J.
 *see* History
Kropotkin, P.
 *see* History
Kuchum, khan
 *see* History
Kumandin people 471
Kurgan 24, 492
Kuril islands 44, 159, 219
Kurosawa, I. 33, 169
Kuznetsk basin (Kuzbas)
 6, 112, 188, 304, 309,
 313, 551, 553, 556
Kuznetsk 309, 556
Kyakhta 47, 56, 59, 263


L

Labour 13, 125, 260, 272,
 486, 557, 560, 562,
 565, 576, 579-80, 590,
 640, 650
Languages 29, 314, 316-17,
 319, 325, 344, 398-405,
 724, 730, 732
 *see also* Altaic
 languages;
 Paleosiberian
 languages; Uralic
 languages
Lattimore, O. 113, 311,
 385, 517

Law 489, 576
 *see also* Administration;
 Crime; History:
 political; Vagrancy
Ledyard, J. 25
Lena river 52, 59, 64, 74,
 201, 664, 667
Lehman Library,
 Columbia University,
 New York 344
Lenin, V. I.
 *see* History
Leningrad, Museum 327
Leskov, N. S. 683
Lesseps, J. B. de 26
Libraries 209, 709, 726
 *see also* Lehman
 Library; Minnesota
 University Library
Literature 368, 497, 596,
 652, 656, 668-705
Little BAM 653


M

Macao 18
Mackinder, H. J. 214
Magadan 514, 524, 533
Magnitogorsk 553, 559
Mail 630
Makarii (Glukharëv)
 454-5, 466
Mammoths 23, 177, 181
Manchuria 38, 46, 82, 110,
 215, 342
Mangazeya 238
Mansi people 194, 202,
 315, 335, 337, 416-17,
 434, 445, 480, 677,
 680, 689
Maps 94, 117, 127, 132-40,
 166, 531, 592, 614, 621
 *see also* Town plans
Mariinsk 515
Maritime region 64, 157,
 159, 163, 182, 547
 *see also* Amur river;
 Artëm;
 Blagoveshchensk;
 Khabarovsk;

Maritime region *cont.*
Nakhodka; Okhotsk
region; Ussuriisk;
Vladivostok
Markov, G. M. 684-6, 703
Medicine 5, 17, 73, 172,
278, 351, 462, 521, 561
*see* Food supply;
Sanitation
Mensheviks 493, 496, 729
Mercantilism 128
Messerschmidt, D. 29
Military issues 11-12, 29,
63, 80, 162, 228, 248,
265-302, 580, 657
*see also* Cossacks;
Crimean War; World
War I; World War II
Minerals and mining 5, 61,
67, 71, 73, 79, 89, 99,
105, 109, 113-14, 139,
149, 158, 171, 187,
232, 255, 270, 291,
306, 309, 312, 525,
528, 546, 579, 592,
618, 620, 622, 703, 710
*see also* Physical
geography; Resources
Minnesota University
Library, James Ford
Bell Collection 27
Minusinsk 72
Minusinsk depression 48,
109
Modern Humanities
Research Association
32
Mongolia 35, 41, 49, 57, 70,
282, 292, 342, 459, 706
Mountains
*see* Altai; Dzhugdzhur;
Physical geography;
Salair; Sayan;
Tienshan; Urals
Müller, G.-F.
*see* History
Munzuk, M. 169
Muravëv-Amurskii, N. N.
*see* History
Museums 490
*see also* British Museum;
Leningrad, Museum;
Peabody Museum;
Smithsonian
Institution

**N**

Nakhodka 95, 163
Nanai people 36, 319, 331,
334-5, 339-40, 384-5,
408, 434, 475, 483,
680, 689
National minorities
*see* Peoples
Natural history
*see* Fauna; Flora
Nenets people 315, 323,
329, 335, 338-9, 386,
416-17, 475, 610, 680,
689
Nerchinsk 20, 64, 75, 506
Nganasan people 202, 329,
335, 387-8, 417, 434,
475, 483
Nicholas II
*see* History
Nivkh people 36, 58, 60,
64, 106, 259, 330-1,
334-6, 340, 350, 389
434, 440, 445, 479,
483, 598, 677, 680,
689, 695
Nomadism 194, 196, 203,
205, 207, 212, 218,
220-2, 226, 337, 394
*see also* Herding and
stockraising
Non-conformism 52, 64,
451, 456, 459, 462,
467-70
*see also* Skoptsy
Norilsk 535
North Atlantic Treaty
Organization 588
Novgorod, republic of 213,
223
Novosibirsk 6, 70, 97, 113,
117, 120, 123, 528, 551

**O**

Ob river 52, 57, 70, 170,
194, 491, 608, 639,
663-5
Oil and gas 13, 87, 125,
131, 147, 308, 546,
560, 592, 610, 613-14,
617, 619, 623, 656,
689, 703

Okhotsk 18, 26, 44, 51-2,
59
Okhotsk region 51, 96,
243, 458
Old Believers 13-14, 672,
701
*see also* Avvakum
Omsk 56-7
Oregon Historical Society
22, 235
Oroch people 93, 202, 326,
334-6, 340, 408, 479,
483, 689
Orok people 13, 202,
334-6, 339-40, 390,
410, 479
Orthodoxy 13, 42, 64, 71,
77, 86, 213, 251, 452,
454-5, 457-8, 460, 461,
464-6, 472, 669, 672,
682-3, 700

**P**

Peoples 3, 5, 13-14, 20,
28-9, 42, 51, 54, 79,
84, 94, 100, 125, 131,
195, 221, 226, 247-8,
258-9, 306, 314-97,
460, 579, 592, 637,
689, 716, 718, 720,
728, 730
*see also* Ainu; Altaian;
Burkhanism; Buryat
Mongols; Chukchi;
Colonialism;
Cossacks; Dolgan;
Enets; Eskimo; Even;
Evenk; Folklore;
Germans; Gypsies;
Itelmen; Jews;
Karagas; Kazakh;
Ket; Khakass;
Khanty; Kirgiz;
Koreans; Koryak;
Kumandin;
Languages; Mansi;
Nanai; Nenets;
Nganasan; Nivkh;
Oroch; Orok; Physical
anthropology; Poles;
Prehistory; Samoyed;
Selkup; Shor; Social

anthropology; Soyot;
Tatars; Teleut;
Tofalar; Tuvinian;
Udegei; Ukrainian;
Ulchi; Yakut; Yukagir
Pacific Ocean 27-8, 211,
234-6, 248
Paleosiberian languages
357-8, 377-8, 396,
398, 418-28, 718
Pallas, P. S. 27
Paris 26
Pavlov, P. N. 210
Peabody Museum of
Archaeology and
Ethnology 203
Peasants 14, 39, 56, 73,
278, 310, 354, 429,
433, 487, 489, 507,
514, 541, 543-5, 558,
596, 675, 682, 690-1,
700-1
*see also* Agriculture;
History: settlement
Pennant, T. 27
Perestroika 366, 581, 599
*see also* Gorbachev,
M. S.
Permanent International
Altaistic Conference
(PIAC) 415
Pérouse, la 26, 28
Peter the Great
*see* History
Petropavlovsk-Kamchatskii
84, 264
Peyton, B. 261
Physical anthropology 194,
326-7, 354, 378, 385
Physical geography 14, 52,
127, 129, 131, 139,
145, 148, 150-4, 159,
166-7, 201, 613, 710,
714
*see also* Mountains;
Rivers; Vasyugane
Planning 546-8, 552, 557,
562, 564, 568, 577-8,
580-2, 586-91, 593,
606, 624-5, 650
Poles 63, 69, 292, 336, 391,
453, 498, 505, 521,
525, 536
Polevoi, B. P. 210

Population 159, 162, 237,
341, 538-65, 579-80,
590
Potanin, G. N.
*see* History
Prehistoric and ethnic art
191, 194, 196, 199,
204-5, 207, 334, 368,
389, 703
Prehistory 191-208, 219,
225-6, 327, 369, 602
*see also* Archaeology;
Nomadism; Peoples
Prokopevsk 551

### R

Railways 5-6, 38-40, 45,
49, 53-4, 58, 61, 68,
71-2, 79, 82, 92, 97,
104, 112, 115, 117,
119, 122-3, 139, 157,
254, 260, 283, 496,
515, 524, 528, 539,
541, 545, 592, 629-30,
632, 634-44, 647, 649,
654, 659
*see also* Baikal–Amur
railway; Bering Sea
tunnel scheme; Little
BAM; Turksib;
Tyumen–Surgut
railway
Rasputin, V. G. 94, 671,
675, 691-2, 703
Red Cross 40
Religions 5, 445-85
*see also* Buddhism;
Burkhanism;
Christianity; Islam;
Shamanism
Remezov, S. U.
*see* History
Resources 12, 130, 166,
183, 588, 590, 615-16
*see also* Energy;
Minerals and mining;
Physical geography
Rivers
*see also* Amur; Anadyr;
Angara; Enisei;
Indigirka; Irtysh;
Kolyma; Lena; Ob;

Physical geography;
Tom; Water transfers
Roads 5, 20, 39, 41, 56-7,
64, 70, 72, 75, 81-2,
89, 157, 516, 542, 592,
629, 662
Roerich, N. 442
Rozen, A.
*see* History
Rubtsovsk 522
Russian Geographical
Society 253, 257
Russo-Japanese war 69,
80, 643
Rytkheu, Y. S. 103, 674,
681, 693-4

### S

St. Petersburg 30
Sakhalin island 43, 58, 60,
64, 75, 79-80, 100,
108, 145, 159, 166-8,
208, 219, 308, 336, 695
*see also* Ainu; Nivkh
Salair mountains 82
Samoyed peoples 333, 386,
416-17
*see also* Enets; Nenets;
Nganasan; Selkup
Sanitation 267, 552
Sartakov, S. 696
Sarychev, G. 28
Sayan mountains 111, 145,
196, 292, 515, 602
Science 11, 587
*see also* High technology
Sects
*see* Non-conformism
Selenginsk 17
Shamanism 7, 93, 321-2,
343, 351, 357, 367,
371, 376-8, 382, 385,
388, 395, 424, 445-6,
451, 471-85, 550, 674,
698
*see also* Folklore
Selkup people 323, 329,
335, 339, 416, 475, 689
Shchapov, A. P.
*see* History
Shor people 331, 335, 434,
441, 471, 733

215

Shukshin, V. M. 679, 701,
    703
Siberia and world affairs 2,
    12
    see also Military issues;
    Trade
Siberia: eastern 5, 9, 14,
    29, 35-6, 55, 67, 72,
    77, 79, 91, 100, 108-9,
    124, 157, 201, 274,
    304, 368, 515, 619
    see also Angara; Bratsk;
    Enisei; Eniseisk;
    Krasnoyarsk;
    Transbaikaliya; Tuva;
    Yakutiya
Siberia: northeastern
    see Chukotka;
    Kamchatka; Yakutiya
Siberia: western 2, 5, 14,
    29, 34-5, 44, 72-3, 77,
    87, 124, 170, 194, 227,
    315, 320, 362, 600,
    611, 613-14, 617, 629,
    639, 664-5
    see also Abakan;
    Akademgorodok;
    Altai; Dudinka; Irbit;
    Irtysh; Kemerovo;
    Magnitogorsk;
    Novosibirsk; Ob;
    Prokopevsk; Tobolsk;
    Tomsk; Tyumen;
    Verkhoture
Skoptsy 71, 76, 181, 184
Slavery 488
Slavin, S. V. 9
Smithsonian Institution 327
Social anthropology 194,
    327
    see also Peoples;
    Religions; Social
    issues
Social issues 2, 8, 13, 52,
    57, 64, 68, 71-3, 87,
    89, 92, 94, 98, 102,
    104, 106, 157, 167,
    169, 320, 393, 486-91,
    552-3, 575
    see also Alcoholism;
    Consumers; Crime;
    Education; Family;
    History: settlement;
    Housing; Labour;

Medicine; Peasants;
    Population;
    Sanitation; Slavery;
    Urbanization;
    Vagrancy; Women;
    Young people
Socialist Revolutionary
    Party 272, 274, 513
Soviet Far East 2, 5, 8, 33,
    45-6, 63, 69, 91, 119
    127, 129-30, 145,
    158-63, 184, 201, 203,
    219, 236, 243, 248,
    262, 265-6, 270-3, 277,
    279-81, 287-8, 301,
    305-6, 331, 362, 452,
    457-8, 525, 542, 545,
    547, 558, 580-1, 583,
    588, 590, 615, 620,
    648, 708, 711, 720,
    732, 735
    see also Amur region;
    Artëm; Far Eastern
    Republic; Kamchatka;
    Khabarovsk; Kolyma;
    Magadan; Maritime
    region; Okhotsk;
    Petropavlovsk;
    Sretensk; Suchan;
    Ussuriisk; Vladivostok
Soyot people 292, 322, 335
Sparwenfeld, J. G. 134
Spathary
    see History
Speranskii
    see History
Sretensk 82, 117, 496
Stalin, I. V.
    see History
Strahlenberg, P. J. von 29
Suchan 163

T

Tatars 314, 322, 335,
    392-3, 436, 471
    see also Golden Horde;
    Kachin; Kumandin
Telegraph 5, 42, 45, 62
Teleut people 540
Territorial production
    complexes (TPCs)
    125, 578, 585-7, 590,
    595, 615, 624, 657

Thomas, A. 132, 136
Tienshan mountains 111
Tobolsk 17, 18, 24, 52, 64,
    138, 246, 269
Tofalar people 471
Tom river 199
Tomsk 18, 39, 51-2, 56, 59,
    64, 75, 117, 491
Tourism 6, 95-6, 101, 104,
    111, 117-23
    see also Air transport;
    Railways; Travel
Town plans 5, 117, 121,
    123, 564
Towns 23, 118-19, 138,
    237, 539, 543, 546,
    549, 553, 555, 558, 728
    see also Abakan;
    Akademgorodok;
    Artëm; Barnaul;
    Biisk;
    Blagoveshchensk;
    Bratsk; Chita;
    Dudinka; Eniseisk;
    Golchikha; Irbit;
    Irkutsk; Kemerovo;
    Khabarovsk;
    Komsomolsk;
    Krasnoyarsk; Kurgan;
    Kuznetsk; Kyakhta;
    Magadan;
    Magnitogorsk;
    Mangazeya; Mariinsk;
    Minusinsk; Nakhodka;
    Nerchinsk;
    Novosibirsk; Okhotsk;
    Omsk; Petropavlovsk;
    Prokopevsk;
    Rubtsovsk;
    Selenginsk; Sretensk;
    Suchan; Tobolsk;
    Tomsk; Tura;
    Tyumen; Ussuriisk;
    Verkhoture; Vilyuisk;
    Vladivostok; Yakutsk
Trade 11, 45, 52, 57, 65,
    71, 110, 114, 118, 130,
    158, 169, 227, 233,
    239-41, 246, 250, 252,
    262-3, 266, 285, 290,
    303, 311, 365, 579,
    590, 605, 609, 615,
    617-28, 637, 642, 647,
    654, 731, 735

Transbaikaliya 50, 55, 67,
 108, 139, 159, 248,
 298, 342, 354, 367, 492
 *see also*
 Blagoveshchensk;
 Buryatiya; Chita;
 Khabarovsk; Kyakhta;
 Nerchinsk; Selenginsk
Transport 2, 5, 11-12, 14,
 39, 42, 47, 64, 125,
 159, 252, 304, 579,
 629-67, 714, 725, 728
 *see also* Air transport;
 Railways; Road
 transport; Travel;
 Water transport
Travel to Siberia
 32-123, 156, 160, 163,
 170-1, 177-8, 181, 183,
 723
 *see also* Transport
Trotsky, L. D.
 *see* History
Tura 368
Turksib railway 92, 97,
 632, 660
Turner, F. J. and frontier
 thesis 216, 220
Tuva 169, 292, 394, 599,
 602
 *see also* Tuvinian
Tuvinian people 314, 331,
 335, 394, 434, 471,
 475, 599, 602, 677, 706
Tyumen 57, 59, 87, 523,
 656
Tyumen–Surgut railway
 656

U

Udegei people 331, 335,
 677
Ukrainians 544
Ulchi people 319, 326,
 334-5, 408, 411, 689
Umanskii, A. P. 210
Ungern-Sternberg, baron
 *see* History
USSR Academy of
 Sciences Siberian
 Section 9, 209, 221,

225, 471, 486, 567-8,
 594
United States and Siberia
 2, 12, 25, 38, 45, 56,
 144, 217, 261, 265,
 273, 277, 279-81, 283,
 297, 303, 305, 308-9,
 311-12, 327, 338, 364,
 463, 635, 638, 642,
 659, 731
 *see also* Alaska
Ural mountains 41, 57, 59,
 63, 194, 214, 309, 553
Uralic languages 398,
 416-17
 *see also* Khanty; Mansi;
 Nenets; Selkup
Urbanization 13, 237, 315,
 319, 384, 558, 575
 *see also* History:
 settlement;
 Population; Towns
Ussuri region 257, 262, 543
Ussuriisk 163

V

Vagrancy 221
Vampilov, A. 692, 703-4
Vasyugane swamp 87, 689
 *see also* Oil and gas;
 Tyumen–Surgut
 railway
Verbitskii, V. I. 433, 455
Verkhoture 57
Vilyuisk 462, 506
Vladivostok 58, 64, 102,
 111, 113-14, 117, 157,
 163, 182, 257, 279,
 283, 287, 297, 301,
 524, 581
Volkonskaya, E. 504

W

Wallace. H. A. 113, 517
Water transfers 125, 142,
 146
Water transport 13, 20,
 56-8, 64-5, 68, 70-1,
 75, 81-2, 97, 117, 157,
 285, 491, 524, 528,

542-3, 592, 629, 637,
 663-8, 696
Waxell, S. 31
West Siberian Historical
 and Ethnographical
 Expedition, University
 of Omsk 320
Windt, H. de 50, 75, 358,
 638
Witte, S. Y.
 *see* History
Women 7, 493, 498, 504,
 507, 518-19, 521-2,
 529, 535-6, 680
 *see also* Volkonskaya, E.
World War I 40, 57, 275,
 294, 502, 687
World War II 113, 306-7,
 526, 528, 668

Y

Yadrintsev, N. M.
 *see* History
Yakut people 52, 76, 93,
 171, 181, 202, 225,
 314-15, 326, 331, 333,
 335, 337, 344, 359,
 395, 407, 409, 433,
 471, 475, 483, 490,
 513, 600, 680, 689, 706
Yakutiya 2, 6, 44, 47, 51,
 74, 86, 108, 124-5,
 145, 159, 171, 181,
 225, 300, 311, 315,
 366, 513, 530, 590,
 594, 600-1, 667, 682
 *see also* Anadyr;
 Indigirka; Vilyuisk
Yakutsk 18, 59, 64, 74, 91,
 113, 462, 501, 667
Yamal-Nenets
 Autonomous Region
 94
 *see also* Nenets people
Young people 315, 563,
 650, 656
Yukagir people 74, 330,
 333, 335, 338-9, 396-7,
 422, 432-3, 445, 473,
 475, 598, 600, 677,
 680, 688-9

Z

Zurich 22

# Map of Siberia and the Soviet Far E

This map shows the more important towns, railway lines and other fea

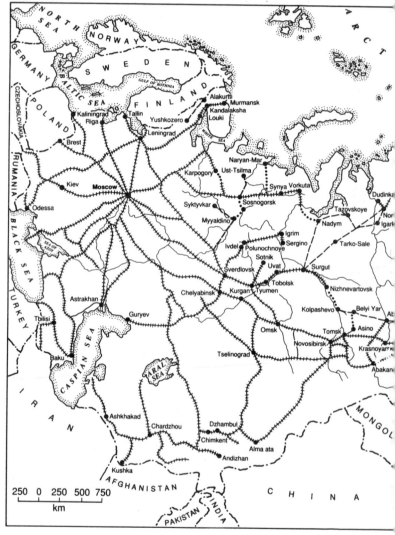

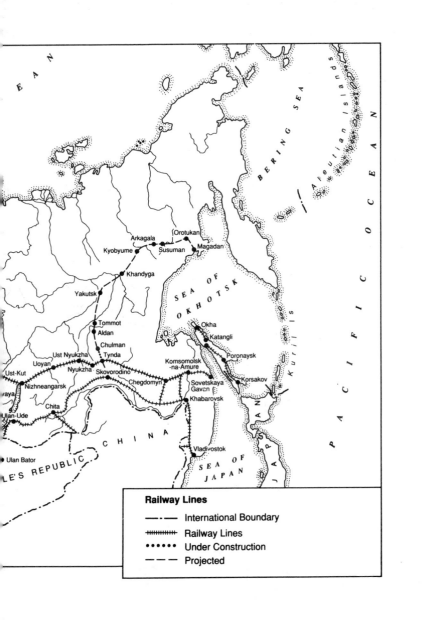

**Railway Lines**

—·—· International Boundary

+++++++ Railway Lines

•••••• Under Construction

— — — Projected

# Native groups in Siberia and the Soviet Far East.

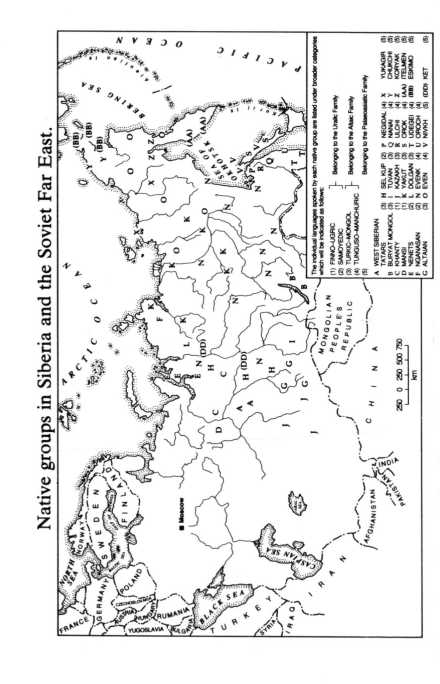

The individual languages spoken by each native group are listed under broader categories which will be indicated as follows:

(1) FINNO-UGRIC  
(2) SAMOYEDIC  ⎤ Belonging to the Uralic Family  
(3) TURKIC-MONGOL  ⎤ Belonging to the Altaic Family  
(4) TUNGUSO-MANCHURIC  ⎦  
(5) Belonging to the Palaeoasiatic Family

| | | | | | | |
|---|---|---|---|---|---|---|
| A | WEST SIBERIAN TATARS | (3) | H | SEL'KUP | (2) | P | NEGIDAL | (4) | X | YUKAGIR | (5) |
| B | BURYAT MONGOL | (3) | I | TUVAN | (3) | Q | NANAI | (4) | Y | CHUKCHI | (5) |
| C | KHANTY | (1) | J | KAZAKH | (3) | R | ULCHI | (4) | Z | KORYAK | (5) |
| D | MANSI | (1) | K | YAKUT | (3) | S | OROK | (4) | (AA) | ITEL'MEN | (5) |
| E | NENETS | (2) | L | DOLGAN | (3) | T | UDEGEI | (4) | (BB) | ESKIMO | (5) |
| F | NGANASAN | (2) | N | EVENK | (4) | U | OROCH | (4) | | | |
| G | ALTAIAN | (3) | O | EVEN | (4) | V | NIVKH | (5) | (DD) | KET | (5) |

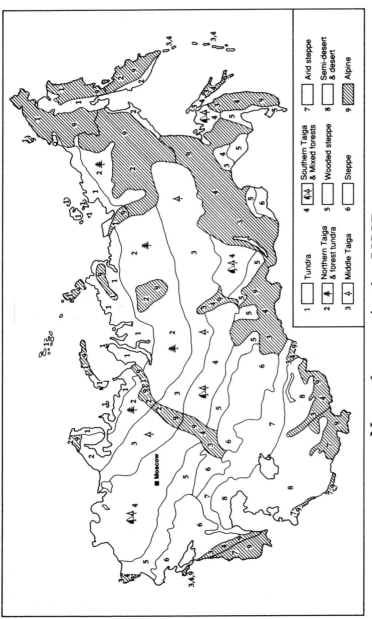

## Natural zones in the USSR.

**Legend:**

1 Tundra
2 Northern Taiga & forest tundra
3 Middle Taiga
4 Southern Taiga & Mixed forests
5 Wooded steppe
6 Steppe
7 Arid steppe
8 Semi-desert & desert
9 Alpine

■ Moscow